VIEWER'S GUIDE TO FILM

ARTS, ARTIFICES, AND ISSUES

A VIEWER'S GUIDE TO FILM

ARTS, ARTIFICES, AND ISSUES

Richard M. Gollin

University of Rochester

McGraw-Hill, Inc.
New York St. Louis San Francisco Auckland Bogotá
Caracas Lisbon London Madrid Mexico City Milan
Montreal New Delhi San Juan Singapore
Sydney Tokyo Toronto

This book is printed on acid-free paper.

A VIEWER'S GUIDE TO FILM

Arts, Artifices, and Issues

7 8 9 10 11 12 13 14 BKMBKM 9 9 8 7

ISBN 0-07-023700-X

This book was set in Palatino by Arcata Graphics/Kingsport.
The editors were Peter Labella and James R. Belser;
the production supervisor was Richard A. Ausburn.
The cover was designed by Fern Logan.

On the Cover: This image shows rainmaking in Chicago's Wrigley Field during the shooting of Frank Capra's *Meet John Doe* (1941). The rain is backlit so that it can be seen, the stadium is empty except within camera range where it is crammed with extras holding umbrellas, and Gary Cooper, as "John Doe," waits on the speakers' stand for an opportunity to explain that he is not a fake.

Library of Congress Cataloging-in-Publication Data

Gollin, Richard M.
    A viewer's guide to film: arts, artifices, and issues / Richard M. Gollin.
        p.   cm.
    Includes index.
    ISBN 0-07-023700-X
    1. Motion pictures.   2. Motion pictures—Terminology.   I. Title.
PN1994.G585   1992
791.43—dc20
                                                                91-26627

ABOUT
THE AUTHOR

The founder, and for twenty years, director of the University of Rochester's Film Studies Program and of its film resource center, Richard Gollin
has taught many different kinds of film courses, lectured on film to
civic and professional groups in the United States, Canada, Britain,
and Japan, and written on film for such publications as the *Quarterly
Review of Film Studies* and *College English.* He received his Ph.D. from
the University of Minnesota, studied at Oxford University and later
briefly at the American Film Institute School for Advanced Study, and
taught at the University of Minnesota and Colgate University before
coming to the University of Rochester, where he is a Professor of English
and Film Studies.

Earlier he taught and published in Romantic, Victorian, and modern
literature and drama as well as film, and he has also directed doctoral
dissertations in those fields. He has served as a consultant to other
institutions seeking to institute their own film studies programs, has
twice served as a program director of the Rochester International Film
Festival, has twice been a juror in annual CINE competitions, and once,
memorably, served as an expert witness in a film obscenity case. He
has received Fulbright, Ford, Wilson, ACLS, and Rockefeller scholar-
ships and fellowships, and a major grant from the National Endowment
for the Humanities to develop film studies at Rochester in conjunction
with the International Museum of Photography at George Eastman
House. His next project is a book on screen comedy.

CONTENTS

AUTHOR'S NOTE

This handbook might also be titled "Everything You Always Wanted to Know about Movies Everyone Else Thinks You Already Know." The book contains in compact form many things film viewers, students, and self-educated buffs should know but often don't and many things others think they know but don't. *A Viewer's Guide* can supplement other textbooks or stand alone as a primary text or guidebook. Like other such books this guide says some obvious things and some not very obvious, always in the language commonly used by filmmakers and film critics rather than the specialized discourses developed by theoreticians and scholars. The critical issues implied by film terminology are discussed not in alphabetical but in functional order, in a form fit for launching readers into more advanced studies, other courses, their own further readings in film magazines or journals, or their own readings of dense films previously thought boring or baffling.

A Viewer's Guide has a strong humanistic base. Although the book acknowledges and illustrates that images moving in rectangles provide our primary knowledge of ourselves and each other in this century, it does not assume that films create that knowledge. Rather, the book explains how actual experience underlies most filmic conventions, stressing that film viewing is not passive but highly interactive, guided by accustomed visual and dramatic conventions that constitute the materials of a major art form. *A Viewer's Guide* is always concerned with how films affect us while we watch them, with what they say by how they say it.

The films mentioned range widely but are mostly limited to the mainstream commonly discussed in universities and found in video stores as well as on late night TV. This is not to deny that other times, countries, and filmmakers also make films that provide equally apt illustrations and examples nor to imply that this main range of reference represents anything other than a sampling of well-made, well-known films. The films discussed are those often mentioned in anthologies and journals, cited for their familiarity. Because this book helpfully supplements other kinds of information and analysis, only occasionally does it refer to films outside the mainstream. For better or worse the film conventions which are our subject are, with very few exceptions, nearly universal in the world's filmmaking cultures.

To be dense yet clear, and brief yet useful, this handbook stresses primary meanings and uses of terms and techniques, not their many alternatives. Thus the text seems often to speak categorically, even dogmatically. But once its basic discriminations become habitual, readers can freely refine or correct these judgments, as they should, from their own observation of their own actual experience at the movies.

Faculty and others approaching film from their own interests and disciplines often ask me for this kind of information for themselves as well as their students, to found or supplement other purposes. This handbook is the result—just long enough to say what needs saying.

PREFACE

Film is the first new art form to emerge since Greek times, or the second after its immediate predecessor photography. Film is also the most inclusive of the earlier arts, heir to painting, sculpture, architecture, music, drama, dance, rhetoric, and photography, all of which are part of any film. Meanwhile it has its own unique concerns: with images that move within flat rectangles, with the way the images are arranged, and with their implications when projected on screens before audiences.

Narrative films made for large audiences are also the most expensive art form to emerge since Greek times. Only architecture is similar in the costs and supervisory approvals required before creative work can begin, especially when films are made to the highest technical standards (called in the industry "production values"). Movies are big business. Perhaps 300 to 500 feature-length films, running between 80 and 140 minutes, are made annually in the United States. In 1987, the 13 largest U.S. film companies made 186 films (of 511 altogether) to fill 22,721 screens, investing in each an average of $16 million plus $9 million for their marketing and earning $4.2 billion in box office receipts in this country. (In 1990, over a billion theatrical admissions brought in more than $5 billion.) Video exploitation of theatrical films doubles this income, and overseas income adds another third to the total. With subsidiary sales (toys, records, etc.) added in, a single blockbuster's gross income nowadays can approach a billion dollars all by itself. A "major" motion picture will cost $35 million to make and another $15 million to market. Even Spike Lee's shoestring first big venture *She's Gotta Have It* (1986) cost nearly $200,000 in borrowed money, mortgaged houses and businesses, and deferred fees. The 1988 remake of the low-budget horror film *The Blob* (1958) cost the industry average for a film that year, $17 million, 100 times the cost of the original. Yet, in 1958 the original cost more than 100 new automobiles, or ten new houses. Such numbers soon sound meaningless. But each dollar is someone's real money.

No one puts up such large sums for Art's Sake. Investors hope for high returns to compensate for the very high risks. Industrial, commercial, and educational films are paid for in advance by the clients who commission them, serve specific short-term purposes, and are not expected to earn their own way in the world. Avant-garde films explore filmic ideas within whatever lean budgets their makers can muster, personal money sometimes supplemented by grants from foundations. But narrative films are like sporting events in our culture. They compete with other such events to provide primary leisure-time "entertainment" in the marketplace. Like sports they meet a persistent human need for shared perception of extraordinary human capability in conflict with itself; and like sports they are contemporary forms of the public rituals all cultures develop for themselves, attended as religiously. But films are made as financial speculations, with venture capital, by people who hope that large numbers of other people will pay to see them. Films don't need to be original or profound. They need to be popular.

Any film's popularity depends on intricate but customary visual, auditory, and narrative conventions which help audiences understand what they see and guide their responses. Some films use these conventions in traditional ways, and some innovatively. Both can become box-office blockbusters, and some films like *Casablanca* (1942), thought at first to be one kind, turn out also to be the other. Painting and the other traditional arts within motion pictures also depend on their own various conventions, which provide a kind of common language, familiar yet fresh when recombined. Films tend to use these other conventions, along with their own uniquely cinematic coventions. With them, films can express extremely subtle and powerful things, yet remain accessible to audiences who merely want to be entertained. Even entertainment films—the most expensive kind, therefore necessarily the most popular, and therefore necessarily the least venturesome or perplexing—use intricate but familiar conventions to satisfy audiences who want to feel gratified, amused, or moved, without being baffled.

Audiences know much more about these conventional languages than they think they know. Some films even parody film conventions knowingly, especially as they recur in the mannerisms of certain genres or directors, and regular film goers immediately get the joke. This handbook attempts to make that knowledge systematically available to the deliberate critical perception the best films require and reward, to help viewers become more discriminating in both senses of that word. Though the handbook emphasizes the customary, it does not deny that many films use customs in unaccustomed ways, with a truculent or cheerful perversity or with bold originality; nor does this book deny that other cultures and subcultures may use different codes when formulating their own public displays. Some theory-conscious filmmakers try to evade the supposedly built-in ideological implications of some codes, but their survival over many decades is itself evidence of their effectiveness as dependable ways to create significant experiences for large numbers of people. Within the international culture that film itself has created, the customs persist. We all go to the movies, and we all understand them. Mostly.

ACKNOWLEDGMENTS

A book presenting basic ideas with some subtlety is indebted to many people. The Museum of Modern Art's early screenings eventually made me what I am today, as they have many others. A seminar once conducted by the American Film Institute School for Advanced Study in Beverly Hills, under a Rockefeller grant, informed me what films are to the people who actually make them. Some former graduate students who are now seasoned scholars will recognize their own ideas here and there, including Marshall Deutelbaum, Allen Fischler, Joe Gomez, and Sidney Rosenzweig; when film studies was not quite academically respectable we all acted as if it were, until the legend became the fact. Two decades of undergraduates provided the first occasions for the notes elaborated here; many know who they are and know that I know. Friends and previous or present colleagues whose passion for films or for ideas about films, or whose books, articles, or conversations, have all entered and affected this book, include Skip Battaglia, Bob Carringer, David Cook, Janet Cutler, Ron Gottesman, George Grella, Ed Jahiel, Dan Kimmel, John Kuiper, Julia LeSage, Sam McElfresh, Sylvia Moukous, John Mueller, Sean Nolan, Connie Penley, Lee Poague, Andrew Ross, Kaja Silverman, John Waters, and Hayden White, among many more. These I hope will find this book useful as well as familiar, though of course not all will agree with all things in it. I especially want to thank readers of an earlier draft, who did not agree with all of it, and whose suggestions were always welcome and often adopted: Rick Altman, University of Iowa; Robert Carringer, University of Illinois; Mark Charney, Clemson University; E. Michael Desilets, Glassboro State College; Joseph A. Gomez, North Carolina State University; Frances Kavenik, University of Wisconsin–Parkside; John Kuiper, University of North Texas; Phil Skerry, Lakeland Community College; and Janice R. Welsch, Western Illinois University.

The archive of the International Museum of Photography at George Eastman House challenges any film scholar and chastens those situated in Rochester. Its first curator, Jim Card, first showed me its enormous potential, which in turn urged on us the creation of the University of Rochester's Film Studies Program. Its present curator, Jan-Christopher

Horak, and his associate, Paolo Cherchi-Usai, are also colleagues in that program, who understand contemporary film scholarship and its needs and contribute to both. The Film Department's Robin Bolger is another dedicated archivist who has been unfailingly helpful and courteous. The frame enlargements from *High Noon* are as abundant as they are in this book because their splendid print was available. Nearly all the illustrations in this book are by the courtesy of the George Eastman House archive and its curatorial staff; the few exceptions originate in the URFSC collection.

A brief comment on those illustrations. Most are copies of production and publicity stills, poured forth when the films were released to provide free publicity, made when the films were made but often angled, framed, and lit differently, and often posed rather than acted. They show much, but their analytic uses are limited. Some pictures in this book are, however, enlarged individual frames of actual films. They too show much. But because films compose their dramatic meanings in sequences, with

The publicity still from *High Noon* (1952) opposite, shows Mrs. Will Kane (Grace Kelly) shooting a gunman in the back (A). The same moment in the actual film is more bewildering because only part of an edited sequence. We earlier had seen Mrs. Kane enter the building and peer anxiously out the window, a huge gun on the wall ignored in the foreground. Later we see a gunman reloading his pistols, hear a gunshot, and see his body fall forward to reveal a window with a woman in it apparently watching (B). Only then comes an explanatory reverse shot from inside the building, showing Mrs. Kane standing sorrowfully by the window with a gun in her hand. Audiences cheer when they finally comprehend what this means.

B

shots in motion following one another, no one frame can serve all analytic purposes adequately either. Nor can videotape or videodisks, which show movements and sequences but lack scale and detail and provide no sense of audience. Whatever the fit uses of illustrations, even when we confront the real thing in a theater an alert eye and critical tact remain indispensable.

A

This book is dedicated to the development of such eyes and minds. It is dedicated as well to all the people mentioned above, who are all similarly dedicated. Also to Kathy, Michael, and Jim, for hearing me out on movies no matter what, and to Steve and Jill for hearing them out. Also to David, for whom films are still magical, and to Emma, for whom they are still sociable. Above all to Rita, who shares with me all her own life, mind, and feelings, not only about movies.

Richard M. Gollin

1

Making and Viewing Films

PRODUCTION

Movies are manufactured collaboratively by closely coordinated artists, managers, technicians, and workers. As when a house is being built, some artisans appear only when the project requires specialized skills, and others remain with the project from start to finish. Actual filmmaking occurs in three distinct stages: preproduction, principal photography, and postproduction.

Preproduction includes all the preliminary creative, developmental, and planning stages, from the first gleam in a scriptwriter's eye, or a producer's first decision to purchase the film rights to a novel, through selecting of the principal artists and negotiating of their contracts with their agents, to the building of studio sets and preparing of locations for the first and all subsequent days of scheduled shooting. Preproduction lasts often more than two years and rarely less than three months.

Principal photography includes all phases of a film's actual "production"—the creating of the basic acted film footage with accompanying recorded dialogue. This production period usually lasts thirty to eighty

In a room which is not a room but a dressed set on a sound stage, James Stewart acts, Alfred Hitchcock watches, and the camera crew shoots *Rear Window* (1954) from outside the window, occupying space the film defines as midair. All this Hitchcock planned with his usual care during months of preproduction.

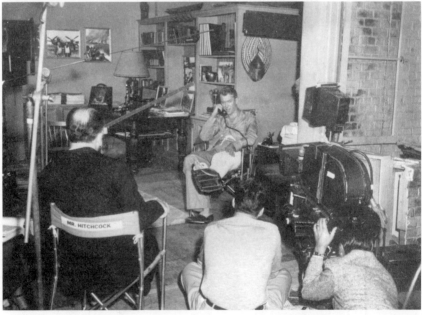

days, each long day covering perhaps 3 pages of script and generating perhaps two or three minutes of final used footage.

Postproduction includes all reshooting of particular shots, editing, dubbing or looping of voices, mixing of sounds, creation of the music track and adding it to the mix, completion of special effects shots, previewing, and fine-tuning of the film. This process takes from a tight three months to an additional year. These three stages end with a complete negative ready for printing; full production costs are therefore called **negative costs**.

DISTRIBUTION, EXHIBITION, AND MARKETING

The general public still does not know the film exists, although tipster fan magazines may leak "insider" information about it. Films made speculatively by individuals can end up "on the shelf" at this point,

Erich von Stroheim directs ZaSu Pitts and Gibson Gowland in one of the scenes from *Greed* (1924) that actually survived the studio's infamous postproduction re-editing, the final version cut from ten hours to five, then to four, finally to a mutilated but commercially acceptable two hours.

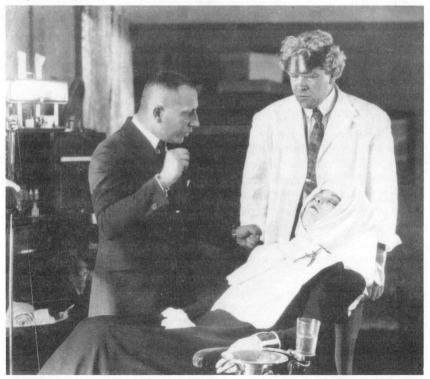

awaiting festival screenings, foreign or cable TV sales, or perhaps a studio distribution contract—Claudia Weill's first feature *Girlfriends* (1978) got such a contract after it was made, as did Michael Moore's documentary *Roger and Me* (1989). But even a studio-sponsored film with big stars may be buried by one of the industry's frequent changes in top management; new studio chiefs may not be willing to risk money and prestige marketing someone else's films. Or despite expensive stars the film may turn out to be a dog not worth further investment. Or the studio may decide the film is a dog even if it isn't. Some films eventually turn up in video rental stores or on cablevision. Some take on new life by word of mouth. Many merely disappear.

Without another way to distribute a film, an eager independent filmmaker may decide to **four-wall** a film's first screenings, renting a complete theater in a major city, ushers and all, outright, so reviewers can notice its existence and perhaps celebrate its virtues. This happened with Joan Micklin Silver's first feature *Hester Street* (1975), a fine film at first ignored, about adult Jewish immigrants at the turn of the century, shot in black and white, and directed by a woman; distributors looked at these as three strikes against the film until it opened under its own auspices and found its own audiences.

A commercially funded film, however, will usually receive the **distribution, exhibition,** and **marketing** appropriate to its income-producing potential. This process includes the printing of **projection positives** for screening in contracted theaters, perhaps only a few in selected cities ("markets") to build the film's publicity portfolio, but perhaps 2000 such prints to saturate theaters across the country all at once. The distribution process includes contracting with theater owners for maximum ensured exposure of the film to potential customers and a maximum ensured share of the box office receipts. These theater owners, like Loews or General Cinema, may control hundreds of screens. At first they usually keep only 10 percent of the box office receipts themselves and profit only from the overpriced popcorn and soft drinks. To be sure they have attractive "product" for their screens, especially during school holidays, exhibitors will sometimes agree to **blind bidding** for an unseen film still in production or agree to **block booking** of one very attractive film in a package with others (though often illegal, neither practice is rare).

Marketing also requires preparation of **publicity materials.** These include short **trailers** or "coming attractions" shown earlier in theaters, at times designed by people who have not seen the film, short **commercials** to saturate TV when the film is released, and long *The Making of . . .* documentaries for time-fillers on cable TV. There are standardized **newspaper** and **magazine advertisements, press kits** laden with glossy photos, biographies of the stars and artists, plot summaries, and sample favorable reviews, and posters and lobby cards. Marketing also includes the negotiating of **subsidiary sales;** such sales of related records and tapes, clothing, franchise foods tie-ins, or toys are now a big business in themselves. Feature articles about the film are planted or encouraged in newspapers and fan magazines, with junkets carrying journalists to hospitable interviews with the stars. The film's famous names are booked onto local and national TV talk shows, which they lend their celebrity while publicizing the film as earlier contracted. All-in-all a major film is always floated to the public on great waves of "hype" (hyperbole, exaggeration).

These marketing costs often amount to half again the original negative cost and can cost more than the negative if the film's producers are intent to buy the audience to protect their original investment. Films made for TV rather than theatrical release are shot perhaps three times faster, often prepaid for by the network and tailored to appeal to a given demographic segment of consumers. Advertisers then use these films to attract audiences to their commercials.

SCREEN CREDITS

Most of the people responsible for whatever appears on the screen are credited, the important ones in the **main title credits** at the film's beginning, the others in **end credits.**

Screen credits bore most audiences, who endure the opening displays naming major artists because they must and who turn their backs on end credits listing lesser collaborators in order to get to the parking lots. Audiences may know the stars' names and perhaps the director's, but they usually don't care about the others. Yet credits are essential to the industry's view of itself. They fulfill legal obligations; and they constitute the individual artist's or technician's signature on his or her work as well as its official certification, a prideful acknowledgement in the presence of one's peers. Credits are also a form of payment, carefully negotiated, the highest-valued coin being a lone name on the screen "above the title," in letters as large as the title's.

Graphic styles and behind-the-title shots are carefully considered and designed and are themselves credited. The film is after all under way as soon as the studio logo appears and music or a significant silence fills the theater: A receptive mood is being created, a predominant visual style begins to establish itself, and often narrative information is conveyed until the last opening credit—these days the director's—allows the audience to watch the film undistracted. The old postcard views of Martinique behind the main titles of Euzhan Palcy's *Sugar Cane Alley*

(1983) establish an ironic but affectionate attitude toward the island's shabby gentility, and the canceled postage stamps seen here and there on the images convert the whole film into a kind of postcard from the past. We then settle in to watch.

A story ceases when end credits begin rolling up from the bottom of the screen, the final mood supported by accompanying music, the words "The End" nowadays rarely needed. Sometimes rejected takes or sequences can be seen behind the end credits, as in *Citizen Kane* (1941), *Being There* (1979), or *Married to the Mob* (1988), confirming that the film is a made object, a parable, or a shared experience, not a mere photographed event.

Some credit sequences—Saul Bass's for Alfred Hitchcock, or Jean-Luc Godard's for his own films—are themselves artful and worth separate study. Not all credits speak the whole truth: The last director of several may end up with the sole screen credit, like Victor Fleming with *Gone with the Wind* (1939) or Stanley Kubrick with *Spartacus* (1960); and sometimes major artists help out in ways inadequately credited. But as viewers grow more sophisticated, they attend more closely to the lists of various jobs, artists, and technicians who helped solve a film's problems, and they remain especially alert to the way the credits are presented. In this century and especially in this "postmodern" era of mixed media, art often includes words, which signify in different ways from images. How a film's main title and end credits are designed, the rhythms they create while rolling past, and the collaborative efforts they signify, are all part of the film.

Despite the film community's general liberal feelings, nearly every name mentioned in the credits will belong to a white male. Many credited names are a legacy of the marginalized turn-of-the-century Jewish immigrants who first developed this once-vulgar branch of the entertainment industry. Until recently, black filmmakers never really prospered, though established studios gestured occasionally toward satisfying black concerns. A few superb cinematographers have been black (Gordon Parks), or Asian (James Wong Howe), and some members of film crews have always been Chicanos.

Few or none have been women. In fact, movie ads in newspapers still reveal only a sprinkle of women's names among the major credits reproduced there in microscopic print. In mainstream filmmaking, women are often scriptwriters, costume and set designers, and editors. Some are directors: Perhaps a half-dozen in this country now make features regularly, every few years, and perhaps another half-dozen in Europe. More are producers or co-producers, and one headed a major studio for a short time. Films have always had actresses of course, though some now call themselves "actors" in an attempt to make the

In Joan Micklin Silver's *Crossing Delancey* (1988), Amy Irving and Suzy Roche converse easily with each other at a bar; like the woman one seat over, they are in possession of their own space, more relaxed and themselves than when men direct such scenes. Possibly male directors are not comfortable with the idea of women sitting at bars on their own.

term gender neutral (they note that no woman director is a "directress"). But when a film's credits seem to contain a noticeable proportion of women's names, or those of a suppressed minority, usually someone has deliberately employed such people. Despite decades of raised consciousness and expectations, films are still made mainly by men, using women, and films still present what men hope will attract audiences, including women.

Studios

Until the 1950s single large corporations made movies, each providing the management, financing, script development, trained actors and technicians, laboratories, set construction facilities and production stages, and marketing frameworks for a few or perhaps fifty feature-length films each year, of "A" (high budget), "B" (lower budget), even of "C" and "D" quality to keep salaried employees busy. Growing out of the early fly-by-night days of the film industry, and often consolidating with each other, each studio developed its own stable of contracted "stars," artistic personnel, and technical and crafts personnel, and each studio's head was a "mogul" exercising total control over his studio's "product." Factories attempting to maintain a steady flow of profitably marketable commodities, the studios were nevertheless uneasily dependent on intangibles such as talent, temperament, and creativity. The ability to organize artists to serve corporate purposes was highly honored.

The "majors" were Metro-Goldwyn-Mayer, Twentieth Century Fox, Paramount, and Warner Brothers; the "minors" were Columbia, RKO, Universal, and a shifting group of smaller secondary studios (Chaplin, Keystone, Goldwyn, Selznick, United Artists, Disney, Republic, Hal Roach, Monogram), many located on Gower Street in Los Angeles, which became known as Gower Gulch, or Poverty Row. The major studios and some others owned or were owned together with certain theater chains; thus the studios needed to make films to fill seats in those particular theaters, some large and prestigious, some not. Most studios developed particular styles and subjects. MGM was known for sophisticated quality dramas about people who were—or behaved— upper middle-class, Warners for tough working-class conflict films and occasional "prestige" costume dramas, and Republic for cheap action films. Much of their work was carried on by subsidiary production units; the "Freed Unit" at MGM for example was responsible for many opulent MGM musicals during the forties and fifties.

Since the 1950s, studios have been owned by larger industrial conglomerates and occupied mostly with contracted TV production for independent producers and networks. Some studios have disappeared or sold their land to real estate developers (the old Fox back lot is now the high-rise Century City complex). Others provide only financing, distribution, or production services. Many studios contract with independent producers for a stated number of pictures and have relatively little influence on the final product.

Filmmaking arrangements and their corporate structures tend now to be unique for each film, a "bankable package" of principal artists and a script assembled and conditionally contracted by a producer or agent, financed by an investment group (some combination of commercial banks, foreign investors seeking tax shelters or foreign distribution rights, insurance companies, studios, and individuals), and eventually made at hired production facilities. The confusion of many names now introducing or "presenting" a film represents an intricate archaeology of business deals often impossible for the uninitiated to uncover. A studio logo preceding the film—the MGM lion improbably framed by elegant Latin declaring that art is its own reward, the forbidding Warner's shield, Paramount's mountain haloed by stars, even Tri-Star's dreamy Pegasus—may nowadays acknowledge no more than a marketing agreement reached after the film was completed. Even "Hollywood"—a section of Los Angeles where some films were made in the old days— now signifies no more than "planned in the United States," since studios can be owned by foreigners and films can be financed overseas, shot on location anywhere, and then finished in Canada, England, or Italy to save money. Many originate in the New York City area: the Astoria Studio across the East River was built by Paramount during the twenties for films starring Broadway performers and is still in heavy use.

Producer

The **producer** is the chief business executive responsible for the film's corporate management (financing, business planning, insurance, contracting, hiring, renting, cost-control, and so forth). Once, as in the days of David O. Selznick, of *Gone with the Wind* (1939), or Hal Wallis, of *Casablanca* (1942), producers could imagine themselves the creators of their films because they hired, advised, approved, fought with, and fired the people actually making the film. These days producers only occasionally exercise creative judgment over a film. Rather, they will trust that the "talent" are performing as expected and will work to keep the film's costs within the projected budget. In this sense a producer is the film's *impresario*, the organizer of the occasion for creating it, responsible for providing its means. An **executive producer** may exercise this role, or a producer may be an administrator overseeing the business problems of a particular film day by day for an executive producer (a line producer). Producers maintain staffs of accountants and assistants, down to the people who arrange lunches and transportation for the cast and crew when on location (these too are credited). Sometimes contractually a star, director, or writer will receive a producer credit of some kind, especially if that person's money underwrote key decisions or that person's participation was part of the film's bankability. Now, as in the old studio days, some directors get the freedom to make a film their way by also producing it.

Script Writer

The **script writer** may create the screenplay and attempt to market it or may be hired to write one based on a **concept** (story idea), a **treatment** (story outline of several pages or more, with character descriptions), or an **adaptation** of a novel, play, or short story. In general, the greater the literary work, the less cinematically satisfying the film, because the work's original qualities may be untranslatable or because the script writer feels too intimidated to make essential changes. Great films often originate in potboiler novels or short stories. A film based on an enor-

Alfred Hitchcock explains the compositional strategy of a shot from *Strangers on a Train* (1951), drawing it as if for the film's original storyboard.

mously popular novel such as *Gone with the Wind* or *The Godfather* is said to be presold, already well-known, and the novel's best-remembered scenes must be written into the film even if unsuitable. Usually film rights to popular novels are purchased well before the book is published.

Written in a prescribed format, a **screenplay** will average 120 to 140 typescript pages containing fifty to sixty master scenes, each scene numbered and marked "interior" or "exterior," "day" or "night," with all the dialogue provided (some scripts prescribe every shot, but directors rarely welcome such incursions into their own prerogatives). The director or other writers may revise the screenplay (*Citizen Kane*'s shooting script was the seventh draft, called the "third revised final"). The director and art director may also create a **storyboard** resembling a comic strip for each sequence of shots, especially for difficult or expensive sequences

(Alfred Hitchcock and David Lean are famous for storyboarding every-thing). At some point script deficiencies may be repaired by an unac-knowledged script doctor, a specialist skilled at solving other people's problems. The Screenwriters' Guild will adjudicate any arguments about proper crediting.

Screenwriters' talents provide the basis for everyone else's work, including usually the odd twists of story and character that make the film seem fresh and perceptive, the memorable lines, and the film's profound point if any. Yet producers tend to think of these creative men and women as mere suppliers of raw material for the product, essential to begin with but to be used and then dismissed. Like novelists, playwrights, and poets, screenwriters work mostly alone. They are rarely known to the public. The best are appreciated by being very well paid, but many move to direct their own scripts as soon as they can.

Director

The **director** is the film's primary creative authority at least during actual production, ultimately responsible for virtually everything that appears on the screen. Once a director was expected to decide on camera posi-tions, block the actors (direct their movements during the shot), elicit their performances, deliver the resulting footage on schedule, and then move on to another project (though some did much more). More recently, directors have claimed the status of superstars or *auteurs*, total artists involved in the project from early in its script development through its final release to the public, even its afterlife on the video screen.

Such a director tries to contract for the power to determine or veto *anything* from casting through set design to **final cut** (though few ever achieve this ultimate power), so the film can express that one person's judgment and sensibility in every particular. The resulting film is, as a pretitle announcement nowadays informs us with varying degrees of truth (e.g., "An Amy Heckerling Film"), *that* person's personal expres-sion. Others may suggest, propose, or insist, but the director finally decides; and if the director is often praised for other people's contribu-tions to a film, he or she also bears blame for any of the film's deficiencies. Usually the director will meet early with the cinematographer, the pro-duction designer, and other major artists and technicians to discuss and settle together the film's basic visual style and strategies.

There are also **first assistant directors** and **second assistant directors** to assist with cast and crew management, crowd control and coordina-tion, and even a **DGA trainee** apprenticed to the picture by the Director's Guild of America who can serve as a gofer. Someone close to the director will concentrate on **continuity** (formerly a script girl), making sure that

For *The Maltese Falcon* (1941), his first directorial job after a decade of writing scripts for others, John Huston directs his father Walter how to stagger mortally wounded into a private eye's office carrying a mysterious black bird, while Humphrey Bogart watches half-hidden by the camera. Like his heroes, Huston at times overreaches, but many of his films are as memorable as this first one; in a unique accomplishment of sorts, Huston directed his father Walter, his daughter Anjelica, and himself among others, to Academy Awards.

an actor's clothing, ongoing gestures, mussed hair, or props are the same in different shots made at different times of supposedly continuous action. An ambitious film may also have a **second unit director** simultaneously shooting certain necessary shots elsewhere, when principal actors are not involved. A producer may replace a director during shooting while keeping the usable footage, although this is risky and rare, and the director may have a play or pay contractual guarantee making it uneconomical as well. After winning many Academy Awards with *The Deer Hunter* (1978), Michael Cimino was signed to a nearly unbreakable contract for *Heaven's Gate* (1980). His extravagant perfectionism then bankrupted United Artists.

Cast

The **cast** includes the players and walk-ons who constitute the dramatic characters, the **stars** most people go to the movies to see, and the **support-**

ing players they see whether or not they notice them. A star's personality and celebrity can provide a film's bankability. It is difficult to recall that these stellar presences are nevertheless and primarily actors doing a day's work day after day, that they are merely highly visible, talented people whose images have been inflated by fantasy into other things altogether.

The position and size of an actor's name in the credits is negotiated by the actor's agent. Usually actors will yield their own sense of their roles to a director's judgment, since only the director has weighed how all the dramatic roles will play with each other (a hero may confront silly or tough heroines in different ways, with comic or melodramatic effect depending on the director's sense of the picture); often only the director holds in mind how the role should develop sequentially when— as is customary—shots are made out of sequence, while sets still exist or certain performers are still available. Some actors are stubborn ("difficult") about their performances, while others compliantly do whatever they're told (sometimes brilliantly). But often a scene represents a collaboration between the director and the talented, experienced players who each contribute interpretations, movements, and ideas, the director reserving final approval. Supporting players are usually reliable performers who are hired to do what they are known to do well. They may share a main title credit with other lesser actors but often are listed only in the end credits. For their own reasons well-known stars sometimes make **cameo** appearances in lesser roles and are often not credited at all.

Lesser performers or **bit players** and uncredited **extras** are usually provided by a separately credited **casting agency.** Extras are ordinary-looking people hired to fill out a street scene, hotel lobby, or crowd (real passers-by might unwittingly attract attention, look at the camera or crew, or recognize a star walking alongside them, ruining the shot). If extras speak briefly, like the then-unknown Alan Ladd in *Citizen Kane* asking "Or, Rosebud?", or the then-unknown Richard Dreyfuss in *The Graduate* (1967) asking "Shall I get the cops?", they are paid more for their day's work. Dangerous shots are made with **stunt doubles** for lead players and other **stunt men** and **women** who crash the cars and take the falls, their equipment and planning overseen by a **stunt coordinator.** The stars each also have **camera doubles** or stand-ins of the same build and complexion who stand in the stars' places and endure the tedium while cameras are focused and the set lit; these are never seen in the final film. Sometimes an uncredited professional dancer will double for a star who can't dance well enough, as with Jennifer Beals in *Flashdance* (1983), and not infrequently an uncredited dubbing actor or singer will provide the voice for a major player, as with Rita

A stunt man substitutes for the actor Steve Railsback, who plays a stunt man supposedly substituting for another actor, in *The Stunt Man* (1980). The godlike director (Peter O'Toole) of the film within the film, named "Eli Cross" to underline the point, manipulates various ostensible realities to thrust the stunt man through ritual scenarios toward his own redemption, while the audience is frequently tricked about which world it is watching, the one it sees filmed or the one it sees created by film.

Hayworth's famous "Put the Blame on Mame" in *Gilda* (1946); this common phenomenon provides the comic climax of *Singin' in the Rain* (1952). Sometimes an uncredited body double will provide intimate glimpses of a character's body when a main performer is unwilling or inappropriately endowed.

Director of Photography

The **director of photography** or cinematographer is the artist and technician responsible for the photographic look of the film, its lighting, color values, visual texture, and framing. This person must do the job flawlessly, since reshooting ruined footage can be hideously expensive and even impossible, and must provide especially difficult shots if wanted, such as silhouettes in mist against a setting sun. The credit may note membership in the American Society of Cinematographers (A.S.C.), the small self-selected guild of experts who shoot most high-budget U.S. films and TV programs, and who advise each other about difficult photographic processes (in Britain, the B.S.C.).

A cinematographer has three principal assistants: the **camera operator** (sometimes called the **cameraman** in the credits), who actually operates the camera; the **focus-puller,** who rides the front of the camera to change its focus as the camera or the action move closer or further away; and the **clapper-loader,** who appears at the beginning of each shot with a chalked clapboard identifying the film, shot, take, etc., so that thousands of takes can be each tagged and synchronized with the recorded sound; the clapper-loader also sees that the camera is loaded with enough appropriate film stock.

The cinematographer also oversees lighting of the set as the director, the set designer, and long personal experience may dictate. Some cinematographers have their own distinctive lighting styles, opulent or stark, and some a considerable range from richly sculpturesque to flat-lit home movie (Raoul Coutard has provided Jean-Luc Godard with both kinds). Some are in fact responsible for bravura compositions usually credited to the director. The technical crew for lights includes a **gaffer** or chief electrician (theater jargon for "the old man," Grandpa), a **best boy** to serve as the gaffer's chief assistant, **grips** led by a **key grip** to haul heavy lights around, and many others.

Production Designer

The **production** or **set designer** (or **art director**) is, along with the director and the cinematographer, responsible for the look of the film, primarily responsible for designing and creating each set according to the budgets and expected strategies for each shot. When studio production predominated, the art director might assign a particular subordinate to each film. Each of these in turn would draw or commission sketches and architectural drawings of rooms, buildings, facades, huge flat paintings used as backdrops, or even whole streets, all with due regard for mood, period, dramatic necessity, room for required technical equipment, and camera angles; each subordinate would then supervise construction of these sets (or selection and preparation of the "real" location if actual buildings and places are being used) according to the shooting schedule. The studio's art director would then take primary credit, as Van Nest Polglase did with *Citizen Kane,* though his brilliant assistant Perry Ferguson in fact created the sets. Now, the person credited is the person responsible.

Some set designers are associated with particular kinds of films (Harry Horner with atmospheric period films for example, or Richard Sylbert

A

B

Harry Horner's production design for *The Heiress* (1949), based on Henry James's novel *Washington Square,* includes a sketch of a grand staircase with a huge mirror on the landing, for camera angles showing the heroine entrapped in the elegant prison of her father's house (A). The staircase in the film elaborates this intention (B).

16

with the suave decor of Mike Nichols or Warren Beatty films). Much attributed to the director's visual style may be the designer's. In theater most sets are three-sided, the audience peering through the invisible "fourth wall." In film sets can be any-sided, scaled down or scaled up (or with forced perspective both); and two adjacent rooms or the walls of a single room can be in fact miles from each other, depending on the shot's necessities. The art director usually oversees the dressing of the set as well, the assemblage of **props** ("properties") making up a convincing yet appropriate clutter of furniture, curtains, lamp posts, or parked cars (**property masters** with their own assistants are in charge of these); part of many sets are the huge paintings of distant sunsets or skylines glimpsed through windows. The art director may also oversee special photographic effects, such as the glass or matte paintings used to substitute for huge buildings, cliffs, or space ships. Those who supply the props or create the more elaborate **special effects** are separately credited, along with the coordinators and labs hired to provide these specialized services. Like lights, sets can be heavy. Grips supervised by a chief grip or key grip haul the equipment and segments of sets wherever needed.

Costume Designer

At a minimum, the **costume designer** selects the clothing worn by the players in different parts of the film but often even designs that clothing with due regard for the required action (rough fighting, comic tearing, or vigorous dancing), for the period and for the social pretensions or moods of the characters implied by their clothing. Life's elaborate dress codes and rituals signal significant information to us about people who conform or assert their eccentricity while seeming to conform, and these codes carry even more elaborately into films. Even rags must be designed, and can seem clean or dirty, disgusting or picturesque. Audiences often take cues for their own clothing from costumes in films they have seen (as with the *Annie Hall* look), spreading the film's fame or notoriety; costume designers know they are often creators of popular fashions and try for subtle distinctiveness. Designers of teen flicks need to lead changing teen dress codes, which all teenagers understand implicitly, so the film won't seem dated when it is released a year later. The costumes are looked after and provided according to the day's shooting schedule by **wardrobe;** the costumes for extras and for low-budget films are rented or perhaps supplied by the player.

Composer

The **composer,** or **music director,** composes or selects music to be heard during the film, classical or popular, symphonic or guitar, traditional or modern. If there is **source music** in the film (a song played, sung, or hummed by a character), the composer will provide it early, and the composer is usually hired early in the film's production, when the expected strategy for background music can be discussed with the Director. But usually work on the score does not begin in earnest until the film has reached late stages of editing, so the synchronizing of music and dramatic action can be precise. Then the composing, timing, orchestrating, and assembling and conducting of instrumentalists, bands, choruses, and orchestras must be done quickly, so a completed tape master can be delivered for mixing with the sound track before the film's release. A sound track album with scores and songs created or assembled for the film, or modified from the film's sound track, is now a routine part of a film's subsidiary sales and income. End credits listing old songs, performers, and groups on the track of a nostalgic film can roll endlessly.

Editor

As do cinematographers, those especially distinguished by guild membership list an acronym after their name (A.C.E. for American Cinema Editors). An editor receives the footage as shot and rough-assembles the selected takes according to the film's **cutting continuity,** a special script created for the purpose, so that soon after the film is shot a **rough-cut** or complete assemblage of all the shots in their proper sequence can be seen from beginning to end. The film is now complete, except for titles, retakes, special effects or second-unit shots, the fine-tuning of individual shots, and later decisions about the timing of sequences or reediting or elimination of whole scenes (which end up on the "cutting room floor" or literally, in film vaults preserving them for later inclusion perhaps in a foreign release or videocassette version). The laboratory keeps the negative uncut in pristine state in its vaults but provides a **work print** the editor and various assistants can cut and splice, each shot logged and each frame coded so the lab can eventually duplicate the completed work print with the original negative (even the "negative cutter" is credited). The lab then provides an **answer print,** except for color balancing the finished film, printed with an optical sound track fit for standard theater projectors.

Editing being one of the primary arts of film, the director often works closely with the editor, and good editors have saved many dull or awkward sequences with artful or ingenious cutting. *Jaws* (1975) lacked a shot essential to its continuity showing the shark-hunting boat starting to be pulled backward; the editor Verna Fields looked into her waste barrel and made one out of another shot run backward. By his own account Woody Allen's longtime editor Ralph Rosenblum radically re-shaped *Annie Hall* in the cutting room; when he was replaced by his assistant Susan Morse, Allen's films took on more sedate rhythms, per-haps not coincidentally.

Sound

Not usually included among the main title credits, and more technicians than artists, the sound recorders, boom operators (who hold micro-phones on long poles above the camera's field of vision), sound editors, mixers, balancers, dubbers, and re-recorders provide the complex aural environment which *is* the sound track. The dialogue is recorded sepa-rately during shooting (in studios more often than on location), or it is later dubbed by **ADR editors** who work with automatic dialogue replacement equipment. Sound editing is especially important when sound is being used expressionistically to comment on or heighten dra-matic effects. With constant upgrading of home-audio standards and therefore of audience expectations, demands for higher-quality sound tracks never let up (Dolby stereo, digital recording, and Lucas's multi-speaker THX theater systems are now commonplace). Films may use this improved sound quality dramatically (for example, to create ambigu-ous sounds which *clearly* could be *either* a woman's scream or a tire's screech, the audience as uncertain as the characters), but most films only sound better than they once did.

A sound editor's services are often hired by contracting with the companies they work for. These maintain recorded libraries of thousands of common sounds and noises to modify, mix, modulate, and synchro-nize onto the film. Some editors called **Foley artists** (after a well-known sound effects editor) know how to make new sounds. Footsteps on gravel or wooden floors, in mud, closets, or haunted castles, must sound right if they are to be heard at all; and in martial arts films legs must whistle through the air with impossibly devastating speed, sounding like whips, which in fact could be providing the sound we hear. A Foley artist or editor can substitute selected sound effects for the inade-quate noises actually made on the set. In Brian DePalma's *Blow Out* (1981), John Travolta plays a sound editor looking for a terrified scream to dub into a horror film when the actress can't do one; he is finally horrified to find one.

Other Credits

Many more are credited, ranging from crucial consultants through armies of accountants and auditors to luncheon caterers, even car rental agencies. The end credits for the independent *sex, lies, and videotape* (1989) include its lawyers, insurance company, and completion bond company, no doubt all essential contributors. The end credits for *Memphis Belle* (1990) refer after long lists of names to "120 other craftsmen" who contributed, men and women who might have been credited by name in a less labor-intensive film.

Many states and municipalities maintain motion picture coordinators to help with the licenses, releases, and permits needed for shooting on location (for police blocking off streets, for example, so paid pedestrians can substitute for real ones), hoping to publicize the city, share in the glamour, and encourage film companies to spend money there. Recent films set in Vietnam have been shot in the Phillipines, and Biblical deserts can be Spanish, Algerian, or Californian. Where the film was shot may explain peculiarities of period and locale and is stated late in the end credits. Film artists and technicians travel when they must, though nearly all would rather go home nights.

Independently produced, underfunded narrative and documentary films may be made with many small donations of cash, props, and expert or unsolicited advice from friends, relatives, funding organizations, townspeople, and local stores, each of them eventually thanked by name in long end credits. The less "front money" used to make the film, the longer the acknowledgements roll by.

FILM VIEWING AND AUDIENCE PARTICIPATION

People go to the movies for many reasons, elemental and sophisticated. Above all, they go to engage in imaginative play with their own identities and circumstances. Theatrical films offer audiences communal public recognition of their own private desires and fears, shared in the safety of a dark room and each other's presence. Films also offer privileged personal engagement with other lives, safe from responsibility for the consequences. So powerful is the desire for these experiences that most film goers would rather not think of a film as an object made by many different skilled individuals, each credited, each of whose professional decisions are visible on the screen. Rather, we prefer to think of a film as an induced state of mind, a place we go to "get away," to be taken out of ourselves and brought somewhere else.

Vicarious Experience

A common reason people go to the movies is that in fantasy, movies extend our personal experience into places most of us never travel, dramatizing events or ordeals most of us never confront or would wish to confront as ourselves, in worlds inhabited by people more fascinating or amusing than their counterparts in our own lives. Usually these people have extraordinary traits or capabilities: exceptional beauty, courage, or cunning, or exceptional ugliness, cowardice, or stupidity. Even ordinary familiar characters are usually more lively and personable than those we know in life. How we imaginatively enter into their worlds is extremely complicated and not well understood. Despite our "realist" assumptions, we know that a movie presents us with an artificial world only superficially resembling our own, an "authentic artifice" where highly styled or improbable adventures can take place without straining our will to believe or to suspend disbelief. Every child knows that "Once upon a time" really means "Never at any time," a ritual invitation to enter into purely fictive worlds, made up of elements of our own but altogether reconstructed. There we explore alternatives to the world we inhabit as if they were extensions of that world, as if a film were merely evidence of things not yet seen.

Whether or not filmmakers and their audiences conspire to believe that prosperous suburbs, dusty cow towns, Park Avenue mansions, or Brooklyn ghettos resemble the versions portrayed in films, the pretense is sufficient to stimulate and satisfy our curiosity about ostensible persons, places, and events beyond those of our customary rounds. Films take us where we can't go ourselves. We can believe the experience literally "educational" or broadening, the movie a kind of travelogue revealing exotic times, circumstances, people, and adventures elsewhere. Or we may not care whether those places are accurately portrayed, as long as they are colorfully different. Sometimes, like the salesman played by Steve Martin in Herbert Ross's *Pennies from Heaven* (1981) or the housewife played by Mia Farrow in Woody Allen's *The Purple Rose of Cairo* (1985), we need bright movie worlds to break the monotony, perhaps to help make a drab existence more bearable.

In another important sense film fantasies provide us with marvelous surrogate experiences, journeys into other kinds of places. Films allow privileged entry into a world of significant events, unlike our own in that everything matters, conflicts have issue, moral or psychological dilemmas can be identified and resolved, ultimate purposes are revealed or confirmed, and whatever happens "means" something which may or may not reflect whatever meaning we find or impose in our own lives. In the movies, at least, there are always reasons for things. Even apparent chance or coincidence finally reveals itself to be part of a larger design, significant, not accidental, and usually reassuring. Even an existentially constructed film like *L'Avventura* (1960), seemingly arbitrary and exploring a world without essential meaning, reaches finally a profoundly meaningful view of our human predicament in that world as its main characters themselves arrive at it. In films, as in novels and dramas but not in life, ultimate reasons finally reveal themselves.

Identifying and Role Playing

Another common reason that people go to the movies, especially young people, is to become other people. Critically sophisticated viewers know that characters on a screen are really essential dramatic functions embodied by actors, phantasms required by the story. But we rarely think of them that way. In the situations presented on film, and in the presence of screen characters creating or responding to those situations, we find our own possible states and characters elicited, sometimes our "best selves" but also other selves, tentatively reintegrated as those other people or as ourselves responding to them. We test out in the dark what it would be like to be, or be near, Dirty Harry, Scarlett O'Hara, or the Cookie Monster, and we become aware of our own similarities and differences accordingly. We test out what it might be like to be in the presence of the actors as well as the characters they play, and the traits they reveal elicit our own similar inclinations. As them, like them, or with them, we share their feelings as their dramas develop.

How we "relate" to characters on a screen varies, as how we relate to people in life varies. We say casually that we identify with them. But this can mean different things:

1   The least intimate way is merely to recognize that character's traits and capabilities, perhaps only in passing, without understanding, sensing, or caring to know about inner motives, feelings, or compulsions. The character may resemble others we have known, as we superficially "identify" anyone who looks familiar measured against memory. We maintain our distance. Secondary characters whether comic or villainous are adequately known this way, as are the type characters who recur in particular film genres, gun molls in gangster films or wisecracking best friends in romantic melodramas. So too those handsome matinee idols and fetichized glamour queens audiences use for companions in their own private fantasies; the less specifically delineated they are as characters the more easily they serve our other purposes.

2   More intimate is understanding how that character thinks and feels, as from past similar experiences we think we understand other people's inner lives. Whether they are imperious bullies, self-amused detectives, defiant streetwalkers, anxious mothers, timid clowns, or whimpering victims, we know these characters well enough and can surmise how they feel when we see what they do. Our sense of their inner purposes may be crucial to understanding the dramatic action, but even so we are not tempted to join them in feeling what they

seem to feel. When uncertain how they will respond to a situation we study their faces intently for clues, and the filmmakers usually oblige us at such moments with a close-up.

3   We may find ourselves sympathizing with characters, caring about them, our personal concerns briefly enlarged to include theirs. We share feelings to some degree with many people in life. But when we are watching movies, mere shadows, we indulge our generous or sentimental feelings much more freely. When we suffer or celebrate with the defeated or victorious Rocky, or the much-tried but finally well-rewarded women of *Working Girl* (1988) and *Pretty Woman* (1989), that's what we want to do; in fact no film without such characters or moments ever does well at the box office. Chaplin's tramp gained increasing audience sympathy as over the years he changed from an amusingly ingenious, street-smart survivor to someone more helpless and pitiable. Melodramas provide many such moments, and thrillers some, though comedies avoid them, because too-close sympathy generates pathos instead of the distanced amusement we need for viewing a buffoon's deficiencies. Berthold Brecht despised dramas providing such gluttonous feasts of

In John Ford's cavalry Western *She Wore a Yellow Ribbon* (1949), a sternly amused John Wayne disciplines an insincerely repentant Victor McLaglen, the camera close enough for us to see, feel, enjoy, and share in the affectionate respect they maintain for each other.

sentiment, and Godard disrupted them ironically in his films, but few films apart from comedies provide us a distanced or estranged space for viewing everyone with detachment. Joel and Ethan Coen's films such as *Blood Simple* (1983) or *Miller's Crossing* (1990) distance us with a tight visual style and characterization bordering on caricature. But in general the medium itself works against it.

4   More intimate still is empathizing with a character, really *as* a character, intensively imagining ourselves in that character's shoes and situation, seemingly projecting ourselves into his or her temperament and trying it on (more accurately, introjecting that temperament as implied by various overt expressions of it), and then feeling what that character feels (that is, attributing to the character what we then feel, cued by the character's responses). The relationship is highly interactive, much more so than when we are absorbed by our own imaginings while reading a book. But intermittently, or even the whole time, we remain aware that we are ourselves, role-playing. When this happens in life with people we know intimately, we seem to share their inner lives, and we suffer or celebrate as them as well as for them, oscillating between the two. Such "bonded" shared feeling is common among close members of a family, as with lovers, children, pets, dolls, and anthropomorphized cartoon creatures, and with screen characters we care strongly about. We lose ourselves at the movies because we carry fewer inhibitions into a theater. There, like children playing with dolls, we can play games of domination and submission, sublimation, transference, and projection without feeling restrained by real-world consequences.

5   Finally, for brief hallucinated moments we may become that character in imagination, reintegrating ourselves as the screen image and suppressing all irrelevant personal traits, momentarily losing our usual sense of self, feeling instead a heightened sense of our latent possibilities as elicited by that moment in the film. We then "imagine" we are the person we see, briefly unaware that we are not. We altogether lose ourselves. Much important film theory assumes that this degree of identification constitutes our usual relationship with the figments of human beings we see on the screen (and has assumed as well, also wrongly, that such rapt out-of-body experiences never cross gender lines). But this illusory ego transference remains rare, fleeting and privileged. We may seek and find it in life or art, but we are quickly enough dispossessed and back where we were.

However we shift among these states, we are cued especially by facial expressions seen close up (often a close-up is an invitation to upgrade our involvement) and by body language. In movies people seem novel or unique, but they are always far less complex than any of the real people in the audience. Often they are barely more than the clichés required by their genres. Actors fill screen characters with their own traits and try to make them credible, and we recognize and add other traits, along with suitable motivations from ourselves if not the movie. Then the characters seem as real as we are, briefly.

Contemporary film theory is especially concerned with how film "texts" "construct" our subjectivity, guiding the way the person who is watching the screen feels while watching, in effect creating their own spectators. Certainly identifying with screen characters is one way we define our own selves and ego ideals, even a means of self-discovery. Men and women "identify" in differing senses with wimps, gunslingers, shy heroes, brassy heroes, perverts, parents, children, victims, or whores with hearts of gold, each as each will, depending on individual temperament and situation. We are all these things or contain enough of their traits to reintegrate ourselves tentatively as one, then another. Feminist controversy over *Fatal Attraction* (1987) arose over who one should identify with and how: the overly dependent career woman who hounds a man to prolong their brief affair (from her point of view deserted too casually by that man), the man appalled to find that her pathological persistence threatens his family, or his threatened wife. There is no question that the film's structure expects us to collude finally with the husband and then his wronged wife in the career woman's doubly violent death. Yet at different times, especially early in the film, we identify in one sense or another with each of the three.

Most of the time people go to the movies to enter the lives of those other people on screen, to find self-justification or different selves in their screen presence. We like who we find we are at certain movies with certain actors and characters and do not like who we are at other movies, for many of the same reasons we like being with certain people in real life and not others. We feel more fully "ourselves." Young people especially attend films to test and discover those selves, through "role playing" to create what they can be. Many of the arts of film conspire to heighten and intensify these kinds of audience participation in the worlds created on screen.

Yet, the other arts within film provide many additional ways for us to participate, enjoying those arts and appreciating what they signify, with our minds as well as our feelings, critically as well as instinctively. The shapes and meanings built into films can be retrieved for our own contemplation if we can remain alert to those other arts and to their cumulative effects upon us. We can then move beyond our fascination with films as surrogate states of mind, see more, and discriminate much more.

2

Camera Conventions: Dramatic Space

I. Camera Placement
   A. Distance from Subject
   B. Angle to Object
II. Camera Movement
   A. Horizontal Movement
   B. Vertical Movement
   C. Interior Movement
III. Camera Speed
   A. Fast Motion
   B. Normal Motion
   C. Slow Motion
   D. Freeze Frame
IV. Lens Effects
   A. Focal Depth
   B. Focal Length
   C. Special Effects Lenses
V. Lighting, Film Stocks, and Filters
   A. Lighting
   B. Film Stocks and Lens Filters
VI. Frame Composition
   A. Aspect Ratio
   B. Open Compositions
   C. Closed Compositions

Because cameras photograph something "out there," viewers sometimes assume that what is photographed is "real" in some sense, that it ostensibly existed and was recorded, and that a film can therefore be judged for its fidelity to "reality." This notion confers a peculiar authenticity upon screen images; we tend despite ourselves to assume that any photograph is evidence of something that was photographed. Even the first Lumiere films (1895) are thought of as virtual documentaries or "home movies" despite the obvious care with which their subjects were chosen (usually irreversible processes), the care taken to decide when to turn the camera on or off (just before a process begins and just as it ends), and the strategic positioning of the camera and therefore viewer (usually so the action moves diagonally from rearground to foreground, not as in the Edison films horizontally across the picture plane). Moreover, many of the events recorded were obviously "set up" in advance, performed in order to be photographed. Screen reality is more usefully thought of as an artful construct, created rather than recorded. That artfulness is always evident in the image, whatever the claim that the image merely records another reality outside itself.

What we see is a screen or picture, a two-dimensional, patterned rectangular flat design, like a full-page newspaper advertisement or an abstract painting. But we also see what looks like a framed three-dimensional space, a window. No film ever ignores centuries-old esthetics for the organizing of flat rectangular areas, but most camera conventions depend on our seeing the screen as a window opening out into a world of its own, one which peculiarly resembles the world we inhabit no matter what its other peculiarities. Camera conventions all derive from the ways we see our own world and the people in it and from our customary proximities to people.

What cameras photograph is another world created by artists and technicians, seemingly familiar but made to be seen in particular ways. Cameras become our eyes and generate our responses by implying them in their own. Cameras create the on-screen texts that "construct"— as some critics say—their audiences. We see what we are meant to see, and we see it the *way* we are meant to see it.

CAMERA PLACEMENT

Distance from Object

While showing us what we see, cameras establish how much of it we see, from how far away, and what fills the intervening spaces. With different positioning or lenses a camera can seem to place the viewer further away (wide angle) or nearer (telephoto), whatever the actual proximity of camera and object being photographed. The problem of distance for the filmmaker is of physical and psychological relationships within the shot: how much should the audience see, in what relation to the background, feeling how close.

A **long shot** (or **establishing** or **cover shot**) shows full human figures, head to foot, placed in visible surroundings in clear spatial relationship to each other, as characters defined by their other possessions and attributes such as horses or luxurious hotel suites, also visible, creating opportunities for each other or constricting each other's prospects. The figures seem potentially free to move about and reorient themselves within the larger still-visible world, although they won't seem to get very far unless the camera moves to follow them and the shot is of very long duration. Distances in a long shot can vary from thousands of miles in space to the length of a room, and the field of vision can vary from vast panoramic landscapes to a single person seen all at once from top to toe.

The space between the camera and its primary object allows for intrusions of other objects partially blocking our view or for shooting through

A high-angle long shot from Billy Wilder's aptly named *Ace in the Hole* (1950), later called *The Big Carnival*, provides a shocking panorama of crowds reveling in their sensational proximity to a breaking news story about a man trapped in a cave. The scene reveals all at once the circus atmosphere that substitutes for sincere human concern, the passing train seeming to add to the festivities.

obstructions to give a sense of separation as well as distance, affecting how we see the character. This is the most traditionally remote or "theatrical" view, because it holds the audience physically apart from the action and in possession of its own mind, observant, speculative, perhaps appreciative or disapproving. Because much of what happens in films assumes that there are ongoing relationships between characters and settings not visible in any one shot, a long shot is often used for the master shot, which is the entire continuous dramatic scene photographed uninterruptedly. In the final edited version, a master will be broken up by inserted close-ups, cutaways, or other differing shots variously analyzing the action in detail for its significance, the audience remembering what lurks offscreen unseen and the actors playing to it.

A **three-quarter shot** (or **American shot,** so-called by the French when they noticed its frequency in U.S. studio films), shows the human figure from the knees up, evidently free to move within visibly defined space and choosing whether to do so, meanwhile doing other things. This distance imposes on the audience an easy familiarity with the character but provides neither intimacy nor detachment. The three-quarter shot may be used for a **one shot** (a single individual alone on screen), a **two shot** (two people seen together in the frame, a kind of small social entity in a discourse of consent or disagreement), a **three shot** (three such people), or even more. Because legs are visible, any character seems able to walk away from any other at any time; none seems trapped or transfixed.

A **medium shot (mid-shot)** shows the figure from the waist up, acting or reacting in place, usually standing or sitting still in space defined only by what is close at hand. This shot implies for the audience a comfortable, perhaps strained, but certainly privileged intimacy, and for the moment little physical action (though an action shot can seem especially energetic or violent as the character or a fist careens across the screen). Although frequently used for conversations in two shots, three shots, etc., this shot sometimes implies a lone character's isolation even in a crowded room, as in the final shot of Elaine May's *The Heartbreak Kid* (1972), whose character is conversing with another off-screen character, who may be similarly isolated in alternating shot/reverse shot. An **over-the-shoulder shot** provides the sense of shared presence inherent in a two-shot while preserving a medium shot's concentration on one individual's reaction. The brilliant final sequence of Chaplin's *City Lights* (1931) is an exchange of over-the-shoulder shots ending in a close-up. Oddly, the tramp's arm position differs in the over-the-shoulder reversals, and this accidental mismatch enforces a sense of the characters' alienation from each other despite their supposedly shared space, greatly complicating what the film means as it ends.

In a **close-up,** the head is isolated from its spatial environment and even bodily postures in order to concentrate a viewer's attention on a character's facial expressions or other subtle responses to a situation. This shot usually creates a strong sense of intimacy or empathic identification especially if of long duration, and a close-up can strengthen the force of an eye-line if the character is looking off-screen. A close-up is often used in **shot/reaction shot** sequences (showing a character looking, then at what, then how that character reacts). A close-up on any object (such as a hand, with or without a gun in it), immediately confers special significance on whatever is seen. If the top of the head and perhaps the chin are cut off by the frame in a **choke shot,** the effect is powerfully claustrophobic, implying great contained emotional intensity.

Extremes and mediums of all the above shots are commonplace, for modulation or special emphasis.

Angle to Object

A shot's angle to object establishes perspectives and audience relationships appropriate to superior, equal, or inferior beings, immediately generating additional attitudes toward whatever is seen. A **high angle** (looking down) is the most aloof, superior, detached, or indifferent point of view, showing characters on their ground, perhaps pinned to it and puny (especially in long shot), perhaps amusing, relatively helpless. Frequently the last shot in a movie is a high-angle long shot, because it separates the viewer from the action. An **extreme high-angle shot,** nearly straight down, can be the most vertiginous and—because it provides the least familiar way we can look at another person—the most dehumanizing. In Hitchcock such a shot often signifies that the character so seen is about to die. Scorsese ended the climactic bloodbath sequence of *Taxi Driver* (1976) with such a shot, perhaps in homage.

From **mid-angle** (looking across, as if from a sitting or standing position at someone similarly positioned), the viewer is placed equal with whatever is being scrutinized, involved or perhaps merely observant. A person so seen usually appears fully but merely human, strong yet fallible. Whether the camera is chest-high or waist-high further affects how we feel toward that person; the camera is rarely head-high, as we normally see people when standing. The Japanese director Ozu places his camera at eye level near the floor while his characters sit on the floor to converse with each other or with the camera as if it were the other; we share their directness.

From a **low angle** (looking up), the viewer tends to feel intimidated and relatively helpless, and whatever is seen seems strong and dominat-

Despite the difficulty of lighting sets covered with ceilings, Orson Welles insisted on showing them in many sequences of *Citizen Kane*. Here, in the last shot of the breakfast sequence depicting the fate of Kane's first marriage, a low angle reveals the couple sitting under two different archways separated by a heavy beam, the ceiling serving to image their estrangement down below.

ing, grandly heroic against the sky, though perhaps oppressed and delimited by ceilings, a hollow titan like Citizen Kane on election night. Because this angle of vision is imprinted by our childhood, it induces a subtle sense of helplessness in the viewer and perhaps the awe appropriate to staring at a statue on a high pedestal or at a parent.

A **canted angle** (the camera set off-vertical on its tripod) usually implies a world awry and out of plumb, with customary horizontals such as horizons and curb lines seen sloped and customary verticals such as trees and the edges of buildings seen angled diagonally. Canted angles are commonly used in horror films to suggest a character's disorientation and to disorient the viewer, as in George Romero's *Night of the Living Dead* (1968), or to suggest a world peculiarly unfamiliar and perhaps menacing, as in Sir Carol Reed's *The Third Man* (1949). In a frame with no strong horizontal or vertical elements, a canted camera can have other expressionistic purposes, to imply the difficulty of struggling uphill though on ostensibly level ground for example, or to create a feeling of ease when a character walks seemingly downhill toward some desirable goal.

A **subjective** (point of view or camera eye) angle presents the point of view of another character, as if the camera and viewer had momentarily become that other character. Called "POV" in scripts, the angle provides an intense implication of the audience with a character's state of mind when it is used sparingly (as Hitchcock uses it during especially suspenseful moments), but otherwise POV shots can seem somewhat factitious, too obviously manipulative (as with the horror movie cliché in which the camera momentarily takes on the vision of a mad slasher approaching a victim). Most of Robert Montgomery's crime film *Lady in the Lake* (1946) was shot from the main character's POV (we see him when he looks into a mirror), as was an episode of the TV *M*A*S*H*. But our own shifts of attention when, say, we first walk into a room are usually sharper than a camera's. Orson Welles once planned a version of Conrad's *Heart of Darkness* seen entirely from the narrator Marlowe's POV and might have solved its problems with discontinuous consciousness, but that film was never made. POV shots are most frequently used in shot/reaction-shot sequences to show what a character sees just after we see that character see something.

CAMERA MOVEMENT

Three kinds of movement are created or implied by motion pictures. First, the viewer's eye searches or scans the screen, as when we look at paintings or still photographs, led by so-called lines of action and deflected by the composition from following the screen's corners and edges out of the frame altogether. Second, characters or objects move across the screen within the fixed frame, like stage characters within a fixed proscenium arch. Third, the camera moves across, into, or away from its own field of vision, the entire framed image moving accordingly, perhaps to follow a moving character or perhaps for other reasons altogether.

The last movement is unique to cinema and in turn creates a unique effect. As the whole image moves, it defines an "off-screen space" in the viewer's peripheral vision, unseen but held in memory, not visible but nevertheless present and part of the potential for dramatic action (characters will often talk to other characters supposedly off screen). A static shot from a **tripod** holding the camera steady in one place can impose a sense of immobility or implacability on whatever it sees; a moving camera implies a more malleable and changing world. Moreover, the basic effect when a camera moves is of an observer's head

A ballet of the bad guys from *High Noon* (1952). While the three gunmen wait for their leader to arrive on the noon train, their slow, limited movements express their patience, boredom, and unity of purpose; repeatedly the gunmen form intricate patterns, then pause. Here one man walks into the frame and then stops to look back, one holds a baroque slouch over his harmonica, and, braced against the right side of the frame, one raises and lowers a liquor bottle.

turning, or moving to another part of the scene, following the action as if entranced or entrapped by it. For any camera movement, the rate of change—swift or sedate—creates its own further meanings and effects.

Horizontal Movement

A **pan** is a slow horizontal pivoting of a camera fixed in one place, a panoramic inspection of the setting as a potential field for action, like a head turning slowly to inspect the scene systematically, casually, or curiously, without apparent personal engagement. A pan can also follow an object moving across the picture plane such as a car or a person running. A rapid movement is a **"swish pan"** or **"flash pan,"** the field of vision blurred by the speed with which images seem to cross the screen, sometimes used for transitions between shots (as in the *Citizen Kane* "marriage montage"), often produced unintentionally when amateurs pan their home movies too fast. Since the early days of D. W.

Griffith's Biograph films, with sets opening to an outer world on the right and an inner chamber on the left, a pan to the left often seems to complete and confirm, while a pan to the right often seems to discover and surprise, perhaps because we also read from left to right, though why is not clear. The resting point at the end of a pan carries special significance, as if one had finally arrived somewhere; having arrived, an audience closely examines where.

A **tracking shot** (also **trucking** or **travelling** shot) is a linear movement of the camera alongside a moving subject, or along an extended background such as a row of buildings, often on tracks actually laid down on rough ground for smooth camera motion. The audience is committed to an involved and continuing relationship with whatever is followed in motion, or else it is committed to changing its field of vision. If the tracking follows a moving person, that person remains fixed in our sustained inspection, though seemingly free and unobserved. At the end of Francois Truffaut's The 400 Blows (1959) a boy escapes from reform school and runs down a road in a very long tracking shot, imprisoned by the picture's enclosing frame even though apparently liberated; and at the end of the battle in Kenneth Branagh's Henry V (1989) a very long tracking shot follows the King carrying a dead boy across the devastated battlefield, which we see at length, the King always centered and bearing the burden of what we see at length. A moving car can be followed down the street by a series of pan shots, each showing it approaching, passing the camera, then moving away, or the car can be followed by a single sustained tracking shot taken from a vehicle moving alongside. Each creates a different relationship and meaning for the audience.

Vertical Movement

A **tilt shot** involves the slow vertical pivoting of a camera fixed in one place. As with upward-turned eyes, a tilt up can imply aspiration, ascending thought or curiosity, or perhaps fearful revelation of something above one's line of sight, the camera and viewer remaining transfixed. A camera rehearsal on board ship early in King Kong (1933) has Fay Wray slowly lifting her eyes and head, seeing something horrible as directed, and screaming—prescient of many such actions to come. Truffaut's early Les Mistons (1957) ends with a tilt from a young woman to the trees above her, in an attempt at a transcendent resolution of the mystery of desire and loss. Contrariwise, as with lowered eyes or head, a tilt down can imply humility, depression, or increasing curiosity about things beneath ordinary notice.

Crane (also **boom**) movement sends the camera vertically or diagonally up or down, liberated in space, so the viewer can inspect a large object or collection of objects (or people), or a tall building, as if a privileged voyeur exempt from the law of gravity, all the while in a continuing relationship with whatever is shown. Some cranes are several stories high, like those used in skyscraper construction; others are short pivoting camera platforms on wheels used also for dollying, with a vertical range of only a few feet. A crane shot can also move horizontally across, diagonally up and away, or down and into the field of vision, maintaining the comparatively fortunate viewer's sense of separation from a character's implied immobility or entrapment. Helicopters are often used to create extreme "crane" shots, moving from just above the action to a great distance away, as in the Bay Bridge shot of Mike Nichols' *The Graduate* (1967), or vice versa, as in the elaborate Statue of Liberty to Staten Island Ferry first shot of his *Working Girl* (1988); the effect is often spectacular.

Crane shots can be extraordinarily eloquent. A rising crane shot in *Gone with the Wind* enlarges the field of vision crammed with more and more wounded Confederate soldiers, until the numbers grow unbearable. In Fred Zinneman's *High Noon* (1952) a crane shot abandons the sheriff, moving from a medium shot to an extremely long high-angle shot, even the viewer seeming to abandon him to confront the killers on an empty street alone. Rene Clair's *Sous les Toits de Paris* (1930) and John Ford's *The Informer* (1935) each begin with a crane shot moving across rooftops (or models of them), implying that the drama we are about to watch is only one of many. Brian DePalma, in early films such as *Carrie* (1976), uses slow crane movements to lull the viewer just before something shocking occurs. A famous crane shot near the end of *Citizen Kane* surveys the vast accumulated detritus of Kane's life to arrive finally at the film's climactic revelation.

Interior Movement

Dolly movement (which may be combined with modest craning) is a smooth rolling movement into or out of the field of vision, created by a small wheeled camera dolly or hand truck. A **dolly-in** usually generates a sense of curiosity gratified, but also of spatial intrusion, increasingly privileged but vulnerable as the viewer enters space previously only observed. As we move closer to the point of greatest interest within the image, that point of interest grows larger and so gains in importance. The effect on the viewer is reciprocal as the dolly proceeds—what the camera tells us deserves closer scrutiny seems to deserve it, and coming closer, we want to see more. Other objects in various depths of the frame change in perspective as the viewing camera approaches them

A

B

Not only do cranes provide liberated motion across large numbers of people assembled on crowded sound stages, but once in place they can be used as instant scaffolds for static shots. The cranes seen here provide both complex motion and raised platforms, for the grand banquet scene of Michael Curtiz's *The Adventures of Robin Hood* (1938) (A) and for the John Doe Convention of Frank Capra's *Meet John Doe* (1941) (B).

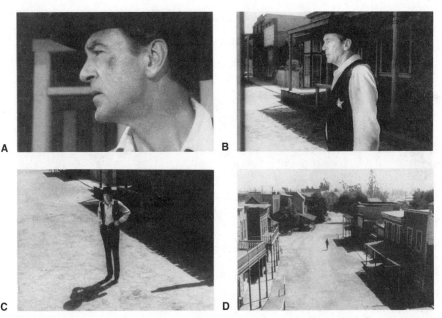

Just before the gunfight begins in *High Noon*, abandoned by everyone including apparently his own wife, Sheriff Kane steps into the street to meet his probable death. There is a brief close-up establishing maximum audience empathy with his feelings of entrapment and desperation (A). Then with an extraordinary crane shot (B), (C), and (D), we too abandon him, and he turns to walk away from us, utterly alone. Meanwhile the background music plays insistently the film's theme, "Do not forsake me. . . ."

and disappear off-screen as it passes them. A **dolly-out** similarly generates the meaning it assumes, a sense of abandonment, leavetaking, or escape which seems self-justifying. With notable exceptions, nearly all films end with a dolly or crane out, as if bidding farewell and disengaging our interest, though they may also end with an ironic or self-preoccupied movement of the main characters away from the camera, abandoning the viewer. Or, as if by mutual consent, with both movements.

A **zoom shot** is not a camera movement but a less costly lens effect approximating the visual effects of a dolly-in or dolly-out. It was used frequently during the 1960s but sparingly since. When the focal length of a specially designed "zoom" lens is changed, the field of vision widens or narrows while the size of the frame remains the same. The result for a zoom-in is an enlarging of part of the image with loss of its peripheries off-screen and for a zoom-out the reverse, a diminishing of the original image as off-screen information enters the edges of the frame to surround what had previously occupied the entirety. A zoom approximates the camera approaching or retreating from the object.

A

B

Behind the main title credits for Francis Coppola's *The Conversation* is a single, extremely long zoom shot, from a distant view of a square in San Francisco (A) to a close, flattened, and foreshortened image of Gene Hackman walking along the square as if only one more pedestrian (B). As it turns out, the shot precisely matches the trajectory of a bullet microphone aimed from the same place, implicating us from the beginning in the film's subject, surreptitious surveillance.

But not quite. Perspectives and parallax do not change in a zoom, as they do with a dolly, and spatial relations in depth (background to foreground) flatten with a zoom-in instead of growing proportionally deeper as with a dolly-in. The effect created by a zoom is not really of physical movement into a visibly defined space; rather it is more psychological, more of concentrated attention increasingly given to one part of the image, which grows to fill the frame as if filling the viewer's consciousness. Amateurs and some video artists enjoy "tromboning" their zoom lenses in a meaningless inflating and deflating of visual rhythm.

"Hand-held" camera movements approximate the rocky, weaving movements of a participant in the action. Hand-held movements—actually, a heavy camera is shoulder-held—are frequent in newsreel and documentary photography; the shaking usually confers a sense of immediacy and authenticity on whatever is seen, especially if the events shown are unpredictable and dangerous to the observer (as with war scenes or street riots), or are vigorously spontaneous (as with all-out dancing). In Stanley Kubrick's *2001: a Space Odyssey* (1968) Astronaut Bowman's fury as he moves to dismantle HAL's brain is signalled for the audience by the hand-held camera following him; all earlier movements were smooth, even somnambulistic. During the boring Buddhist funeral service in Itami's *The Funeral* (1984), the camera idly follows a public address system's loudspeaker wire through loops on the floor and on out of the room, as if seeking distraction.

In recent years a one-person counterweighted camera and harness called the **Steadicam** has been used to eliminate the shaking of hand-held images or the costs of complex dolly or tracking setups (and the risks of showing dolly tracks accidentally); a Steadicam can achieve smooth, fluid, studiolike movements even when the camera operator is running down stairs to follow a bobbing and weaving actor. In Hitchcock's *Frenzy* (1972) a Steadicam shot backs slowly down the stairs and then across the street, as if regretfully but discreetly abandoning an unsuspecting woman to her strangler. A Steadicam shot lacks the spontaneity of hand-held photography; its effect is more like that of a short, dollied crane.

CAMERA SPEED

A motion picture camera moves strips of film past a lens at a given speed, pausing periodically so a shutter can open and expose the film to light from the lens, then moving the film a notch further and pausing again, so again the shutter can open. What results when the film is developed is a long strip of still pictures, each "frame" differing slightly from the previous. A motion picture projector does the same thing in reverse: The film moves through the projector at a given speed but intermittently, pausing periodically while a shutter opens to allow light to shine through the frame held still momentarily in the projector's "gate." The light passes through a lens and out onto a white screen (in early days a "silver screen" but now beaded and treated for intensified reflection at any angle). What the screen shows is a series of still pictures, each differing slightly from the previous, with darkness between them. But the neurological phenomenon called "persistence of vision" prevents anyone from seeing this if the frames are changing faster than about 12 frames per second. What the eye and mind "see" is a continuously moving image, perhaps flickering (hence the British and later American slang term for movies, "flicks").

During the silent film period hand-cranked cameras ran at variable speeds, usually 16 to 24 frames per second, but more or less as the filmmaker saw fit, and projectionists sometimes similarly varied their speeds. Synchronized optical sound tracks since 1928 have required that film speeds hold constant, and they are standardized at 24 frames per second (fps) (though greater clarity is available at higher speeds). Many solemn early dramas shot at 16 fps are now improperly projected at 24 fps, the actors racing through their paces with spastic energy. Silent films of sufficient historical or artistic significance were once "stretched" or "step-printed" during reprocessing to reproduce their original pace and rhythm, every other frame printed twice. But variable camera speeds combined with invariable projector speeds provide filmmakers with options for certain kinds of in-camera special effects.

Fast Motion

Fast (undercranked) motion shoots fewer than 24 fps but projects at 24 fps, artificially speeding the action. In comic action, such motion provides zany, dehumanized activity (as in silent comedy chases), need or greed propelling the participants to absurdly superhuman effort, their desire visibly outrunning their humanity. Especially in Mack Sennett comedies, characters may collide without consequence (since their velocity is anyhow illusory); their pride goeth before their pratfalls but with no implied risk of injury to taint the audience's amusement at their folly. In an extreme form films may be **pixillated,** most frames per second cut out altogether to show people acting as automata in the frenzied grip of their own compulsions, as in the orgy in Stanley Kubrick's *A Clockwork Orange* (1971) or the rising antagonisms in Norman McLaren's *Neighbors* (1952).

Fast motion provides energetic action and can heighten a sense of tension or purposive efficiency in high-pressure business or newspaper offices, for example. Such action can increase the sense of danger in a car chase or other scenes showing machines gone out of control (decreasing the danger to stunt men on the scene). In dialogue scenes the effect needs to be approximated, for example by rapid-fire overlapping speech as in Howard Hawks's *His Girl Friday* (1940).

Fast motion can produce surreal action, in which the material world as we know it behaves strangely, its natural rhythms accelerated by stop-motion photography, perhaps a frame per minute or hour instead of 24 per second: Flowers break ground, grow, and blossom in smooth, swift ramification; clouds gather and race strangely across the sky; or automobiles flow down highways and across intersections like rivers through rapids, as in Godfrey Reggio's much imitated *Koyaanisqatsi* (1983). The familiar appears beautifully or dangerously unfamiliar, sometimes willfully exhibiting a mind of its own. Stop motion photography can also animate objects such as disembodied shoes marching up stairs, or tennis balls rolling into formations spelling out their manufacturer's name, but here the effort is to achieve normal-seeming tempos.

Normal Motion

What we consider "normal" in our experience of tempo is highly variable, subject to attention, distraction, impatience, boredom, retrospection, etc.; no two moments in any one life seem to flow at the same pace. Films reproduce or attenuate these subjective states for dramatic purposes by varying the actors' rates of speech and movement, by accompanying the action with music, or by shot and editing strategies (a distant action seems slower than one thrust at the camera, a long take can seem interminably longer still, and several short shots spliced together seem faster than a single continuous shot if continuity is maintained). Even the obvious artifices of speeded or slowed motion can seem normal if customary, apt, and unobtrusive. But most films, most of the time, do not call attention to their temporal states as such, and we accept their tempos as equivalent to the experience of duration as we otherwise know it—unexceptional, that is, normal.

Slow Motion

Slow motion (overcranked, or "slomo") shoots faster than 24 fps but projects at 24 fps, slowing down the action. For expressionistic and esthetic purposes, slow motion can present a dreamlike world, languorous, lyrical, ecstatic, interminable, sodden, or horribly entrapping in time as well as space. The tendency of things to seem to float or to frustrate effort when their usual velocity is slowed opens innumerable possibilities for the conversion of normative experience into prolonged esthetic experience (movement enjoyed for its own sake), or into fractured subjective states (unnatural movement correlating with desire or fear). To dream that one can run only excruciatingly slowly from danger is commonplace. Violent death filmed in slow motion became a hallmark of Sam Peckinpah's action films, because it implies both daydream and nightmare, what is feared in fantasy and yet what occurs, and it allows the inevitable to seem in its own way beautiful.

For perceptual purposes, some actions simply occur too fast to be seen and need to be slowed for proper dramatic effect. Explosions are often climactic in a dramatic action, but real explosions are over very quickly, almost before they are noticed; fast cars driven off cliffs may seem to hang in the air too briefly to gratify an audience's pleasure or apprehension in the prospect of seeing the machine wrecked or a character at risk. The climactic collapse of a house toward the end of *Lethal Weapon II* (1989) happened almost all at once when it was being photographed. But the event was shot at 60 fps, slowing it 2 ½ times, then slowed still further by insertion of various detailed close-ups in slow motion, creating a much more satisfying pseudo-event.

Slow motion can be stopped altogether to produce a freeze-frame, that is, when a selected single frame is reprinted on the film repeatedly and then projected, the moving image, with its potential for change, "freezes" into a still photograph, a record of the moment fixed for all time. Our sense of time as the revelation of significant process is arrested, then eliminated altogether. The effect resembles a Victorian *tableau vivant*, an estranging stage convention wherein actors suddenly hold their postures, allowing the audience to contemplate the dramatic implications of the moment, or actors deliberately imitate the still-life of paintings, costumes and all, for the effect on an audience enchanted to see life imitating art. Freeze-frames have been much used since Francois Truffaut revived them in 1959 for their cinematic artifice and expressive advantages.

In an **initial freeze-frame,** a still photograph establishes itself and then begins to move. Often an apparently drawn picture or sketch takes on photographic detail and then becomes a motion picture (by reverse processing), implying a bookish origin for the narrative to follow (in some such films each separate "chapter" of the story begins in this way). The artifice is especially suitable for highly styled films [such as George Roy Hill's *The Sting* (1973)], or for folk tales, whether or not the stories originate in actual novels.

In a **medial freeze-frame,** the movement pauses at an especially significant moment, allowing the audience to savor and contemplate that moment, then resumes, as with the meeting of two friends after long absence in Truffaut's *Jules et Jim* (1961). The sudden estrangement of the audience from the film's world of illusion can become one of the film's shared pleasures.

In a **terminal freeze-frame,** the final image of the film ceases all movement, converting the lives of the characters into parable, as in *The 400 Blows* (1959), into art, into historical legend, as in George Roy Hill's *Butch Cassidy and the Sundance Kid* (1969), or into the changelessness of death, as in Bo Widerberg's *Elvira Madigan* (1967), translating the characters out of time and distancing the audience in an invitation to meditate on the meaning or impermanence of all that has gone before. A terminal freeze-frame is now also a common device to put TV story segments on hold just before a commercial.

LENS EFFECTS

Lenses are optical systems with differing characteristics, each producing a different kind of photographic image. Which lens is chosen for a particular shot depends upon the dramatic effect desired. No lens precisely reproduces "what the eye sees," since much that the eye "sees" the mind ignores anyhow, or reprocesses in the act of seeing, no camera can move or refocus as deftly or as reflexively as the human eye, the mind meanwhile unaware that anything intricate is happening. Camera lenses can do both more than the human eye's physiology allows and less.

Focal Depth

For each lens, depending upon the amount of light available, objects are sharply in focus for certain minimum and maximum distances from the camera and out of focus otherwise. Anything being photographed must remain within that range or else appear blurred. During a shot a camera may be refocused (**rack-focused** or "racked") to keep an actor's image sharp as the action or the camera moves closer or further, but only as preplanned. Which lens to use of what focal depth given the brightness or dimness of the scene's lighting is part of the shot's planning.

In **shallow focus,** the image is sharp only a particular distance from the camera, only within a narrow range (perhaps only between 3 and 4 feet from the camera, perhaps only between 3 feet and 3 feet, 2 inches), and is otherwise blurred. The depth of field in sharp focus being shallow, the action must take place parallel to the picture plane, at all times the same distance from the camera (unless the lens is refocused during the shot to follow a character). A shallow lens concentrates an audience's attention on the most significant details in the frame (the rest being blurred). If a two-shot conversation takes place in depth, foreground to background, only the speaker or the listener will be in clear focus at any one time, not both; if in a single take, refocusing from speaker to listener on-screen guides and redirects the viewer's attention. Woody Allen's *Interiors* (1978) emphasizes the characters' self-concern in isolation from each other while we examine each in turn.

So-called **deep-focus** (really **"depth of field"**) photography shows clearly almost everything within the camera's field of vision regardless of distance, privileging everything in the physical universe (as do the "photo-realists" and some surrealists). Theoreticians like Andre Bazin convinced many others that the effect is "realistic," as the eye sees. In fact the effect is unreal, unaccustomed, even hallucinatory, privileging the film viewer. The human eye has a relatively shallow depth of field, seeing little with clarity though constantly refocusing itself. But "deep focus" reveals everything all at once whatever the depth. The hard-edged, cameo-cut world of "deep focus" photography can provide great quantities of visual information in each shot. Moreover, such photography allows for framing and blocking of the action across several planes in depth simultaneously, in turn allowing dramatic tensions and ironies to express themselves as spatial relationships within the image. Deep focus was so used frequently in Welles's *Citizen Kane,* and occasionally in William Wyler's *The Best Years of Our Lives* (1946), both films photographed by Gregg Toland. But because deep focus cannot isolate in sharp focus only the most significant elements of the image (foreground or background), it risks sensory overload or irrelevance. This technique has been the subject of considerable discussion as used by Jean Renoir and Orson Welles.

Focal Length

Each lens system is designed to refract (or "see") a wider or narrower field of vision although the camera remains the same distance from the subject. Most lenses are thought of as "normal," in that their images exhibit no peculiar qualities calling attention to themselves. We are accustomed to snapshot cameras equipped with either 50-mm or 35-mm lenses, both serving to record memorabilia, the 35-mm lenses providing a somewhat wider image. Unlike a human eye, a lens has focal "breadth" on its peripheries; details on the edge of an image are as clear as those in the middle, although the edges are then masked to form a rectangle.

Since the motion picture screen's rectangle remains the same size

This frame enlargement shows one of the few moments in William Wyler's *The Best Years of Our Lives* (1946) when "deep focus" foreground and rearground relationships function dramatically. At the end of the film, while the couple to the right are being married, Dana Andrews and Teresa Wright look steadily into each other's eyes through the shot's depth of field, and without a word spoken agree to marry. Their intensity of feeling registers in part because they remain this way through most of a lengthy shot, 56 seconds, even after the ceremony ends and other guests come forward to congratulate the bride and groom.

whatever the focal length of the lens used and the area seen, the field of vision filling the screen will be wider or narrower according to the lens chosen. The images will therefore appear smaller or larger on the screen, as if in long shot or closeup. Changing a lens can be a fast, inexpensive way to simulate changing a camera's distance from the action; but the images created are quite different and affect the viewer differently, and the two complement rather than substitute for each other.

Wide-angle (short) lenses open out distant spaces enormously, creating an impression of greater distance still; if used for close shots, they distort whatever is very near the camera, with grotesque and horrifying or ludicrous and amusing results. For shots at any proximity, wide-angle lenses tend to exaggerate a sense of depth even while providing a wider field; what is further back seems much further back because much smaller in a larger field of vision. Thus, for a medium shot in which the background (the rear wall of a room or a line of trees) should be far back and low on the horizon, emphasizing perhaps the character's open options or empty past, a filmmaker would choose a wide-angle lens and place the camera a bit closer to preserve the required waist-to-head framing. An extreme wide-angle (or fish-eye) lens will curve horizons and bend verticals (such as skyscrapers) as well as distort the proportions of whatever is near; an intrusive nerd close to a girl's face in POV can seem a gargoyle, and in horror films, a threatening face can become horribly distorted as it looms closer. In Lina Wertmuller's *The Seduction of Mimi* (1974) the man who has plotted to seduce an overweight woman seems to cower in the distance at the far end of the bed, while at the near end close to the camera, gargantuan buttocks climb onto the bed and wallow toward him.

   Telephoto (long) lenses bring distant images closer and make close images seem enormous, but diminish distances in depth so that buildings or trees far behind a character will seem to loom close, the character seeming to be up against a wall which is in fact blocks away. The effect of such flattened rear-ground closure can be decorative or oppressive or both, as in Walter Hill's films. Another effect originates in the foreshortening of great distances in a telephoto image: A sheriff's posse some distance from the camera and riding toward it would seem to be much nearer than it is, but the riders would seem to be gaining little ground even at full gallop. In Nichols's *The Graduate* (1967), a young man runs interminably down the street toward the camera, hoping to

A man here seen as a small face barely visible upper center is determined to avenge his honor by seducing his wife's seducer's wife, in Lina Wertmuller's *The Seduction of Mimi* (1974). Her use of a wide-angle lens converts that moment of macho triumph into a ludicrous ordeal.

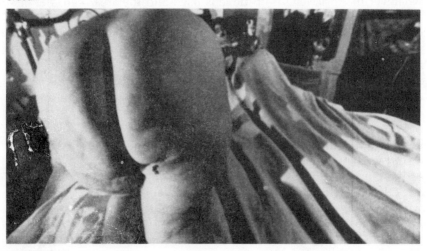

stop his girlfriend's wedding, and his desperation seeming to get no-where becomes a condition of the audience's perception of him.

Anamorphic (cinemascope or "scope") lenses, compress the photo-graphed field of vision horizontally to fit on standard gauge film then expand the field again in projection. Thus on the screen the field of vision appears much wider than higher, 2.35 times wider in fact. This ribbon-shaped rectangle (once called useful "only for parades and snakes") was part of the industry's attempt to win early TV viewers back to the movie theaters by producing spectacular extravaganzas on a vast scale; scope images filled the eye horizontally if not the mind. Like depth-of-field photography, scope images can provide considerable information to the viewer, although they are rarely used to invite an audience's searching inquiry of the screen. The size allows overwhelming panoramas and extensive backgrounds even in medium shots to reinforce by sheer mass and replication of detail the mood or meaning of a situa-tion. A scope image allows conversational two shots even in close-up without necessarily implying intimately shared space, because the faces may remain some distance from each other. In general, a scope shot invites longer takes and less editing; quick-cut scope shots in close-up can stagger the eye, as when a bank's iron bars and gates slam shut at the beginning of *Butch Cassidy* (1969); the effect is abrupt, almost brutal. Scope is compositionally difficult to manage: often only half the screen is needed and the rest is filled with nondescript props, and cross-diagonal compositions across the picture plane impact gently rather than stressfully on each other.

When a scope film is shown in a reduced "scan" or "flat" print for limited 16-mm projection, or to match a TV screen, nearly half the image is missing. What may have been the fully visible facial expressions of two people conversing across the screen in a two-shot must be replaced with alternating one-shots, or with one visible speaker listening to off-screen replies. The full scope image will not fit on TV unless the upper and lower parts of the TV screen are left empty. Such "letterboxed" images irritate many viewers, who can too-readily decide that their TV or the broadcast signal is defective. Thus scope films are rarely broadcast as such, though main titles and end titles must be letterboxed or shown in squeezed scope format so all the words can be read. By contract Woody Allen's carefully composed film *Manhattan* (1979) is broadcast in scope or not at all.

Special Effects Lenses

Special lenses meet the special needs of particular shots. Such lenses provide distorted images for horror films or dream sequences, kaleido-

A

B

C

In Stanley Kubrick's *2001: a Space Odyssey* (1968), two astronauts chat while strolling down the aisle of their space ship, a centrifuge to maintain artificial gravity. Scanning from the picture's right edge for a 1:33 aspect ratio (A), the frame's left edge runs down the pillarlike axle, unbalancing the composition so the upper and lower curves seem to whirl dizzyingly out and up. With a 1:85 ratio (B), space to the pillar's left is reopened, and some balance or near-symmetry is restored but not the whole frame's ironically reassuring sameness and emptiness. With a 2:35 ratio (C) Kubrick's image speaks precisely.

scopic special effects, or star bursts to any on-camera sources of light, such as street lamps or stage spotlights (a common effect in rock concert films). **Three-dimensional images** can be approximated by shooting the same scene simultaneously with two lenses set apart the same distances as human eyes (between two and three inches), discriminating each image with differing polarization or color filters, then projecting the two images together on one screen while the audience views the projected result with differentially polarized or color-filtered glasses.

But three-dimensional viewing remains a marketing novelty despite its potential for dramatic engagement of the viewer. Since eye focus and eye convergence are called into unaccustomed relationships while watching "3-D" (each eye focuses steadily on a screen always the same distance away, while both eyes together move to follow images seeming to move closer or further), a sizable proportion of the audience watching a "3-D" movie will always develop headaches.

LIGHTING, FILM STOCKS, AND FILTERS

Lighting, film stocks, and filters are large and largely technical topics in the primary dominion of the director of cinematography. Needless to say, no theatrical film exposes home movie film stock by whatever the available light or by a single flood light perched on the camera, as amateurs do, unless a home movie effect is desired, as in the color sequences of Scorsese's *Raging Bull* (1980), or the family party of *Up the Sandbox* (1972)—which adds amateur zoom tromboning as well.

Lighting

Lighting creates the way we see while it also defines what we see. Available light is used in documentaries when artificial light sources or artfully placed diffusers and reflectors would be distracting to the participants, although such light is usually flattening outdoors and dim, fluorescent green, or incandescent orange indoors and rarely appropriate except to a sense of documentary authenticity. Available light falls as it may, not necessarily where it should to highlight a scene's significant details or effects. Although lighting strategies are infinitely variable, three primary styles are commonly used for lighting a set or augmenting the available light of a location.

Natural light attempts not to call attention to itself by simulating the familiar lighting of different situations even while dramatically augmenting the scenic effects and preserving the film's established visual style. Close attention is paid to ostensible light sources (lamps, windows, even candles) which are not too noticeably violated as other studio lights substitute for them. Various lights—at least three—provide a sense of modeled three-dimensionality: A **key** light angled from the front picks out the actor or the most significant part of the frame and may provide a gleam in an eye; a **back** light shines on the actor from the rear, high up, providing a visible border separating that person from the background and perhaps giving hair a romantically haloed edge; and a **fill** light softens the contrasts between lit and unlit areas. In addition there can be base lights to raise the general level of illumination, set lights to pick out notable architectural details, and special lighting to create specific additional effects: A man's face may look roughly textured and weathered and a woman's glowing and smooth, even though they both share the same ostensible light in the scene, since in fact different lights shine on each. Large filters and umbrellas or huge metallic-sheet reflectors further distribute bounce light as desired.

Low-key or "hard" lighting (so-called expressionistic light) strongly contrasts illuminated and shadowed areas, with mysterious or ominous pools of darkness. This lighting implies large areas of the unknown in the film's world, with a certain moral force and simplicity dividing the characters and their predicaments. The center of interest in the frame may be the most brightly lit spot (as in Josef Von Sternberg's films) or may be an unreadable shadowed face against an illuminated background (as when Charles Foster Kane first reads aloud his "Declaration of Principles"). Low-key lighting creates a visual effect approximating and inducing awareness of the fears and dark areas of the mind, as in twenties' German expressionist films and horror films since, although low-key lighting's mysteries can also enhance romantic scenes. Such lighting is common, almost mandated, in the *films noir* of the forties and fifties. Highlighted areas of the screen (faces and hands when clothing and backgrounds are dark, for example) can become powerful compositional elements when photographed in black and white. When in John McTiernan's *Die Hard* (1988) Bruce Willis finally appears in a doorway to confront the last of the terrorist-thieves, their nemesis finally revealing himself, he is blindingly backlit, the apparition of a pagan god. The extra-terrestrials in Steven Spielberg's *Close Encounters of the Third Kind* (1977) are treated the same way, pools of bright light replacing the more usual expressionist pools of darkness.

High-key or "soft" lighting (so-called realistic light) provides an evenly lit world, usually without surprises (except in the implications and outcome of the plot) and often without strong moral distinctions (the characters may all be fallible but forgivable). Frequently high-key lighting is used in the world of musicals, comedy, domestic drama, and even crime detection films when the criminal poses no special threat (as in some police procedural films). That which can be known is known or soon will be.

Film Stocks and Lens Filters

Film stocks and lens filters have varied in their characteristics over the years, and many choices (with a wide number of further options for processing) remain available to cinematographers. **Black-and-white** film (and, of course, many shades of grey) was the standard until the early 1960s, when public preference for color TV and color films gradually ended choice. Black-and-white photography is virtually its own art medium: It can be sumptuously fine-grained, with delicate densities of grey implying a refined and sophisticated world, or it can be coarse-grained, as in newsreel, documentary, and documentary fiction ("mock-doc") or neorealist films. Until recently, the more light-sensitive the film, the grainier the image; newsreel stock sensitive enough to be shot in whatever the available light established an esthetic in which graininess seemed more authentic and finer tones more artificial. Early orthochromatic stock was not sensitive to red, and so actors needed heavy makeup; in 1928 panchromatic stock emerged; and in the late thirties a sensitive fine-grained film made depth-of-field photography with low-key lighting possible.

Black-and-white photography emphasizes compositional harmonies and dissonances, and certain directors (Woody Allen, Martin Scorsese, or Jim Jarmusch) occasionally use it today despite its enormous financial disadvantages, to create a formal elegance of image not possible with color, or to associate their films with older films, presumably older modes of experience. Various filters can further affect the mood of the image: A polaroid filter creates an even-toned sculptured effect; a yellow filter brings clouds and reflected light into high contrast; black-and-white stock shot through a red filter makes even a sunny day look ominous; other filters can heighten key-light glare so that a face in a passionate moment seems radiant and glowing (because it is).

Silent films might be tinted, toned, hand-colored, or stenciled, and a "two-strip" color process was used in the twenties, but richly saturated "three-strip" Technicolor became available for special films in the mid-thirties, and other processes have been adopted since. Although black-and-white film continues to imply old-fashioned film or else documentary reality, color implies all other kinds of reality for its audiences. In Victor Fleming's *The Wizard of Oz* (1939), Kansas is a drab monochrome sepia, but Oz, as everyone knows, is not; Butch Cassidy and Sundance ride from old-fashioned monochrome into full color as, presumably, we move our own imaginations back into their turn-of-the-century present. Originally color films required high light intensities, but now any kind will serve. Color stock needs more careful light exposure and "balancing"—matching of shades from shot to shot—than black and white, and better-planned compositional integrity, because bright or hot colors can dominate the frame even when intended for the background.

With filters color film stock can present subdued pastel worlds, candy-cane or comic-book worlds, worlds bleached of color or meaning, drab dark tones, a world bejewelled with neon commercial signs, or a world cheapened with them. Color film can also code its ostensibly colored worlds toward one color, color-code themes and meanings—as do Godard's *Pierrot le Fou* (1965) and Hitchcock's *Vertigo* (1958), or darken daylight exposures to resemble night (using **day for night** filters).

The recent practice of **colorizing** older black-and-white films to increase their appeal to general audiences places these decisions in the hands of electronic technicians rather than visual artists. Apart from the drab colors of colorized film and the absurd monotony of flesh tones of the same shade whether in sunlight or lamplight (implying a cheerful daytime even in bleak *film noir* night scenes), colorizing masks subtle grey tonalities and wrecks an image's compositional strength. The effect may not be bothersome in loosely composed spectacles such as Michael Curtiz's *Yankee Doodle Dandy* (1942), but tightly organized compositions such as Busby Berkeley's kaleidoscopic choreographies or John Huston's arrangements of enclosed characters in *The Maltese Falcon* (1941) lose much of their dramatic force.

FRAME COMPOSITION

The screen presents us with a flat rectangle generating three-dimensional space, together with the qualities such as tension or serenity pertaining to these two quite different sets of interior relationships, especially as they relate. A screen shows simultaneously a "picture" in the darkness at the front of the theater and a hole in the audience's world with another world beyond. Many people are not tuned to the esthetics of two-dimensional space, the difference between a painting and a picture, or in photography a picture and a snapshot. Such people look at the screen only as if through a window. Yet many characteristics of rectilinear composition affect everyone.

The Aspect Ratio

The aspect ratio, or ratio of the rectangle's width to its height, has varied since television entered the media marketplace during the early fifties. The wider the rectangle relative to height, the more dominant the side action across the picture plane, and the less significant are depth, action from the rear, or diagonals (since a line from a lower left corner to an upper right is more shallow, and a steep diagonal line occupies only part of the frame). Wider images can provide a feast for the eye, but they can also distract from centers of attention.

Academy ratio, or 1.33:1, was standard before 1950, and remains standard for TV, for most 16-mm nontheatrical projection, and for Super-8 home movies. This "golden mean" of 4 to 3 invited compositional compression of the images and strong conflicts of diagonals across the screen matching those of the action. For a sophisticated director or cinematographer (and many are), the academy ratio opened access to the compositional strategies of six centuries of painting, especially those of this century, when abstract relationships have dominated. Now, if used at all in theatrical films, the ratio implies that the images belong to an old movie.

European widescreen ratio, or 1.65:1, was adopted during the film industry's struggle to retain audiences gone to TV, preserving some of the advantages of academy ratio while gaining some of the advantages of widescreen format. Some 16-mm prints preserve this ratio with "frame bars" blacking out the tops and bottoms of the screen.

American widescreen, or 1.85:1, became the U.S. response to competition with TV, and is now standard for films shot in this country, with some of the advantages of cinemascope and fewer of the disadvantages.

The **cinemascope** ratio, or 2.35:1, became the single-camera, simpler way to approximate the spectacular effects of "Cinerama," the early 1950s widescreen system with three cameras each simultaneously projecting one-third of a single scene, the images matched at their edges to provide the audience with a wraparound visual environment. Cinerama was too ungainly and expensive to become more than a novelty, and cinemascope—an anamorphic lens-generated extra-wide-screen ratio with other trade names such as "Panavision"—became and remains a standard alternative to the 1.85 widescreen format. The ribbon-shaped scope screen can provide a plenitude of visual imagery and of space—implied freedom—for the characters, overwhelming audiences when sets and character movements are designed to fill the horizontal dimension effectively, as in Truffaut's *Jules et Jim* (1961), a film itself about freedom. Often, however, the scope screen provides mere additional sensation for the eye and potential distraction from the significant parts of the screen. See the discussion above about lens effects for other aesthetic problems associated with this now common and popular ratio.

Open Compositions

Open compositions are the most dynamic and apparently liberated way to organize screen space, implying a larger three-dimensional world the viewer explores through the "window," a world of coded images of recognizable forms representing their real equivalents, images of automobiles as automobiles, the faces of people as the presence of people.

The viewer's concern is with the image's signified "reality," mostly with looking at "things." The camera is often in motion, and the off-screen spaces are revealed to be open and extensive. The structures of spaces within the window are not significant as such, but what we see is nevertheless by design, usually of the set and of vectors of movement within the frame. The space two-thirds of the way up the frame, where eyes usually appear in close-ups, tends to be especially privileged and is inspected first. Italian neorealist films often create the impression that they are as open in their compositional elements as newsreels, but in fact they are often tightly composed, as elegantly sophisticated as any "art" photograph.

Lines such as horizontals (as of street curbs or horizons) may stabilize or delimit the action to an upper or lower segment of the frame; verticals (as of tree trunks or door frames) may soar or divide the field of action and separate characters standing on either side; diagonals (as of ceiling edges or railroad tracks) may imply process or change of state, leading attention backward or inward; circles or curves may imply a roundness

Though some shots in Woody Allen's *Annie Hall* (1977) are as formally composed as those in his next two films *Interiors* (1978) and *Manhattan* (1979), some shots seem as open as the film's supposedly casual anecdotal structure. Here Alvy Singer anachronistically revisits a boyhood classroom to defend an early yen for girls, and various classmates tell what they later became. Not the composition but the children's eye lines keep our eyes inside the frame.

or softness threatened by the jagged or linear, as in the famous Odessa steps sequence of Sergei Eisenstein's *Battleship Potemkin* (1925).

The predominant shapes in the image may be delicate or massive, light or heavy, fussy and cluttered or bare and austerely simple, craggy or smooth, lumpy or airy, geometrical or organic, many or few; usually **masses** express visibly some invisible mood or state of mind or characterize a human predicament. But even so, a crowded street is more likely to be seen as such, not as a pointillist pattern of textures.

A frame is **balanced** when masses within it counterweigh each other, though of differing shapes and natures, implying a state of orderly repose (a foreground house, frame left, may be balanced by a distant mountain, frame right). With an open compositional style the image is constantly being rearranged, and balance seems accidental and temporary. **Symmetry** is a rare extreme case: With a symmetrical image the center of the screen serves as an axis—usually vertical but sometimes horizontal—for geometrically similar shapes on either side. A balanced

Human bodies and desert sands together form the textures of a love-in in Death Valley, passion attempting to regenerate death itself. "I visualize ten thousand people making love across the desert," said Michelangelo Antonioni when he first conceived *Zabriskie Point* (1969); when he got to shoot it, open compositions helped imply that more people were there than were in fact available.

Two former comrades-in-arms confront each other as if equals, in symmetry, eyeball to eyeball, parallel to the picture plane, evenly dividing our attention and sense of each one's moral justification. In this shot from *The Best Years of Our Lives* (1946), Frederic March is telling Dana Andrews, a married man, to stop seeing his daughter. The symmetry at first implies defiance and a standoff and then finally their shared fundamental decency; despite the personal cost, Andrews agrees.

composition can be arrived at by the end of a shot, as if a fit state achieved, or can be destroyed in the process of a shot. Because symmetry presents a rational precision of sorts, it can seem reassuring in its predictability or imprisoning in its uniformity, or both, as in the Jupiter mission spaceship of *2001: a Space Odyssey* (1968); because symmetry tends to flatten an image, it can imply a certain deliberate artifice in the shot, creating in the audience a poised detachment for viewing whatever we see as more factitious or amusing than real, as in the would-be gang-rape Alex's gang interrupts for a gang rumble in *A Clockwork Orange* (1971).

A **foreground** may block or filter part of the image, dominating and governing sight of the remainder (as with branches of a tree or prison bars) or may intervene between audience and action, separating and distancing them, as with dust, passing automobiles, or a crystal chandelier. A foreground image can seem to be a condition of a character's state of mind, since we see the character through the image. A close

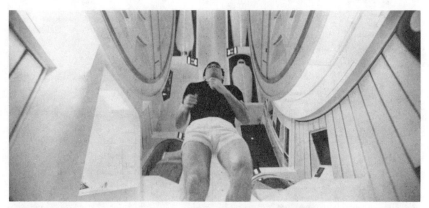

An astronaut jogs along the inner circumference of the huge centrifuge space ship of *2001*, shadow boxing for additional exercise. Despite its heroic implications, this extreme low-angle shot makes him seem puny and his gestures absurd, because of his foreshortened perspective and because of the crushing mass of the two hubs on either side of him. His jogging along on the shot's axis of symmetry further seems to restrict him, and we see him going nowhere as the camera dollies backward to keep its distance.

foreground object forces the impression that the rest of the image is distinctly further back, and so heightens our perception of depth ("Improve Your Snapshot" booklets usually suggest that a bush or tree branch be foregrounded when one shoots into the middle distance).

A **background** also can comment subliminally on the action and the characters' lives. Most obviously, background objects signify what the character owns or lives with, tawdry or elegant. More subtly, backgrounds establish possibilities implicit in their location (deserts, grass-cropped suburbs) and suggest the characters' sensibilities by presenting to the audience's inattention heavily massive or lightly filigreed objects (bulldozers, or flowered wallpaper), closure or emptiness (buildings blocking our view at the end of a street or an open sea with an empty horizon), or listlessness or dynamism (other people standing around or walking briskly). Backgrounds are often flats painted to resemble a credible world, shaded to the scene's mood, sometimes painted with forced perspective to give the appearance of depth to a shallow set. Backgrounds can be parallel to the picture plane (the foreground characters up against the wall) or diagonal to it (implying movement toward or away), and backgrounds can create a variety of textural impressions (smooth, peeling, or jagged with sharp thrusts and outcroppings). Backgrounds reinforce the impression that the action is taking place in a real (or real fantasy) world but function expressionistically as well.

A

B

The traditional sentimental novel's classically opposed heroines, a conventionally virtuous, innocent fair-haired woman and a socially marginalized, experienced dark-haired woman, here confront each other in *High Noon*. Neither Mrs. Kane (Grace Kelly) nor Helen Ramirez (Katy Jurado) respect each other as they begin talking, and their backgrounds reinforce their difference (A). Successive shots change relative backgrounds as they change their minds, and, by the end, when they reach mutual understanding, their positions have been reversed (B).

Some backgrounds function dramatically. In *Do the Right Thing* (1989), behind the delivery boy Spike Lee (who directed the film) and the pizza parlor owner Danny Aiello, we can see—or register without seeing—the photos of white heroes honored by the white owner, though the shop is in a black neighborhood with an all-black clientele. The implicit issue, who has the power to define whose public image, past, and pride, will eventually spark a race riot, and even the artfully evasive "Dodger" will take a stand.

Closed Compositions

Closed-frame compositions invite the most careful and artful use of the medium by controlling the structure of the rectangle and of the pyramidal space within, whether the camera is at rest or is moving with deliberate formality. With the discovery of linear perspective six centuries ago came the predominance of the rectangle as the preferred border of contained picture space; interior lines moving to a vanishing point best create an illusion of depth when they are contained between exterior parallel lines. The world in a closed frame may be balanced or unbalanced but always seems to some extent self-defined and self-contained, displayed and exhibited more than discovered and revealed. The viewer is led, controlled, and informed by many kinds of abstract spatial relations.

The issues of line, mass, balance, foreground, and background men-

A

B

Periodically *High Noon* repeats a view of the iron rails that will bring the noon train and Kane's ultimate destiny, a rigidly formal composition aimed at a vanishing point on the horizon. A high horizon adds to the oppressive feeling that there is no way out (A). When the train finally appears (B), what will be has been accepted, and the lowered horizon is almost liberating.

German expressionism and the psychopathic horror film enter world cinema with *The Cabinet of Dr. Caligari* (1919). A tale supposedly told by a madman with a terrible secret, the frank artificiality of its painted sets, costumes, and faces, and its extravagantly angled shapes and skew lines, accentuate its drama of human beings entrapped by petty motives magnified as grand passions.

tioned in the discussion of open-frame composition take on special relevance, since balance, tension, mass pressures and their release, the relationships between objects and characters, and so forth never seem casual or merely observed by the camera eye but part of a larger deliberate pattern. In Hitchcock's *Psycho* (1960), when an intrusive shadow first appears behind the shower curtain, it satisfyingly and therefore perversely fills out a badly composed image of a young woman showering on one side of an otherwise empty frame. The houseguests bustling in and out of each other's bedroom doors in *Rules of the Game* (1939) seem all the more free, though all the more arbitrary, when they recross at random the severe geometric rigidity of the central checkered hallway floor.

The edges of the frame take on additional importance, since all there is we see, and, at the edges, especially at the corners, the compositional

In Fritz Lang's futuristic *Metropolis* (1926), the new geometry seeks some kind of salvation from the old. A monotonously hyperrational triangle of regimented workers moves itself toward the lofty Gothic archway of a more humane and variegated religious tradition. The carefully closed composition emphasizes that this is not a glimpse of part of another world stretching beyond what we see but a parable—or allegory—defined by what we see and no more.

lines of action turn back in on themselves to reinvite further inspection of the central parts of the screen. Corners are often blocked to prevent the picture's converging edges from leading the eye out of it altogether. High masses seem more oppressive and low masses more stabilized. High detail or clutter can seem more irritating, and low more fitting. Off-screen space seems hidden rather than momentarily not seen.

Compositions gain in dramatic significance since a left area more lightly massed than a right area can imply a needed compensatory

In an uncanny, expressionistically lit street in postwar Vienna, where even vertical building lines seem out of plumb because photographed with the camera canted at an angle, Holly Martins (Joseph Cotten) thinks he sees the shadow of his supposedly dead friend Harry Lyme (Orson Welles) running away. Throughout *The Third Man* (1949), Holly confuses himself and his side of the frame with Harry and Harry's side, and with all each comes to mean.

movement by a character to the left (toward a door perhaps) rather than to the right (toward a gun on a table); the leftward movement seems more "fitting." Character left-right coding, where for example dominant characters may tend to occupy the frame right position and dominated characters the frame left, declares itself to be more than merely accidental when a weak character presumes to occupy the frame right position of his betters, as in Carol Reed's *The Third Man* (1949). A shot may disclose an **internal frame** such as a mirror, window, or doorway, enclosing and posing figures for the audience to contemplate as if a painting yet preserving a sense of open space beyond, unobtrusively in Jean Renoir's films or with elegant artificiality in Max Ophuls's.

Closed-frame compositions can be devastated by TV "scan" prints made from films with wider aspect ratios. If the sides of the frame are

A prisoner in *Brute Force* (1947) breaks jail as a double-triangle bursting out of an enclosing circle, the formal abstract pattern underlying all closed compositions almost visible as such.

missing, enclosing verticals near those sides will be missing as well, and perhaps also vanishing points, those places where in linear perspective parallel lines do finally meet. We are then left with the bare central image stripped of its compositional strength, decor, and commentary.

3

Editing Language: Composing Space and Time

An average feature-length film will consist of 500 to 1500 strips of film of different lengths. Each strip originates in a carefully conceived and photographed run of the camera; each is made at different times, and then all the strips are arranged into a single seamless series of events displayed without interruption, usually in under two hours. This running time was set thousands of years ago, perhaps by physiological necessity, so the entire work's dramatic rhythm would not be interrupted by anyone's need to leave the audience to attend to personal needs. These days it is sustained by economic convenience, the universal desire of theater owners to show a film at least twice each evening.

Film invites elaborate compression and redistribution of the different ways we experience time. One is **real time,** time as we measure it by the unvarying motion of planets, stars, clocks, and watches, natural duration steadily ticking away into the past, which is also the film's running time. Another is **subjective time,** our inner sense of duration, created by the engagement and intensity of our attention, so that minutes may drag like hours and hours seem to pass in the wink of an eye. Yet another is **phenomenological time,** the shifts in our minds from experience of the present to remembrance of the past and anticipations of the future, including recollected past anticipations of the future, all of these memories and intimations entering into the time present of a film's running time. Finally there is **narrative time,** the time supposedly elapsed from the beginning to the end of a story, hours or years. Like novels, films can leap or creep across time in either direction. But unlike the words comprising novels, film images are highly specific. At any one moment films present what appear to be people moving in what appears to be their own real time, and so films absorb us in what seems to be an ongoing experience of time present. Even a "flashback" recapitulation of the past quickly becomes an event seemingly in time present, although a "different" time present from the one originating the flashback.

Here lies a source of our fascination with these guided tours through less than two hours. We edit our own experience by redirecting or suspending our attention, our eyes and minds shifting through varieties of options with twinkling rapidity, the outer world provided by our senses, and the inner worlds provided by our minds; we then recompose our consciousness usually without any sense that we have done something extraordinary. When we watch movies, we witness events in a world which seems unlike any other but which resembles, with far greater specificity, the world we ourselves create in our own heads. Movies liberate us from our own space-time relationships by substituting theirs. Their 500 to 1500 pieces of discontinuous real-time events played end to end make continuous sense to us because the events of our own minds make sense to us in the versions we allow ourselves to notice. One reason movies seem more "real" than stage theater is that they approximate this habitual condition of our waking consciousness. The key art in this process is editing.

Continuity editing provides events arranged in seeming chronological sequences despite the viewer's frequent spatial repositioning as those events unfold, all without calling attention to that repositioning. Things happen one after another while the viewer sees them from different places, one after another. Continuity editing builds an apparently seamless flow of events out of fragments, separate shots, each providing a significant detail or characteristic. But what emerges is rarely the steadfast onward march of real time. Enough real time is provided for events which require it, like uninterrupted conversations, but more often continuity editing tries to produce the rhythms and juxtapositions of subjective and phenomenological time, how things feel as they unfold themselves, jumping from the moments making up one dramatic event to the next moments making up another, leaving out irrelevant moments in between.

This is the common "classical" studio style adopted by Hollywood to provide its audiences with narratives shaped like ongoing sequential realities. This style tends to presuppose what in fact it creates, that beyond the screen's window there is a single space-time continuum within which things happen, one after another, the earlier seeming to cause the later or at least to introduce or augment it for the viewer. Even when there is no such continuum, our minds impose one. This was demonstrated early in this century by the Kuleshov experiment, which showed that the same filmed face seemed hungry following a shot of food but sorrowful following a shot of a funeral. Some theoreticians argue that continuity editing provides only one of many possible ways to organize narratives, the one most manipulative and enthralling of the spectator in the filmmaker's ideological frames of reference. But in its procedures and flexible uses continuity editing reproduces many filmic equivalents of the narrative structures found in the earliest stories of our culture, those of Homer, the earliest books of the Old Testament, and some African tribal narratives, as well as our most recent best sellers. We need to leave Western consciousness altogether and look into Native American tales, for example, to find other ways to tell stories.

Other kinds of editing do everything else. **Structural editing** (sometimes called **"special effects editing"**) can ignore continuity and group objects by what they look like, or what they do, in common or odd juxtapositions; structural editing can display objects as if listing or accumulating them. Many modern novels do this, as do most documentaries designed mainly to convey information. Such editing can present strange dreams, apparently unrelated images associated or driven by some obscure compulsion, or it can fracture and overlap continuous actions into spatially and temporally illogical but thematically sensible cinematic patterns, as in Soviet films of the 1920s.

Structural editing is common in documentary and avant-garde films but is used cautiously in mainstream narrative films. Editing that departs from the accustomed discontinuities of waking consciousness can estrange the viewer by calling attention to itself. This pleases some jaded viewers who want to interpret the medium as part of the message, but such estrangement annoys others who want to attend strictly to the story. It is not uncommon in explosive-seeming fast-action sequences, in current post-New Wave jump-cutting, and in a few non-Western cinematic traditions, such as the Japanese, or in the films of the Senegalese director Ousman Sembene. In the hands of a major artist structural editing can reinvigorate and enlarge the conventions of classical editing. During the 1930s for example Slavko Vorkapich created many special montages for films such as Capra's *Meet John Doe* (1941), overlaying multiple actions, exposures, and dissolves to create a whirling sense of many events taking place simultaneously. His techniques derived from the Russian avant-garde and now seem a cliché of thirties narratives, but they were brilliantly done and still affect us powerfully, as their imitations do not.

We acknowledge that what is "real" includes events which occur apart from our attention to them, events outside of our consciousness. But what matters is the reality we in fact experience. Because movie editing so easily fractures the supposed solidity of space and time outside of consciousness, it provides us with versions of what we have not known as if it were happening now.

FOOTAGE

Footage is the exposed film created while the film is in production, the result of all the activity on the set or on location outside the studio, the filmic raw material from which the final film will be constructed. Everything emerging from the camera—and the synchronized sound recorder—at the end of the day is footage.

Take

A **take** is a single uninterrupted and unedited run of the camera photographing an uninterrupted and continuous action, including the clapper-loader's intrusive slate at the beginning tagging each take with a different number, up to the director's call to "Cut!" or stop acting, stop the camera, and stop recording sound. There can be many takes of each shot, dictated by the director's scrupulous sense of what will do. Each shot usually requires a few takes, more often a half-dozen, and on a bad day when the actors or the equipment aren't functioning properly or the director is relentless, twenty or more. Miraculously, the first take may provide exactly what is wanted, though another will be made anyhow for "protection" in case there is an unnoticed mistake somewhere in the first, or the second comes out better still. Some actors are at their best on the first take and then decline with each repetition; some improve with each repetition; if the two kinds are acting together, the director has a problem. Frank Capra kept performances fresh and apparently spontaneous through multiple takes by changing small details of dialogue in each take; his characters groping sincerely for words to express their heartfelt longings are sometimes played by actors in fact groping to remember which version of a speech is the current one. When a take seems satisfactory the director will call "Cut and Print!" (obviously bad takes are scrapped).

Out-takes are unused takes or segments of takes, including the clapper-loader's slate at the beginning of each take, frames cut from a take because they are not needed in the edited sequence, unused takes, and even whole edited scenes eliminated before final release. A **take-out ratio** is the ratio of exposed footage, including out-takes, to the edited footage appearing in the finished film, rarely less than 5:1, more frequently 10:1, and sometimes 20:1 or more. Film publicists will boast on occasion that a finished two-hour film is a distillation of twenty hours shot, or forty; but such take-out ratios are common because only one take is ever finally used, and that one take is often severely trimmed. **Dailies,** or **rushes,** are the previous day's takes hastily developed for screening and selection of the best take. The director and producer or studio representative always look at them, along with the cinematographer and other artist-technicians, and usually the actors (although a few avoid them, fearing that the sight of themselves acting will make their later work self-conscious).

Shot

The **shot** is the selected and edited take used in the film when the term is used by critics, synonymous with "take" when the term is used casually by filmmakers. A shot's duration may be shorter than four frames or one-sixth of a second, for flashing near-subliminal effect, or a shot can be as long as ten to twelve minutes, the length of a full reel of 35-mm film, for stately and persistent exploration of continuous action by the camera and the audience, as in Jancso's *Red Psalm* (1972) or Hitchcock's *Rope* (1948). Most shots run between five and seventy seconds, long enough for clear recognition of an event but not so long that the mere persistence bores, though one shot's interminable monotony may be as deliberate as another shot's staccato brevity, used perhaps to generate in an audience the boredom felt by a character. In Claire Denis's *Chocolat* (1988), a long final shot merely shows three Cameroon natives at work and at ease with each other against a landscape stretching into the distance, while we puzzle what this may mean; the shot's persistence itself finally informs us, that the black characters' earlier concern with colonial domination has ended and they are relaxed in possession of their own land. Shots when edited may enter on an action already under way, or they may end on an incomplete action, creating a sense of driving momentum carrying the audience through from one shot to the next. Or shots may enclose an action or moment of dialogue in entirety, the containing and framing of the event in a single shot creating a sense of stasis.

A **master shot,** or **cover shot** (also called an **"establishing shot"**) is the entire continuous action photographed from beginning to end, usually in long or medium shot. Scripts are usually written as a succession of numbered master scenes, each a continuous action. Classical shooting first photographs each as a master shot and then breaks up the same action into discrete segments separately shot from different distances and angles, directing the viewer's attention to facial expressions, gestures, or changes in the characters' relationships, and establishing a cutting rhythm appropriate to the action. Parts of master shots are then used periodically in edited sequences to reestablish an audience's sense of dramatic space when a succession of shorter shots might cause confusion, and the "master" may be all there is to carry the story when a lab ruins a more specialized shot.

An **insert shot** is a particular segment of the continuous action usually in medium shot or close-up, a number of these replacing that part of the master shot to accentuate or punctuate the particular action or reaction at issue, until finally—perhaps—very little remains on the screen of the original master.

Composite shots are segments of a completed action made up of separate shots each presenting part of that action, each created for maxi-

---

The first known insert close-up, in Edison's short *The Gay Shoe Clerk* (1903), continuity editing here discovering a primary principle. The shoe salesman is seen in privileged proximity to the young woman's exposed ankle (A), and we then ourselves inspect closely this intimate, erotically charged part of her anatomy (B). The salesman is of course immediately inflamed with desire (C); and the film ends with the older woman whacking him with her umbrella. Not accidentally, the subject of this major event in motion picture history is sexual arousal, and the impulse behind it is a desire to gratify male voyeurism while assuring women they are indeed desirable.

A

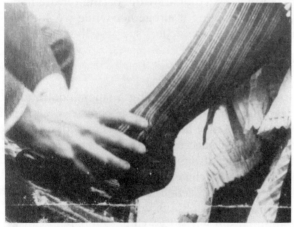

B

C

mum effect despite the fragmentation. Some filmmakers prefer to eliminate the master altogether, conceiving and building the scene shot by
shot into an exacting, carefully planned mosaic of segments, none "inserted" into anything, each linked to its preceding shot. This method
is far riskier, since a single misconceived or missing shot can disrupt
the continuity. *The Deer Hunter* (1978) contains a shot of men dangling
from a helicopter as it flies past, though the sequence shows that those
men are still down below and have not yet grabbed the helicopter's
skids. This mismatch was used probably because an empty helicopter
fly-by shot had not been made and the action required one to seem
continuous. But composite editing opens up spatial and rhythmic possibilities not available to sedate "master shot" editing, with its predictable
spaces and relationships.

Either way, the viewer's sense of continuous action is illusory. With
cuts and inserts a filmmaker will speed or slow the pacing for dramatic
or psychological effect, perhaps halting it altogether while we study a
facial expression in close-up, while the action supposedly continues.

Scene

A **scene** consists of the spliced shots constituting a single continuous
action, whether a conversation or an elaborate car chase with many
smashups along the way. A scene may be a single master shot perhaps
with a few inserts, or it can be a succession of shots each made for
maximum effect and edited together also for maximum effect. A dialogue
may be a succession of one shots in the classical **shot/reverse shot** sequence as each character speaks and reacts in turn, in individual close-
ups or in alternating **over-the-shoulder shots** which provide close-ups
while preserving the communal sense of a two-shot, one person's head
and shoulder visibly framing the other person's face. In news interviews
conducted with one camera, the camera may remain on a speaker while
the reporter asks questions off-camera. Then the camera may be turned
on the reporter asking the same questions again, and registering various
reactions while maintaining an eye-line as if still looking at the speaker.
When these different shots are intercut the audience will seem to witness
an interview, not a monologue. This custom was put to dramatic issue
in *Broadcast News* (1987), where an interviewer later forces tears to his
eyes to create a reaction shot for later insertion into the interview footage,
a form of journalistic dishonesty.

The classical **shot/reaction shot** triad shows a character looking at
something, then what is seen from the character's point of view (a
subjective or POV shot), then the character's reaction. This common
three-shot trope privileges the viewer with a sense of participation and

A

B

A series of reverse over-the-shoulder shots ends Chaplin's *City Lights* (1931), when a blind flower girl now cured recognizes that her former benefactor is not the handsome millionaire she has mistakenly thought him but a demoralized tramp. Four times the camera returns to Chaplin's face while he nervously watches her reaction, holding a flower to his teeth (A). Four times we look over his shoulder at her reaction (B). From her initial shock she moves to full understanding, finally clutching his hand to her breast while saying, "Yes, I can see now." But in a superbly fortuitous editing mismatch, the shots of her face show the tramp holding the flower not to his teeth but at chest level or below. The discontinuity contributes to our uneasy feeling that despite her gesture of acceptance, they cannot come fully together; they inhabit two separate worlds.

Jeffries (James Stewart) is disturbed by what he thinks he sees in *Rear Window* (1954), and we are so accustomed to such reaction shots guiding our own reactions that we incline to think him justified no matter how far-fetched.

yet of impartial observation, and guides the viewer's reaction by providing the character's as in Hitchcock's *Rear Window* (1954), where we watch and also share the main character's voyeurism. In Wim Wenders's *The Goalie's Anxiety at the Penalty Kick* (1972) we see what a character sees and *then* see him looking: The first shot is momentarily disorienting, even bewildering, because seemingly free-floating and unaccountable, forcing us to share for the moment the character's mental disarray.

Any edited continuity usually respects what is called the **"180-degree rule,"** in which a **center line** perpendicular to the camera's line of sight on—say—two characters talking in one shot cannot be crossed in the next, or the two characters will seem to the audience to have reversed their positions on the screen. Directors such as Godard or Antonioni sometimes violate this rule deliberately to suggest the arbitrariness of human relationships and intentions; in *Red Desert* (1964) Antonioni breaches it to show characters departing listlessly in different directions supposedly toward a single prearranged place for an orgy. But "crossing the line" is usually a basic error in filmmaking, confusing the audience. Scene editing is also wary of the so-called **30-degree rule,** which declares that any two shots spliced together should vary their angle to the subject by at least thirty degrees (or else, maintaining the angle, move much closer), or the action will seem **jump cut,** as if intervening footage had been accidentally cut out of the shot and an intended continuity lost. Again, this rule is violated for specific reasons, again especially by sixties New Wave filmmakers, frequently and famously by Godard in his first feature *Breathless* (1959).

Sequence

The spliced scenes—which can be a brief single shot, or a succession of many—making up a significant visual or dramatic unit are a **sequence.** A sequence may include several continuous actions occurring simultaneously, like the ride of the Klan in Griffith's *Birth of a Nation* (1915), or set discontinuously in different times and places but intercut with each other, like holocaust memories in *The Pawnbroker* (1965), but more frequently a sequence consists of a single scene or a straightforward succession of scenes to the conclusion of a dramatic point. The art creating these is called **montage,** the editing, cutting, and splicing of shots for maximum effect or synthesized statement, by juxtaposition, emphasis, ironic disjunction, or temporal wrenching. In the shower murder montage of *Psycho* (1960), for example, Hitchcock claimed that there were seventy-eight shots presented in forty-five seconds; the sequence is no less shocking for there being perhaps twenty fewer shots than Hitchcock claimed.

Most narrative editing employs **analytic montage,** which constructs a "real" world of time, space, and action out of dramatically significant details, with close-ups, inserts, or cross-cutting displaying and punctuating that world. Some special purposes may dictate use of discontinuous **shock,** or **collision montage** sometimes called **"Russian montage"** because it was created and exploited by Russian filmmakers such as Dziga Vertov and Sergei Eisenstein. This kind of editing splices or overlaps violently opposed images, disjunctive actions, abstract forms and textures, and space-time relationships, all without concern for the logical presentation of a single whole world on screen. Rather, shock montage colludes directly with the spectator to induce new ways of seeing meanings and relationships among shots, edited sequences synthesizing in the viewer's mind ideas not obviously portrayed in the film's footage. Eisenstein also used **intellectual montage** in which a shot comments on others by its subject rather than by its relationship to the others' spatial and temporal continuities, e.g., a shot of herded sheep intercut with shots of urban commuters commenting obviously on those commuters.

Film theorists and avant-garde filmmakers alike devote special attention to films which avoid or extend into irony the clichés of classical continuity editing (see Bruce Connor's *A Movie* for example), because as Brecht and later Godard pointed out, stable and continuous fantasy worlds seem to preoccupy viewers who might otherwise act to change their situations in the real world. Such theorists prefer films estranging, distancing, or breaching a viewer's accustomed voyeuristic or fetichistic fantasies. Continuity editing remains nevertheless the primary way films arrange themselves, the equivalent of an ongoing stage action or of linear narrative in novels. Although in fact our senses do not register continuities in actual life, our minds almost immediately impose continuity on whatever we think we are experiencing, because the alternative would seem chaotic. We learn early in life to cleave to the principle that the world is one place, and we suspend that conviction only when dreaming, or when attending certain movies.

TRANSITIONS

Transitions between shots, scenes, and sequences conventionally display the dramatic relationships between those separate units, so the audience can assemble the displayed subject matter in their own minds without confusion (or with calculated uncertainty). With the splicing of separate short shots at the turn of the century, film ceased to be a photographic novelty and entered its long career as a narrative art form; coded ways to signal temporal transitions soon followed. We are now so accustomed to the conventional transitions that when they are used deftly we register their meaning without noticing them, and when they are used clumsily they lurch or register as clichés, overly obvious.

Cuts

A **cut** splices the last frame of one shot to the first of another, the film literally cut so the previously continuous shot changes to another within a twenty-fourth of a second. In effect the audience's positioning with respect to the action changes as abruptly, but certain cues allow instant reorientation. **Match cuts** maintain the temporal flow of action in continuous space but blend different angles of vision or distances, as when a character is seen opening a door from the outside, then seen entering a room from the inside, or as with dialogue carried on in shot/reverse

The spectacular cross-cutting climax to D. W. Griffith's blatantly racist Civil War epic *Birth of a Nation* (1915). Soon after the war, (A) the recently formed Ku Klux Klan rides to rescue simultaneously (B) a town beleaguered by renegade black troops, (C) a woman menaced by an ambitious black politician, and (D) a family trapped by blacks in a rural cabin, the father about to kill his daughter rather than suffer her dishonor when they break in. Griffith cuts repeatedly between these threatened victims and their onrushing rescuers, with powerful cumulative effect. Bewildered by public condemnation of him as a bigot, in his next film *Intolerance* (1916) Griffith made amends by cross-cutting four separate stories of decency savaged by brutality over the centuries.

shot. **Cross cuts** or **parallel cuts** (especially if brief, **cutaway** shots) change to another space and another action presumably taking place simultaneously ("meanwhile, back at the ranch," or "meanwhile, in her other hand . . ."). **Jump cuts** wrench temporal and spatial continuities with liberating absurdity or brutal abruptness, as if time continues to flow while space changes radically—a Beatles' lyric is sung in *A Hard Day's Night* (1964), first on open ground and then on a fire escape, no time elapsed for the Beatles to get from one to the other; or a jump cut can make it seem as if a continuous action were leaping intermediate stages, as frequently in Godard's *Breathless*.

Because all cuts are instantaneous, the effects of preceding shots momentarily carry into successive shots, transferring qualities of energy or mood from one to the other; one may doubt the existence of physiological "persistence of vision," but many physiological reactions and mental states are slower to change than a cross cut, and the mind insists on seeing relationships between shots even when there are none. Moreover, a center of attention in one part of the screen determines the space first seen in the next shot, since the audience's eyes are already fixed on it; action, suspense, and ironic editing alike exploit this "zone" phenomenon. Violation of the 30-degree rule can seem dizzying, and violation of the 180-degree rule can be perplexing; thus a match cut across a center line requires an intervening transitional shot redefining the center line. Traditional shot/reverse shot or shot/reaction shot segments are usually match cut to each other.

Dissolves

A **dissolve** is a quiet major transition from an earlier time to a later one, sometimes with a change of place as well; an earlier shot is gradually replaced by a later shot superimposed upon it for a brief time, so the significance of the earlier action seems sustained into the later (because shots are overlapped on each other, sometimes called a **"lap dissolve"**). The result is a sense of continuous action even while the audience sees that time has elapsed. Dissolves can be swift, scarcely noticeable, although more often they are gradual in their pacing, even languorous. However, dissolves are always precisely calculated (the few or many overlapping frames involved in a dissolve are specifically marked during editing and then overprinted by the laboratory). They inform the audience that time and place may have changed, but a further development or consequence of the action will follow as if without interruption. More recently dissolves have been used to link matched, continuous shots with no time elapsed, signifying rapture (as during lovemaking), delirium, or other feelings of a world in dissolution.

Fades

A **fade** is a major closure declaring that a consequential action has ended and a new event will now begin, usually at a later time, often in a different place. A fade is the cinematic equivalent of lowering the curtain between acts in a stage play. A slow darkening to black, or brightening to white, or to a dominant color as in Ingmar Bergman's *Cries and Whispers* (1972), is a **fade-out;** a slow return of the dark screen to a new image is a **fade-in.** The effect can be produced in a camera or later in a lab. Dramatic tension eases, and an undistracted moment provides for reflection and anticipation of the next stage of the drama. An **iris fade** or **iris wipe** is a circular diminishing of the image until it disappears, common in old films and in recent films to create the feel of an old film.

Wipes

Wipes replace one moving image with another by a horizontal pushing (**line wipe**), flipping as of the turning of a page (**flip wipe**), or other of hundreds of patterns. Wipes are now old-fashioned, with cross cuts or jump cuts used instead, although the wipe has reappeared on television as the electronic technology has come commonly available, and its TV contemporaneity may revive its use in theatrical films. This self-declaring artifice estranges the viewer from the narrative and can be expressive, as can be subtle movements of a wipe, following a train out of the frame for example, or rolling now to the left, now to the right, as when in Kurosawa's *Ikiru* (1952) citizens petitioning City Hall are shunted by bureaucrats from office to office.

Other Transitional Images

Other images can be used transitionally. Clocks with or without dissolves on repositioned hands routinely register the passage of time; in Lubitsch's *Trouble in Paradise* (1932), a man enters a woman's bedroom while the camera remains discreetly in the hall outside, looking at a clock. Or, camera movements such as swish pans, tilts, cranes, or zooms can be used (swish pans across the *Inquirer* building separate the years of breakfasts in *Citizen Kane's* marriage montage). The Japanese director Ozu's custom of using a single recurring shot instead of a fade (a street scene, or a flag flying over a theater) has been widely imitated. **Racking,** or **focus-through,** gradually blurs one shot and refocuses to a different image; this is a common, even clichéd way to signal flashbacks in film noir such as *Sunset Boulevard* (1950) or to show reversion of the depicted world to a character's internal fantasy.

SOUND AND SOUND EFFECTS

All the while editors cut and arrange various shots of the film, they cut parts of the synchronized sound track and mark suggestions for other sounds as well. Sound serves to bind cut images together, to comment on them, and to condition the way they are seen. The full sound track is usually augmented, mixed, dubbed, and synchronized after the edited film has been assembled according to its visual necessities. With animated cartoons this order is reversed, animated images being drawn to synchronize with a preexisting sound track.

Though studios look for very high aural quality in their films, the sound Dolbyized, stereophonic, quadraphonic, etc., most viewers pay little or no attention to whatever they are hearing, even when it affects them powerfully. The sound track seems merely to be "accompanying" the images, even when it is doing far more. But we don't notice. For this reason sound can generate many subliminal effects without disturbing the illusion that an actual world is on the screen; in fact sound contributes to the illusion. Some tracks work subtly, with music or dialogue near the end of a previous shot preparing a receptive mood for the one to follow, or with the sounds of an action lingering afterward like a sweet or a bad memory. Sound may even run counter to an image or a scene, slyly or brutally commenting on it.

Location shots and many studio shots are often made **MOS** (that is, "mitout sound," so-called by German emigré directors working with U.S. crews during the 1930s and now enshrined as shorthand on clapboard slates). Perhaps only **wild sound** will be recorded, the actual voices and background noises during shooting, often not usable: Cameras can be noisy unless heavily "blimped" with soundproofing, and accidental car or jet plane noises can intrude on the sounds of a medieval battlefield. Outdoor dialogue is often dubbed. Italian films are always dubbed into various languages, even into Italian. All singing is dubbed, especially if accompanied by dancing lively enough to affect the singer's breathing; an unfortunate exception to this policy is in Peter Bogdanovich's *At Long Last Love* (1975); he thought that live singing would seem more spontaneous. This dubbing takes place in a **looping studio,** where short loops of the film are shown to actors repeatedly for **lipsynch** re-recording of their voices, aided by **automatic dialogue replacement** (ADR) machines. *Inside Daisy Clover* (1965) shows the process in a climax where a much-burdened Natalie Wood finally breaks down while trying to dub sprightly singing to her own looped image.

The multiple tracks making up the sound track are artfully reprocessed during editing, designed carefully for the sequences they accompany. A foreign film may retain all its sounds mixed on various tracks, with only the dialogue track dubbed into various countries' languages. To the viewer (or listener), sound will seem to be **source sound** (known to some critics as **diegetic sound**), attributable to the world within the film and supposedly created by it, or **unsourced** or **off-screen sound** (that is, **nondiegetic** or **extra-diegetic sound**), outside that world and in some sense guiding the listener's attitude toward it. But both are usually mixed into the film during postproduction.

Human Voices

Immediately identifiable as male or female, mature or childish, voices establish the speakers' moods, social and educational levels, and other clues to their characters and emotional states. Voices are also the signatures of many well-known actors and actresses, carrying known traits attributable to their characters even when their faces are not visible. Until 1928 films developed their arts without voices, using broad or subtle pantomime and occasional written intertitles (for some filmmakers, as few as possible). With synchronized sound, the "talkies" contributed to the audience's illusion that the world on the screen resembles its own, or at least that of naturalistic stage drama. The highly expressive, heavily coded tones of human voices add to the illusion while diminishing opportunities for extravagant editing. Yet even now films say most things without recourse to talk. Characters almost always converse in brief phrases or short sentences, and long dramatic speeches are rare.

Monologue is the sound of one voice speaking whether or not anyone in the film is listening. If attributable to a character we may see that person talking, or the voice may seem to come from offscreen in brief or long reverse shots, while we watch someone onscreen listening and reacting. Or both the speaker and the listener can be offscreen for the moment while we search the image for a source and perhaps locate only an empty room or street, itself commenting on the speech we are hearing, an effect much used by Woody Allen from *Annie Hall* (1977) on. Or the voice may present a stream of consciousness, thoughts overheard while the visible character seems not to be speaking at all, as Olivier arranged Hamlet's soliloquies in the 1948 film.

Recourse to speech in our culture seems to imply some inadequacy or emotional imbalance, a need to be heard or to explain one's self in a search for acceptance. Our male heroes, especially in Westerns, tend to be loners who say little, their silence signaling self-reliance; our female heros talk more readily, as if they had greater access to their feelings and were more at ease socially, and "screwball" women (as played by Carole Lombard or Katherine Hepburn) often talk nonstop, as if to block out their own thoughts and so remain in touch with their unerring instincts. James Stewart's long speeches in Capra's *Mr. Smith Goes to Washington* (1939), or *It's a Wonderful Life* (1946), like Gary Cooper's in Capra's *Meet John Doe* (1941), testify to his character's intense sincerity, long-suppressed convictions finally overwhelming natural modesty and pouring forth. But even these films show the characters to be otherwise spare of speech. Long monologues play well on stage, but on screen they seem excessive. If essential a lengthy **talking head** shot will be broken up with other shots, perhaps of a rapt or an inattentive listener.

A **voice-over** is a voice on the sound track commenting on the action, unattributable to an onscreen character or to one momentarily offscreen. Voice-overs can be the equivalent of a fictional authorial voice, or in documentary a commentator's voice. But voice-overs can also originate in a character narrating or explaining the story as if at some later time. Such narrators impose a sense of purposive significance to the images they are commenting on; we know the story is going somewhere because the narrator is already there. In forties film noir a narrator's voice often introduces a fated movement of the story in flashback toward that moment when the retrospective retelling began, itself entrapped in a plotted circle. Famously or infamously, the Academy Award-winning *Sunset Boulevard* (1950) opens with a voiceover commenting on a body floating in a swimming pool; we learn later that the narrator is that dead person somehow explaining how he got there. The opening of Woody Allen's *Interiors* (1978) shows a man's back while we hear his voice, in what seems to be a narrative voice-over speaking after the film's action has ended, explaining what we need to know before the action begins. Though voice-overs attempt to control audience attitudes toward the events portrayed, the images and the editing will always dominate. In Bunuel's *Las Hurdes,* or *Land without Bread* (1932), the voice-over's remarks are so fatuously inadequate to the awful poverty depicted that they themselves become objects of the film's satire.

Dialogue, or human interchange (or evident inattention), usually observes the convention of completed speech, rare in life but common in drama, where no one replies until the speaker has finished. Sometimes dialogue will interrupt or overlap as is common in real conversations. This is rare in films, though it imparts a frenzied energy to Howard Hawks's comedies, and lends an amusing irrelevance to conversations in Robert Altman's films such as *M*A*S*H* (1970) or *Nashville* (1975). The camera may show a speaker speaking or a listener listening, may anticipate a reply by cutting to the listener before the speaker has finished, or, as at times in Jean Renoir's films, may seem to grow inattentive and drift away from both. If we see alternating one-shots in shot/reverse shot, we sense that the characters, although speaking to each other, are isolated; over-the-shoulder shots maintain a sense of them talking together instead of separately. Voice quality and moods usually contrast heavily in dramatic dialogue, so who is speaking is never in doubt.

Noises

Noises are usually added in postproduction to ensure quality control and precise timing and volume and to allow artists to concentrate on their performances during the actual shooting, no takes ruined by accidental or intrusive noises.

Accompanying or source sounds must be included, such as footsteps, laughter, applause, traffic, crowds, machinery, gunshots, water splashes, off-screen toilet noises in comedies, or other noises obviously originating in the action. Since actors always fake being hit, and the real sound of a blow is anyhow rarely audible, the sound editor must add an exaggerated splat or thud to persuade the audience otherwise.

Ambient or **background** sound contributes to a scene's verisimilitude and dramatic significance. The sound of wind in the trees, birds, various animals "somewhere elsewhere" in the background, passing cars, factory machinery, etc. can punctuate or heighten a mood or key line of dialogue, adding a sense of the mechanical, the mellifluous, the ominous, the serene, or whatever else to the dramatic action. Seemingly terrified horses may neigh during a Western fistfight, as in *High Noon* (1952), emphasizing the scene's animal violence. In Bergman's *The Touch* (1971), an off-screen snarling buzz saw supposedly outside an apartment, but never explained, prevents a scene of sexual coupling from seeming

Sheriff Kane and his former deputy (Lloyd Bridges) fight it out in a stable, the deputy's petty resentment one more of Kane's burdens. Their animal strength is framed and confined by the horse's body and legs, and the sound track's frightened animal sounds help further define Kane's anguish at this moment.

provocative or satisfying. When Kane slaps Susan Alexander during the picnic in *Citizen Kane*, a woman's voice begins screaming unaccountably, supposedly somewhere else while Susan glares silently back at Kane, the background sound expressing Susan's inner outrage. In films by Jean-Luc Godard or Robert Altman, or in the scripts Harold Pinter wrote for Joseph Losey films such as *The Servant* (1963), overheard random phrases spoken by other people in bars or coffee shops may incidentally enlarge or comment on the main characters' conversations or provide a chastening sense that other dramas beyond our concern are also under way. Often even "silence" must be added to a sound-track, since hallways, closets, and prairies each have their own kind with their own resonance, perhaps threatening, perhaps reassuring.

Music

Music is selected, composed, performed, recorded, and added to the track in postproduction, usually last of all, since music can dominate all other sounds and must be synchronized to the edited film, and since it can create, heighten, or comment ironically on the dramatic mood of a scene or sequence especially if the scene itself fails to create an appropriate mood. The strategy for the musical score—classical or rock, single instrument or full symphonic orchestra, sparely used or drenching the entire film—is usually decided and budgeted early; and source music is composed early so it can seem to be performed by characters in the film (as sometimes it is).

Source music (diegetic music) is heard performed in the film's world, by characters, orchestras, radios, or other sources. If the character is a professional entertainer, as in many musicals or biographies of musicians, the origin of the sound is easily understood and its high quality accepted; for *Bird* (1988), original Charlie "Bird" Parker recordings were remastered for the sound track. A helpful convention allows that any ordinary person in love or carrying a torch can sing about personal feelings with a high degree of musical professionalism, with a voice dubbed by someone else if need be. A melodic line or orchestral chord may then become part of the sound track's background musical score. In the final sequence of Kubrick's *Paths of Glory* (1957), a shy girl is forced to sing to a savagely raucous audience of soldiers, and her quavering voice returns to them a sense of their own humanity; the melody then picked up orchestrated on the background track declares that a film about a bitter defeat is also about a triumph. Comedians such as Mel Brooks and Woody Allen have played whimsically with the conventions of source and background scoring. In *Bananas* (1971), apparent background harp music heightening a character's delight at a dinner invitation is revealed ludicrously to be source music played by an impoverished harpist practicing in a nearby closet. In *Chariots of Fire* (1981), a background chorus sings Gilbert and Sullivan's "He Is an Englishman" while we watch the hero at work and play in a succession of shots, as if the film were celebrating his determination to succeed, though with the final shot the music arrives at its source and is seen originating in one more of his activities, a college production of Gilbert and Sullivan.

Background music (nondiegetic music) most immediately originates in Victorian stage melodrama (literally, drama with musical accompaniment). Background music heightens dramatic moods and emotions, part of the theatrical experience but without accountability within the drama. "Silent" films were never really silent but accompanied by music: full orchestral scores, or cue sheets listing suitable melodies, were provided routinely by the filmmakers; in lesser theaters smaller orchestras served; in last-run theaters organists or pianists improvised as they could (even providing sound effects).

During the thirties and forties, Hollywood films were often scored from beginning to end, with different musical leitmotifs, chords, or melodic lines accompanying each character and each dramatic theme, occasionally combining in complex orchestrations as characters and themes combined in the plot, as in Erich Wolfgang Korngold's scores for *The Adventures of Robin Hood* (1938) or *The Sea Hawk* (1940), or in Max Steiner's many scores. In such films even physical movements were operatically accompanied by equivalent movements in the music; the escape of the galley slaves in *The Sea Hawk* is virtually a ballet, each prisoner's every gesture also figured in the music. Cutting shots to a musical beat is called **"mickey-mousing,"** after Disney's practice. It is nowadays avoided as old-fashioned and obvious, although it works powerfully to punctuate the last montage of characters awaiting the noon train in Zinneman's *High Noon*, the musical and editing beats together counting down the last seconds before the train arrives.

More recent films are scored more sparingly, though scored at least behind the main titles and credits in order to establish moods or genre expectations—equestrian rhythms and elegaic ballads for Westerns, whimsical and sprightly melodies for comedies, a deliberate silence behind the main titles to confer solemnity on whatever follows. Nowadays only a few sequences of a film may be emotionally "built" or underscored musically, though some films provide their listeners with a nonstop rock music environment. Suspense, menace, irresolution, or lyrical exaltation can be heightened or even generated by a good musical score; the music tells us how we should feel even when the film otherwise leaves us indifferent. We know that Rocky's various triumphs in the boxing ring are altogether triumphant despite the hid-

The music at this point in *The Sea Hawk* (1940) dips and rises as the galley slaves bend or climb, echoing every move. When finally they seize a ship and set sail "Straight for the shores of Dover," that is precisely what we hear sung in full operatic male chorus.

eous punishment he has endured because the orchestra tells us so. We know that the rape in *Straw Dogs* (1971) is horrible despite the wife's seeming to ask for it, because it is accompanied by horrible sounds. Occasionally the music will comment ironically on the action, as with "We'll meet again" sung mindlessly to a montage of exploding nuclear bombs in Kubrick's *Dr. Strangelove* (1964), or as with mournful operatic melodies peculiarly lamenting Jake La Motta's moments of triumph in the ring in Scorsese's *Raging Bull* (1980). Because music hath charm to invoke feelings of olden times, it is commonly used to establish a sense of period as well as a mood. Scott Joplin's ragtime in George Roy Hill's *The Sting* (1973) was already old-fashioned by the twenties, when the film is set, but ragtime now sounds bygone and playful enough to represent the twenties to modern audiences.

SPECIAL EFFECTS

In traditional film history the Lumières established a realist or seemingly documentary film tradition, and George Méliès a fantasy tradition with stop-action disappearances, double exposures, matte paintings, and other cinematic methods of making an ostensibly real world seem uncanny or miraculous. In fact all cinematic worlds including the Lumières's are created by special dramatic and cinematic effects. Strictly speaking, a female hero's supernaturally flawless complexion or indestructible hair-do is no less a special effect than a werewolf's hairy hand or a character's blood-splattered bullet wound. Even so, certain specular or spectacular marvels often appear on the screen, and appreciating their novelty becomes for some viewers an end in itself. Special effects technicians or artists such as George Pal, Harry Harryhausen, or Douglas Trumbull have become superstars in their own right, and how an effect is achieved now interests many viewers more than how well it is used

A special effect without special effects. As a professional eavesdropper on other people in Francis Coppola's *The Conversation* (1974), Harry Caul tries to achieve physical and moral anonymity. Here, as he phones for an appointment with a client, other people may be watching and listening, and he seems to get his wish. As the camera moves closer and the glass phone booth's vertical edges disappear off the frame, he turns insubstantial among its reflected reflections, and the blank white globe overhead seems the only solid object visible.

in the film. Films are sometimes conceived and made primarily to gratify such technological tastes, the plot an excuse for the spectacle.

Photographed effects are created by makeup, differentiated scale (true size is undistinguishable on a screen), or devices created by expert technicians. These effects include explosions, dummy and stunt substitutions for actors falling off cliffs, scale models framed to seem life-sized, back and front projection of streets racing past cars anchored in the studio (or airplanes in flight seen from alongside), cosmetic and prosthetic masks or amputations, gross-out gristle and monstrous transformations, blood spurts and shattered skulls—the whole range of simulated fantasies that can be placed in front of a camera and then photographed as if real. Recently models in computer-controlled motion have greatly expanded the range of credible effects to be photographed and then combined with other photographs in process shots.

Process effects are created in laboratories, sometimes several labs simultaneously to save time when frame-by-frame processing is required. The techniques are various: multiple exposures, each adding another starship battalion attacking the same planet; blue screens for overlay of images; strange colors or luminosities; computer-generated images or animated drawings on photographed images, such as laser zaps drawn on photographed futuristic guns; doctored sound; and split screens. Split screens can be used well to contrast two events seen simultaneously, as in the family dinner tables of *Annie Hall* (1977), or mistakenly to multiply a kinetic effect when it tends in fact to divide that effect by dividing attention, as in the multiple destructiveness of the climax to *Carrie* (1976). Since photography, editing, and lab processing of chemically coated strips of film are at the center of the art, few illusory events or appearances cannot be created. The issue for filmmakers since Méliès has been to achieve marvelous effects with greater detailed verisimilitude, imaginary gardens that seem real, with imaginary toads in them that also seem real.

But the issue with such fictive experiences since Homer's *Odyssey* has been to reveal ordinary or exceptional human capability confronting mind-staggering, uncanny, disorienting events. The better a story can do this, the less essential to it are high-tech simulated delusions. Effective low-budget horror films such as Don Siegel's *Invasion of the Body Snatchers* (1956) or Tourneur's *Cat People* (1942), with their suggestive indirection, still evoke metaphysical shudders as strong as those of effective high-budget films such as Ridley Scott's *Alien* (1979) or David Cronenberg's *The Fly* (1986); both kinds of films elicit our more profound and profoundly suppressed fears. Yet, young viewers especially enjoy testing their courage or stoicism before marvelously achieved gross-out sights, and they admire candy-colored chromium technologies projected large before them; profound cultural needs are expressed beneath these apparently trivial tastes. Special effects experts will always be essential to filmmaking, but whatever the available special sets, props, processes, prostheses, and budgets, no special effect expert is as effective as a canny director fortunate in the film's script, endowed with imagination, and at work with whatever is at hand.

4

Dramatic Conventions and Screen Acting

DRAMATIC TERMS

Stage conventions vary widely according to a culture's different uses for shared public display. Conventions may draw from religious rituals, bardic chanting, storytelling, philosophical discourses, dances, parades, pageants, spectacles, historical and political celebrations, sporting competitions, wars, or legal procedures, and from their stylized imitations. There is no one kind of drama, even of the kind we think of as drama, the storytelling we watch in theaters and on TV.

By the end of the nineteenth century stage conventions conformed to a narrow **naturalism** designed to create on stage replicas of a separate but familiar world. Almost always the curtain rose on a middle-class living room or upper-class "drawing room," the public areas of private dwellings, and the audience was cast as witnesses to a stage performance of a play and yet also unacknowledged eavesdroppers on an actual domestic event. The drama itself was usually an ironic melodrama or farce; variety entertainment—song, dance, juggling, etc.—survived elsewhere. These dramas reflected bourgeois concerns, usually stresses within family life, even when dealing with the very wealthy or powerful. Despite occasional excursions into other movements, such as expressionism or theater of the absurd, most of our stage dramas still do.

In a naturalistic drama the prime determinants of human action are not God or the gods but heredity and environment, which together determine what a character wishes to do and can do. Yet dramatic actions are usually shaped to display a significant providential order hidden in the most coincidental-seeming events (as presumably in life), with individuals shaped by their past and constrained by present circumstance held nevertheless responsible for their own choices ("character is fate"). Justice in the end is somehow served, if not by some persistent hero or the logic of events then by characters undergoing moral conversions or by apparent coincidences which constitute destiny. In Greek times a happy ending could arrive with a *deus ex machina* or god creaking down on stage machinery to straighten out the messes mortals had made of things. Naturalism requires that these interventions be hidden, supposedly wholly natural, and so accident or coincidence now replaces visible deities. Screenwriters have been encouraged by moral codes if not the Motion Picture Production Code to show that certain kinds of behavior *must* lead to certain consequences, crimes followed inescapably if accidentally by punishments. As this century began novels also preached this naturalistic determinism, some more pessimistically but most similarly revealing a hidden providential dispensation governing human affairs. The motion picture camera and the first "photoplays" came into existence while all these assumptions governed, and most movies still sustain them.

As in many of his films, Preston Sturges satirizes Hollywood habits and pretentions as well as the public's, in this case taking aim at mandatory happy endings. In *The Palm Beach Story* (1942), one deserving character cannot find happiness without marrying Claudette Colbert, nor another without marrying Joel McCrea, but Colbert and McCrea are already coupled with each other. Fortunately, Colbert and McCrea suddenly remember that they are twins, allowing the film to sweep to the altogether satisfying conclusion shown here.

There are key differences between the ways we experience stage and screen dramas. Stage drama presents real performers in real time ("meat actors") enacting fictive characters in fictive time but in space shared with the audience. There is always an element of reenacted performance in theater and of a delimited, persistent acting space. Many plays since Pirandello have used these characteristics as metaphors for the enactments, performances, and limited worlds of our own lives, life itself seen as theater at large. Film, however, presents fictive characters in their own materially different time and space, in a flat world opened up for imaginative participation spatially, temporally, and psychologically, with audiences positioned within those spaces and witnessing events as if they were actually occurring (though we all know they were figured earlier in patchwork by real performers in studios elsewhere). A stage drama often seems to present recreated past events, whereas in film events seem to take place. The "staged" performances within the stage performances of plays like Pirandello's *Six Characters*, Weiss's *Marat/Sade*, Stoppard's *Rosencrantz and Guildenstern Are Dead*, or *A Chorus Line* can be filmed, but on film they lose their meaning as dramatic gestures witnessed by live audiences. Films seem too real to serve such metadramatic or ritualistic purposes, and as theatrical events they are not real enough.

Plot

A **plot** depicts changes of state and fortune undergone chronologically by characters, shown in a sequential revelation to audiences which may not itself be chronological. Aristotle, who founded drama criticism, called all drama "the imitation of an action" (not the mere revelation of characters in action). American films especially are structured and driven by strong lines of action, concern with what will happen next rather than what will next be revealed about the characters, who usually can be understood almost entirely almost at once. An action is usually made manifest by a main character, a **protagonist,** whose initial choices set the plot in motion and whose fortunes we then follow; and so a film seems to be about that character, the plot being the developing situation he or she creates or discovers. "Buddy" films such as *Butch Cassidy and the Sundance Kid* (1969) give us two such protagonists, and films influenced by the parallel plot lines of TV drama, such as *Terms of Endearment* (1983), can have several.

There is usually also an **antagonist,** a character opposed to the protagonist, with resulting dramatic conflict. But a particular protagonist is often not essential to a particular plot, which can be made manifest— perhaps less interestingly—by some other character, perhaps an observer of events others enact. Similarly, the antagonist need not be personified at all; the antagonist can be the situation or life itself conspiring to thwart the protagonist's will. Protagonists may be interchangeable; scripts are sometimes rewritten to change one kind of character into a different kind with greater audience appeal, the basic action remaining intact. Robert Altman's films such as *Nashville* (1975) or *A Wedding* (1978) are often about several different characters forming a social group, not some one leading character.

Linear Plots.   Climactic structures are so common as to constitute patterns of expectation by which a spectator views and comprehends films in process, so that little critical thought needs to be given to a film's narrative structures or strategies. In fact many audiences are confused or annoyed if the customary patterns are violated. In Western cultures all plots are **climactic** in shape, based on some defined **conflict**

between characters, forces, or ideas, some one **plot problem,** or some one **desire** seeking gratification. Plots begin with an **exposition** of the characters and their situation, introducing the conflict or problem (who are they, what has already happened). Plots show **development** and complication of that problem in a rising action. Finally a climax is reached near the end of the drama consisting of some ultimate discovery or recognition, an ultimate confrontation and perhaps reversal of fortune, and always a revelation and perhaps a resolution of the plot problem or at least full comprehension of its underlying nature. A brief **dénouement** follows showing the consequences of that revelation, suggesting some eventual outcome. In screenwriting the climax is sometimes called the "obligatory scene," when all early promissory notes and expectations are paid off.

Climactic structures are especially well-suited to a **teleological** view of human experience, the belief that all human events are meaningfully arranged toward some ultimate purpose eventually revealed (or the desire so to believe) because these structures are themselves teleologically constructed to arrive at a significant event, a climax and resolution of some kind. The opposite would be an **existential** world view, which sees human events accumulating largely by chance, for no essential reason, with no implicit meanings other than those we or our cultures impose on them perhaps arbitrarily. An existential plot shows life lived for its evanescent daily qualities, perhaps reflected upon and savored in memory, rather than life "getting somewhere." Some filmmakers such as Truffaut or Antonioni are existentialists, and their plot constructions avoid apparent purposive movement toward a climactic moment. Climactic revelations to the characters and the audience nevertheless occur by the end of their films.

In most films, what a character wants and what that character finally gets often constitute the primary plot concern, though the thing wanted like the particular character wanting it may be quite arbitrary (Hitchcock called that thing a **"maguffin,"** valuable diamonds, secret plans, power or money, whatever, itself unimportant except for what characters are willing to do to get it). Climactic structures are also well-suited to a deterministic view of human destiny, a sense that we are all imprisoned inescapably in chains of causes and consequences, self-betrayed perhaps by some small original error or accident (see especially U.S. films noir of the forties and early fifties). Some critics believe *all* chronological plots are concerned with chains of causes and their effects. This view oversimplifies: Many plots use chronology for convenience while their main concerns remain with character revelation, or with successive memorable present moments, whatever the plot contrivances used to arrive at them. Causes and their effects, like determinism and free will, were

Cary Grant and Ingrid Bergman discover the "maguffin" in *Notorious* (1946), uranium ore hidden in a wine bottle by well-to-do Nazis established in South America. Any other secret Grant wanted Bergman to find out would have served the plot's needs equally well, and other suspenseful ways to discover this secret might have done well too, though the wine cellar sequence has become a classic. Much in suspense thriller plotting is arbitrary; that the characters think something matters is what matters.

an absorbing concern of our culture during the turn of the century, fascinated as it was by scientific, evolutionary, and literary naturalism as a new way to understand the universe. We now tend to worry about other things.

Episodic plots focus on separate actions—each perhaps climactic in shape but apparently independent of the others—strung out like beads sequentially and unified perhaps only by a single character appearing in all of them, often in process of a journey. If the character is a free spirit acting on impulse and responding to whatever occurs, this is often called a **picaresque** structure (after the Spanish term *picaro*, rogue). Frequently found in novels and television serial dramas and occasionally found in films, episodic plots seen in single sittings are usually nevertheless arranged in climactic order. In episodic "road" films such as Frank Capra's *It Happened One Night* (1934) or Barry Levinson's *Rain Man* (1988), the separate incidents nevertheless carry us toward an ultimate resolution. In films such as Lindsay Anderson's *O Lucky Man!* (1973) or Fellini's *La Dolce Vita* (1961), alternative ways people live are explored in turn and each found increasingly unsatisfactory. The films' structures may seem arbitrary but they are never random: As the two men in Roman Polanski's *Two Men and a Wardrobe* (1961) journey through the city, they encounter various people seemingly in no order, but we can see by degrees first indifference, then sequentially rejection, cruelty, and vicious betrayal. Episodic structures encourage, or readily allow, exploration of an existential world view.

Nonlinear Plots   Films saturate an audience's sense of time present with all kinds of stimulus, allowing little opportunity for retrospective memory or prospective imagination to recall past moments or construct possible future outcomes. Films therefore contain within themselves appropriate occasions for recollecting or anticipating. Some "narratology" discriminates between the **story,** the entire chain of successive events implied by a drama, and the dramatic **action** itself, that which the audience sees in a certain order. An action may present only fragments of a story out of sequence, or may present only its climax, leaving the full story with its implied earlier events to be reconstructed chronologically in the audience's mind afterward if ever. *Citizen Kane*'s story is Kane's, from his early boyhood through a reporter's posthumous efforts to understand the meaning of his death, but its action begins at the beginning of the film with Kane's death and follows the reporter in quest of the meaning of his last word, the audience and the reporter recovering portions of the earlier story from various people (for the most part chronologically, but with some overlapping segments).

Events, characters, phrases and lines of dialogue, props, settings, and shot compositions repeat frequently, enabling the viewer to bind past to present, recall associationally, feel incrementally, and measure the distance travelled since the earlier occurrence. In films as in narrative ballads (as in other forms of oral literature where there is no time for retrospection), repeated refrains, or **recurrent motifs,** gather meaning with each recurrence, and viewers are prepared to comprehend later complex scenes by earlier simpler ones. The term "helots" serves this function in Frank Capra's *Meet John Doe* (1941), and shots from within looking out, framed by doorways, provide recurrence in John Ford's *The Searchers* (1956). In Charles Crichton's *The Lavender Hill Mob* (1951), a larcenous bank clerk in a gold foundry removes a fleck of gold from his shoe with his umbrella tip, and later in a souvenir foundry removes a fleck of lead the same way, shot from the same angle, informing the audience how he can smuggle stolen gold out of the country even before he arrives at that same thought. Moreover, since the earliest Lumières, films have often ended as they began, providing opportunity to comprehend what has changed. The resulting **repetitions** and **sym-**

metrical recurrences are common in "classical" Hollywood films, with their various ironies and self-enclosures. These recurrences can invest any action with meaning when common public symbols or signifying codes become meaningless, by themselves becoming symbols which gather their own meaning within the work.

Flashback is the common nondescript term for the establishment within a film's present time of another earlier time, also experienced as time present by the audience once the flashback transition (such as rack focusing) has ended. An entire film may be a flashback, except for a brief **frame story** containing a narrator whose tale the flashback visualizes. Where stage drama may cautiously present its main action as a flashback, film editing invites such temporal manipulation. So does the human mind, though in life if one is sane the frame story—time present—always dominates memories or fantasies of the past, the real present remaining the place where those earlier events are now again occurring in the mind.

The past may be related to the present in various ways. It can be **causally** related to account for the present, to explain what chain of circumstance has brought the narrative where it is, imposing a dark

Framed. In *Mildred Pierce* (1945), Joan Crawford tells police her version of how a murder was committed, providing a frame for the film's version of her account of that same murder.

fatality on events in films noir such as Billy Wilder's *Double Indemnity* (1944), Michael Curtiz's *Mildred Pierce* (1945), or Billy Wilder's *Sunset Boulevard* (1950). The past can be **associationally** related because the mind of a character, on-screen or implied, is reminded by an event's similarity to earlier events, as in Alain Resnais' *Hiroshima Mon Amour* (1959), where the position of a sleeping Japanese lover reminds a woman of her dead German lover, or in Sidney Lumet's *The Pawnbroker* (1965), when various incidents remind a character of some earlier experience in a death camp. The past shown in a flashback can be **explanatory** to help a character or the audience comprehend the full meaning of the perplexing present, as in Hitchcock's *Vertigo* (1958), where a young woman recalls the true version of events we wrongly thought we already understood, or in Akira Kurosawa's *Rashomon* (1951), where varying versions of the same event compete for belief. The past can be *valuative* to show how the past renders the present especially precious or terrible. **Time-loop plots** in which characters travel into the past, such as those in *Peggy Sue Got Married* (1986), *The Terminator* (1984), or *Back to the Future* (1985), are not strictly speaking flashbacks. These plots are not explanations by the film's storyteller, visualized for the eavesdropping viewer, nor are they replications of a character's memory. Rather, they are usually causal epicycles in an opening chronological cycle, each event taking place *because* of prior events in the story even if we are shown the prior event "later" in the dramatic action. The paradox fascinates, because it implies the past can be as indeterminate as the future.

The **flashforward**—the future as present—is rare in film though common in fiction ("little did she realize that twenty years later she would . . ."), as a device to ease suspenseful tensions (what will happen next? will she escape?) so the reader can concentrate on *how* events develop, not *what*. When a flashforward does appear in films, it is objectively as forestatement to readdress the viewer's curiosity and induce a sense of necessity into ongoing events, as in Brian DePalma's *Obsession* (1976), or subjectively as an anticipatory fantasy, as in Alain Resnais' *La Guerre est Finis* (1966). In the time-loop film *Time after Time* (1979), "H. G. Wells" pursues "Jack the Ripper" from their present into their future (our present) as if into another country; we are amused to see our present customary state as if astonishingly strange, but the future as the end-state of current actions is not at issue.

Unities of Plot Films are self-contained, except for TV soap operas with ongoing overlapped episodes, old-fashioned adventure serial episodes, and a few feature films imitating them (such as the *Star Wars* trilogy). Characters and situations are artfully introduced at the outset with whatever we need to know about their past revealed early in the present action, and the characters cease to exist after the film ends. Since characters usually serve the plot rather than vice versa, sequels with different plots often have subtly different characters even when played with the same name by the same performer (the original Rambo was far more confused and vulnerable than the brooding superwarrior who then usurped the role). Usually we see a single plot problem introduced, developed, and then resolved. Climactic structures impose such **closure** on dramatic actions though rarely in life—when these actions do happen in life, we call the incident "dramatic." But there are other reasons for this sense of self-containment in films. Dramas, like dreams, have manifest and latent contents: They are manifestly about their particulars, but these particulars pose some one universal concern or issue shared by everyone (or else we would care less than we do about what's happening). By the end, something has been said about that concern or issue. The film serves as a specific manifestation of this latent content, which it explores with a thoroughness which seems by the end virtually definitive, complete.

The recent cultural shift called "postmodernism" is impatient with such closure, preferring indeterminate endings and reading even older, superficially self-contained plots for unsettled ambiguities originating in commercial filmmaking's desire to please everybody, or an auteur's uncertainties as to the meaning of action. Many people are no longer charmed by the artifice of a tidy conclusion. But mainstream films still seek out tidy as well as "happy" endings, love conquering whatever the lovers' incompatibilities and the plot's improbabilities, though writers now feel more free to leave characters uncertain about what to do next at the end of a film.

Over 2000 years ago Aristotle observed that all climactic dramas have "a beginning, a middle, and an end." That this statement is profound rather than obvious becomes apparent when we ask about the action, then try to answer, "What is the beginning the beginning of, the middle the middle of, and the end the end of?" Though many viewers seek only vicarious or empathetic experiences in film and are satisfied with whatever the story's ending (some one bad guy is caught, or some one good guy finally wins a girl's admiration and love, or vice versa), an underlying focal issue is usually there as well (can decent persistence finally triumph over unscrupulous malevolence, or can a handsome egotist learn to be concerned for other people, and so become marriageable?). Serious or profound works always have such an issue, and understanding it is essential to any consideration of why the work is as it is. Films "say" things through their resolution of events.

In a unified dramatic work everything works. Any one detail or characteristic is always **indispensable,** functionally and organically necessary to the whole. Each work declares its own rules of inclusion and exclusion, what's in it and what's left out, and then must play by those rules. The best films still contain within themselves the reasons that each detail is as it is, and not some other way, critical analysis revealing why. To see how small or crucial parts and features function, imagine the work without that element and observe what is torn out and missing. What would Joan Micklin Silver's *Between the Lines* (1977) lack without the ruefully cynical Jeff Goldblum character, and what is *he* seen to lack when some fan swipes his jacket? Where in the flashbacks do we first see the glass ball Citizen Kane dropped when he died, and what does this tell us? Similarly, each feature of a unified work is **nontransposable,** always placed where it must be. To see why it is where it is, imagine it transposed to some other place in the work. Suppose in *Kane* that the second Susan Alexander interview had failed, not the first, or suppose in *Rashomon* that the husband's story had preceded the wife's story. Suppose any recently seen straightforward narrative were instead a flashback framed by its end situation.

These rules of **indispensability** and **nontransposability** are sometimes ignored by recent mixed "postmodern" or "poststructural" works, more open and aleatory (governed by chance) in their structures. To show life going nowhere, to escape the tyranny of teleologies (that is, of purposive, goal-directed activity), avant-garde artists in paint, sculpture, "performance art," or film will sometimes deliberately invoke randomness, the way a novelist might publish a novel in a looseleaf notebook, ready for anyone's rearrangement. But however contemporary such works may seem, however liberating from earlier formulaic artistic traditions, they finally register merely as novel or trivial if no underlying essential concern emerges. Any portrayal of merely random events finally says only one thing, that despite our thinking otherwise, life is a random series of events.

But we still seek significant form in art, whatever life offers. Various arguments about TV editing or colorizing of movies always assume that any work has its own economy or "integrity" essential to it, each part the way it is for a reason, and required by every other part, unchangeable. That is, the assumption is that any film should have this rare quality and is a lesser work to the extent it doesn't.

Centuries of misreadings of Aristotle on **unity of time** have generated a "rule" that a dramatic action should cover no more than twenty-four hours. Though Aristotle never said it, and these days it would not matter if he had, many stage dramas still find good reason to conform to a so-called unity of time, with Act I typically "One Afternoon," Act II "That Evening," and Act III, if any, "The following morning." The supposed rule and thousands of plays conforming to it have encouraged playwrights and screenwriters alike to compress their actions. Writers try to find or invent dramatic actions set in relatively brief periods of time, when events of great consequence can be seen to peak and resolve themselves with intense concentration. Life contains many long passages of little consequence and less dramatic interest, signifying nothing much; art cannot. A few films have even attempted perfect unity of time, so that screen time and screening time are the same, for example, Agnes Varda's *Cleo from Five to Seven* (1962), Fred Zinneman's *High Noon* (1952), or Alfred Hitchcock's *Rope* (1948). But whatever the temporal exactitude, such unity of time remains a novelty. Films can be more expansive in time, like novels, and yet maintain the pace of a rising action, because in film any well-placed dissolve can sustain a concentrated dramatic action even while years pass for the characters.

Characters

Characters are people as embodied figments generating or displaying the action or serving as focal areas for synesthetic self-perception. Characters are what most people go to the flicks to see. At the least they feel themselves in the presence of exceptional, or exceptionally attractive, human beings for a brief time, and they enjoy the sense of shared intimacy or privilege. Even more, in certain ways filmgoers **identify** with screen characters. This vexed term was discussed earlier: it implies in part that audiences internalize certain character traits—grace, stoic invulnerability (mainly in men), sensitive vulnerability (mainly in women), courage, anxiety, callousness, sensitivity, superb capability, whatever. Audiences do feel with, feel for, and care about certain characters. Some feminist critics assume "identification" is primarily by gender, men with men and women with women. In fact, as anyone can test, imaginative identification or internalized concern with a screen character is ventured, sustained, or withdrawn in various degrees according to that character's gender, age, race, social class, temperament, intelligence, physical characteristics, capability, incompetence, situation, and intro-spective tendencies (which we are invited to share in close-up), all these potentially for all characters and all members of the audience in a lattice-work of shifting affinities. Morally we sympathize with the oppressed and condemn oppressors, yet we also enjoy being among the privileged, powerful or invulnerable enough to oppress others. As with real people, we enjoy, empathize or sympathize with, admire, observe warily, or detest screen characters as we wish or need; we try on any of their characteristics and roles as acts of self-discovery. This is in fact how

The film version of Eugene O'Neill's *The Emperor Jones* (1933) provided one of the few opportunities until recently for a black actor to take on a complex role, despite the play's stereotypical portrayal of a black man under pressure lapsing into superstitious primitivism. Here Paul Robeson provides a rare image of a powerful black man, cornered, fighting back. With his multitudinous talents and strong convictions, Robeson was one of very few blacks who could refuse servile roles when offered them.

we understand the interior experiences of characters in film or of people of whatever gender in life, if we care about them at all.

A film with no character with whom we can comfortably identify will usually do badly at the box office however profound the characters' dramatic uses. Identification with the nervously evasive main character Harry Caul, the professional electronic eavesdropper in Coppola's fine film *The Conversation* (1974), is too disturbing for comfort for most people, despite his expert superiority at his morally ambiguous trade. Thus the film yielded poor box office returns despite its many virtues, and despite Coppola's earlier great success with the *The Godfather* (1972), a film populated with highly sympathetic Mafiosi. Some plots are written mainly to display a character already proven attractive as a box office draw (Stallone's Rocky or Rambo for example), and some plots exist to explore certain characters' psychological traits. But mostly, characters function as agents of the plot, no more nor less.

Actors who can approximate a character are therefore often interchangeable in an action, more or less satisfactorily: Humphrey Bogart played the tough private eye Philip Marlowe in *The Big Sleep* (1946), and Robert Mitchum played him in that film's remake (1978); other Philip Marlowes in other movies have included James Garner, Elliot Gould, Dick Powell, and Robert Montgomery, each different but all adequately tough with a touch of bitterness. In some plots characters may be altogether interchangeable, businessmen or teenagers replacing powerful kings or spaceship captains in dramas of ambition overreaching itself, or capable women replacing capable men. Ripley in *Alien* was written to be played by either gender, and the ace reporter Hildy Johnson was played by a man in *The Front Page* (1931), a woman in Hawks's remake *His Girl Friday* (1940), and another woman in the re-remake *Switching Channels* (1988). All characters are constructs required by the drama, made up of coded appearances provided by our culture. None are "people" as we are, though they superficially resemble us, and though identifying with them remains one of our primary cinematic pleasures.

Depth   Characters may exist entirely on the surface, defined by their obvious attributes; they are what they seem to be and no more. This kind is common in comedies or in ritual crime dramas, where a frivolous nitwit or a vengeful sadist, like a chess piece, is among the given conditions of an elaborated plot which itself carries its own complexity. Character motivations don't matter and often aren't even minimally supplied.

Characters may be layered, communing with inner lives which move them and determine their behavior. These characters may not reveal their inner nature to other characters or except in rare moments even to the viewer. In *The Maltese Falcon* (1941), Sam Spade seems to be involved in the quest for the black bird out of shrewd self-interest, revealing his highly principled motives only at the end.

Characters may be profound, with a dark mystery at their center inaccessible even to themselves but discernible by behavior sometimes surprising even to themselves. These are rare in any drama, but like Hamlet or Charles Foster Kane, challenging because we sense them to be somehow consistent, even in their inconsistency. Simpler versions of such characters may figure in psychological thrillers: in Hitchcock's

Marnie (1964) we finally learn what early repressed trauma has made Marnie a sexually frigid thief, though we never learn what sadomasochistic streak caused her husband to marry her knowingly, and much critical speculation has tried to explain it. But because the film portrays primarily the rescue of a damsel in distress, the damsel needs only to seem distressed and the rescuer only to seem attractive and dedicated to rescuing her. The rescuer can be a surface character like any fairy tale Prince Charming, a given figure and no more than that, with no further motives necessarily implied (though a strong actor such as Sean Connery has difficulty keeping his performance on that level). Profound characters on the other hand, like real people, sometimes surprise themselves as well as their associates and learn and change during the drama, visibly baffled or deceived even by their own behavior.

Complexity   Single-trait characters can be exhaustively defined by a single characteristic (greed, lust, kindly generosity, sadism), with other traits subordinated or absent. If that one characteristic is grossly exaggerated a **caricature** results, comic or grotesque. Single-traited characters are common and nearly unavoidable in comedy, and in drama are secondary figures who must function supportively without distracting audiences. A "bad guy" may be bad in some one way as a given, because the action requires it, and for no other reason given or implied.

Multiple-trait characters display various motives and internal capabilities, mixed states which may even be divided against each other. In *Casablanca* most of the characters are single-traited or caricatures, but Rick combines tough cynicism with mournful sentiment, and Captain Renault self-interested opportunism with self-amused congeniality.

Types   Types (if highly conventional, **stereotypes**), are characters with familiar clusters of familiar traits, a phenomenon common in all drama as a conventional shorthand needed to establish quickly, with a few deft signals to the audience, a character's recognizable range of capabilities (a novelist can explain an unfamiliar character, but dramatists have no room to do so). Minor characters are often familiar types and no more, and major characters are usually variations on underlying familiar types (the actors often **type cast**). We all instantly recognize the various maverick cops played by Clint Eastwood or Mel Gibson, just as Shakespeare's audiences instantly recognized melancholy malcontents like Hamlet or bragging cowards like Falstaff. Some individual performers can become so familiar in certain kinds of roles that they establish their own types, and audiences assume that their traits are carried with their faces from role to role. For this reason, sometimes they can be **cast against type** to jar expectations, such as decent Henry Fonda cast as a callous killer in *Once upon a Time in the West* (1969). Stock films often turn on stock conflicts among stock types, clever nerds competing with brainless jocks for the pretty high school cheerleader's affections. **Stereotypes** are types already defined by social custom or prejudice and believed by audiences to be actual inhabitants of the actual world outside their own circle of acquaintance, stock notions about real people (e.g., eager yuppies, cool blacks, or dumb blondes), ready-made and available for filmic or political manipulation. **Parody** or **camp** characters are types so exaggerated in their familiar traits that they invite shared pleasurable recognition of their common cinematic, literary, or social artificiality, as in *Blazing Saddles* (1974) or *The Naked Gun* (1988). Parody usually imitates its source with amused affection, and camp originated in the gay community's willful mocking of gender mannerisms, although it now mocks many other kinds of behavior as well.

Functions   If characters exist to figure forth the plot, they contribute in several ways. The most obvious is to *seem* to initiate or respond to the action, and these characters are provided with characteristics and motives sufficient for the purpose. But they carry other functions as well.

Protagonists and **antagonists** form the basis of dramatic conflict, though the antagonist can be something as abstract as "fate" or "society." Characters at odds with each other are often human figments for displaying moral, psychological, or social conflict (e.g., faith versus cynicism, or capital versus labor). The most common in our Puritan-derived culture is the conflict between the saintly and the demonic, good versus evil. In U.S. films characters can usually be tagged easily with one or the other term "good guys" or "bad guys"; almost never—or never—are such quick moral determinations possible in life. Very rarely will a character change from one to the other, and if the change is not carefully prepared and motivated, it appears to all but the most gullible an obvious plot contrivance to ensure a happy or miserable ending. Occasionally characters have mixed traits at war with each other, one of which finally dominates. Though conflicts between good and evil are standard issues in most films, how these moral traits are defined can be both shrewd and original.

A **psychomachia** is a drama externalizing conflicts between certain interior human traits, desires, and capabilities, rational thought versus emotional instinct for example. Ingmar Bergman's early tales of marital infidelity often contain the equivalent of an artist, a doctor, and a housewife—a way to examine stresses in each of us between the ego-consumed but instinctually creative, the orderly and rationally scientific, and the warmly nurturing domestic traits we all carry within us. A psychomachia is a commonplace of medieval allegorical drama, where concepts are personified as characters, and the relationships between those characters inform us of the more abstract relationships between the concepts. For example in *Everyman*, when Everyman must die he is deserted by Fellowship and even Knowledge but not by Good Deeds. Even the nerd/jock/ cheerleader high school plot mentioned above *could* be a way to explore conflicts within us between the demands of mind and body, the problem of reconciling these apparent opposite tendencies in ourselves, and the prize of gratified desire and social acceptance at stake. Plots turning on good guys (selfless, decent to others) versus bad guys (selfish, cruel to others) may be crude psychomachias whatever else they may be as well. Some films turn on pairs or **doubles.** Hitchcock frequently employs this device, one character in *Strangers on a Train* (1951) being the evil form of an opposing character, or one in *Shadow of a Doubt* (1943) the naive form, each pair together constituting the potential of any one human being.

Foil characters reveal traits of main characters which may be at issue (even while fulfilling other functions), by explicit contrast or by providing dramatic occasion for these traits to reveal themselves in conversation or in minor actions. Heroes are often provided with sidekicks embodying extremes, to confirm their balanced normality. Comic pairs (Dean Martin and Jerry Lewis, or Laurel and Hardy) provide foils for each other (the straight and the zany, the timid and the overconfident). Rarely or never will a drama or film contain two characters of the same age, temperament, and physical appearance; scenes between them would seem dully uninformative.

Setting

A **setting** is the named local habitation where an action takes place, offering a specific range of options for characters to choose among but also often serving as an expressionistic reflection of characters' states of mind. The setting may be rich or impoverished, urban or rural, frozen or tropical, sunlit or drenched, crystal-clear or obscured with smoke and steam, frenzied or placid. The setting can also serve as a kind of character, a formative influence on another character, or as an antagonist. The settings for Ridley Scott's *Blade Runner* (1982) curiously combined high-tech and delapidated buildings, gaudy yet drab streets, and new-minted yet also old and worn fixtures, all visible images of a reformulated technocratic world with abandoned and outmoded yet surviving social arrangements and attitudes. Luxuriously affluent Beverly Hills residential and shopping streets appear in *Beverly Hills Cop* (1984) and *Pretty Woman* (1990), where they contrast in each film with the urban slums of Detroit or the decaying rooming houses of Los Angeles. The contrast sets up in turn radical contrasts of style, manners, and social class, with different implications for each film.

Though the characters usually take the setting for granted, no viewer should. The setting provides the primary element in the film's *mise en scene*, the way the film looks as established by its lighting, photography, camera positions, framing, and costumes, even by the weather, virtually everything "up there on the screen," and the setting is always carefully chosen and designed. Every master scene in every script is always labeled "Interior" or "Exterior" at its outset, and "Day" or "Night," information not always essential to the dramatic action, but often to its meaning.

ACTING

Acting is the artifice of imitated human action, simulating the appearances of people and events in a manner appropriate to the genre and character types. Thus successful acting seems "natural" no matter how artificially graceful or grotesque, though performers "cast against type" will create a special illusion of complexity, an unaccustomed violation of conventional expectation which seems "real" in a different sense. Acting requires an extension of the self into a "persona" (the Greek word for "mask"). In other words, acting requires the creation of enough socially coded cues, familiar bodily, vocal, and facial expressions to generate the illusion of a visible "personality" with a private person underneath, with both the outer and inner selves responding to a dramatic situation. Though what matters may be only a few bundled intellectual, psychological, and moral traits, what we see on the screen has the appearance of a whole human being, embodied by the actor. It is difficult to remember that these characters are functionaries, not real people, who exist only because the film requires them and only while it requires them. It is also difficult to remember that the actors are not the characters they play, but people skilled in seeming so.

Production Skills

Because of the way movies are made and seen, screen acting differs from stage acting in several ways, requiring greater concentration and often yielding the actors less personal satisfaction. Screen acting is more restrained and intimate in voice and gesture, since films reveal facial and vocal expressions more subtly, greatly magnified. Even if a stage actor's voice is "miked" (electronically amplified), face and body must nevertheless express feelings visible far back in a theater. Such "projecting" from the stage will seem to be "mugging" or overacting on camera

A

B

Actors act. It doesn't look that way if the illusion succeeds, because we do not see what they are actually required to do. Here in a clutter of production equipment and essential technicians, Robin Hood speaks tenderly to Maid Marian in a dungeon, that is, Errol Flynn and Olivia DeHavilland act in *The Adventures of Robin Hood* (1938) (A); and a westerner takes his bride home to Yellow Sky in an old style railroad car, that is, Robert Preston and Marjorie Steele act in *Face to Face* (1952) (B).

108

(overacting on stage is even more exaggerated, called by actors "eating the scenery").

A screen actor's audience consists of a director who is frequently unsatisfied and alters performances between takes, a jaded and preoccupied crew, and an unresponsive camera; an acceptable take is more like a satisfactory moment in rehearsal than a performance, and the rewards of applause after a superb moment on camera are not to be expected. Without the presence of an audience and its responses to spur them, screen actors require special inner self-assurance.

Most important, and most uniquely, film acting is performed in discontinuous fragments. Since films are rarely shot in sequence, production, and not dramatic necessities, determine when what scene will be shot. As Frank Capra has observed, if a film begins and ends in Alaska, you don't go to Alaska twice. All shots requiring a particular set or location will be made together, after which a set will be struck and another built for other shots, or the cast and crew will abandon the location, go home, and reassemble at a studio or some other location. A crowd may be assembled for several different crowd scenes, dressed in different costumes, used several times, and then dismissed.

All shots requiring a particular performer may need to be made within a few days of each other if that performer is hired for only a few days of work and is otherwise unavailable, regardless of where those shots will appear in the edited film. That performer will need to know only the lines for a particular day's shooting, not the whole script or even the whole role (a director will coach performers on a role's requirements from shot to shot). Some actors never trouble to read the whole script or see the completed film, to find out why day-by-day they were asked to do what they did. Any screen performer must therefore be able to work in short bursts, repeated through multiple takes and matched to other short bursts, with long boring stretches in between of nothing to do. Performances from shot to shot must be matched precisely in facial, vocal, and bodily expression (wolfish grins, looks of steady contempt, and even mussed hair), though photographed perhaps days apart. Master shots and their various insert shots must maintain continuity, and an actor beginning a love scene with an actress may be required to complete it with emotional consistency and rising passion with an off-camera light-stand, the actress nowhere in the vicinity. Movements may not vary from take to take (or actors could move out of focus, or out of the camera's range); actors must "hit their marks" chalked or taped on the floor every time. Performances must be sustained through multiple takes while the director works closely with an accompanying actor, perhaps, seeking the shot's definitive take. The whole role need not be learned all at once (though the performer's conception of the

Even for this publicity still for *To Have and Have Not* (1944), the young and still inexperienced Lauren Bacall must hit her marks. A foot or so short of where she is standing and the mirror behind her might imply that she is two-faced. Yet her body in three-quarter length, like Bogart's seated, implies mobility; like most Howard Hawks heroines she feels free to stay or leave and chooses to stay.

whole role can contribute much), since at most only a single master shot is performed all at once; and the director will remind or inform the actor about the emotions and actions appropriate to each shot made out of continuity. Rarely can an actor work gradually into a character's state of mind and feeling by enacting in sequence the process by which the character arrived there. Nor is time available for lengthy rehearsals. Because the process is in some ways more artificially demanding and yet less satisfying than stage acting, the myth persists that real acting takes place only on a stage with whole roles performed in entirety before live audiences. But screen acting is also real acting, of a different kind. Nowadays, performers learn the separate skills required by each kind.

Acting Techniques

How performers achieve the illusion that they are their dramatic characters can vary with each performer, but certain techniques are taught routinely in acting schools, sometimes with a near-religious devotion. Each technique has its uses, and actors trained primarily in one school will also employ some techniques of others. A skilled performer can be trusted to change his or her mind or mood visibly on camera during a single shot, as evidenced by evanescent changes of expression; a lesser-skilled performer, who may nevertheless create strong and complex characters such as Sarah in *Children of a Lesser God* (1986), may need to be photographed registering one state of mind, then in another shot a different state of mind, with a cutaway elsewhere covering the transition perhaps because the actor can't quite manage it convincingly.

Method Acting   **Method** acting is acting from the inside out. Method acting (variations of the Russian director Stanislavsky's methods) requires a performer to find within emotional states equivalent to the character's, by intensive personal recollection of similar incidents and imaginative re-creation of them in a kind of psychoanalytically reconceived psychodrama, an actor's childhood loss of a dog perhaps invoked to express an adult character's loss of a marriage. Appropriate gestures or extremely subtle facial expressions then occur without the actor necessarily even knowing it. Especially useful for portraying characters alienated from their own inner lives, or lonely people risking self-revelation, or intense or intensely conflicted emotions, method acting such as the young Marlon Brando's is often valuable for intimate effects in close-up, to register strong feeling rigidly masked by impassivity, for example, where minute changes of expression may then loom very large. Always in close touch with the complexity of their feelings, method actors are concerned to know a line's "subtext" or a character's underlying motivations, what purposes to conceal and what to reveal so the audience can sense them.

Technical Acting   **Technical** acting is acting from the outside in. Nineteenth-century actors' handbooks described physical appearances appropriate to every emotion, down to the different kinds of clenched fists required to express rage, grief, despair, or decisiveness. A technical actor now learns from others and from experimentation how to use bodily appearances expressively, which postures, gestures, and tricks of the trade most precisely signal character traits and interior conditions to an audience (how to seem to walk like a lecherous or a weary old man, for example, or how to reveal drunkenness by attempting to conceal it). Some **character actors** can create roles very different from each other by technical means, altered postures and accents, as well as makeup (Dustin Hoffman is a method actor who "stretches" his range with technical acting). A technical actor need not necessarily feel the character's emotions but can register them precisely whenever asked (an especially useful skill for sustaining strong performances through multiple

Errol Flynn, when in character never at a loss for gallant words, here sits on a set for *Captain Blood* (1935), smoking his pipe and studying his lines.

takes), and a technical actor can reveal inner states solely by hand ges-tures in close-up if the shot requires it, or by bodily angles and move-ments if the character is visible only in silhouette.

An extreme artifice of technical acting is **styled acting,** broadly elabo-rated or exaggerated movements whether graceful or clumsy for balletic or comic effect. Styled acting is common in swashbucklers, where Doug-las Fairbanks or Errol Flynn as pirate captains may swing through the rigging to land elegantly poised at the feet of a noblewoman (often Maureen O'Hara), sword and a courteously elaborate speech at the ready. Such acting is central to silent pantomime, where Buster Keaton may take a particularly devastating multiple-stage pratfall, collapsing on his rear, then his back, rolling onto his neck, and then, with a spin, finishing flat on his face, all as if it had just happened accidentally. Appropriate to many adventure films displaced to an earlier time, such choreographed movements seem stilted if set in a realistic present, though they may heighten a climactic moment without the audience noticing. American actors tend to be method trained, as a form of self-fulfillment. British actors who work in repertory companies have greater opportunity to learn varieties of gestures and technical tricks from older actors and usually regard method acting as one more technique.

Improvisation   An exercise used to train both method and technical actors and a technique for generating spontaneous performances, **improvisation** throws the creative burdens onto the actors directly. Given a **premise** or situation (your blind date turns out to be a professional terrorist, or your tyrannical father is now on his death bed), an actor along with one or two others will "make the scene" by inventing the relevant characters and improvising their dialogue, feeling their way through plot complications, and moving the brief action toward some kind of climactic revelation, all the while "in character" and performing. For **dramatic improvisation,** actors must draw unhesitatingly from within themselves the appropriate characters and their characteristics and together discover the form and point of the drama they are creating; for **comic improvisation,** actors usually explore some recognizable social stereotypes, absurdities, or extremities and satirize them cued by each other's ingenuity (Mike Nichols and Elaine May began their theatrical and film careers doing hilarious satirical improvisations together). Actors call on their own inner resources because they have nowhere else to turn, and their responsive attention to each other can provide fresh, often moving results.

In a sense we all improvise our own lives, though in the characters we identify as ourselves, and we discover and stabilize those characters by role-playing them. Some improvisations provide a paradigm for our own enactments. Short improvised dramas or sketches once worked out can eventually become part of an acting company's repertory of set performances, as with the *Second City's* repertory of established improvisations. In films, such directors as Woody Allen, Robert Altman, John Cassevetes, Richard Donner, or Jean-Luc Godard will deliberately encourage performers to improvise certain scenes or to improvise on camera their delivery of certain lines. Some indicators may be overlapping or incomplete speeches, hesitation while a character searches for words (gestures preceding their utterance, as if to help locate them), spontaneous or surprised responses to each other's unexpected behavior, long unedited takes, and an evenly lit set (since the cinematographer may not know where the actors will move, he has to be prepared to follow them wherever).

Performer as Icon

The extraordinary attractiveness or capacity to register dramatic feeling of some actors invites a powerful feeling of intimacy and involvement, even identification. The fascinated self-transformation audiences feel in the presence of certain performers on screen creates the complex commercial phenomenon known as the "star" system, including a vague and unacknowledged intimation that certain of the people who create these screen images are kinds of transfigured spiritual forms, more than mortal, larger-than-life gods and goddesses, or "screen idols" like our own desired alter egos.

Celebrity   A **celebrity's** image is known to millions and becomes, like the weather or the day's news, a figment of our psychic environment, a presence even in absence, a common condition of our shared public consciousness. Once this occurs—originally by some extraordinary notoriety or achievement—celebrities can be celebrated merely for being celebrated, in demand by producers or publicists seeking to capitalize on their fame. Thus they remain celebrities, more than merely themselves in the popular mind, long after the original reason for their fame is forgotten. We feel privileged merely to be in their screen presence; actually to encounter them in the street can be dumbfounding (though also disappointing, because most are after all ordinary people apart from their highly visible skills and notorious reputations). Celebrity can be conferred on other public figures as well, politicians, musicians, or serial killers; their personal lives or some calculated facsimile enters the public domain to become as well known as their public images, aided by gossip columns, supermarket personality magazines, and appearances on TV game shows. We want to know them better, what they are "really" like, as a way of magnifying ourselves or escaping our own anonymity. Many attempted and actual assassinations of public figures are motivated by a nonentity's desire for self-confirming celebrity; Robert Altman's *Nashville* (1975), Martin Scorsese's *Taxi Driver* (1976), his *King of Comedy* (1983), and many other films draw on this unfortunate fact.

Star Quality, Charisma, and Ego Ideals   In ways not understood, certain individuals on screen command attention and rivet the eye by their mere presence; "the camera loves them," and so do their audiences. In part this is a consequence of celebrity, of being already known, stardom conferring stardom. Such viewer response may also involve admiration for celebrities' skills as performers, in which much stardom—but not all—originates. Audiences usually prefer not to notice that an actor is acting, though some performers—Paul Muni, Dustin Hoffman, or

For his German silent film *Diary of a Lost Girl* (1929), as for his *Pandora's Box* (1928), G. W. Pabst cast the U.S. actress Louise Brooks, because she radiated an air of uncorrupted innocence, yet of knowing sensuality. When hardly any respectable women could, Brooks conducted her own life, chose her own bed partners, and defied studio moguls when it suited her, until she ended up blackballed. Here, her seduced and abandoned character Thymiane is exploited by a world of gross physical self-indulgence (personified by Kurt Gerron) yet preserves a childlike sprightliness.

Meryl Streep—stretch into such different character roles from film to film that they demand appreciation for their acting, and one can never see their characters without also seeing their performances.

But in part star charisma results from the intensity with which certain performers project desirable human qualities, real or implied, sensed by an audience whenever that performer appears on the screen: a hint of interior lives as interesting as their exterior manner, perhaps, or the implication of character traits at cross-purposes (self-assurance covering momentary bewilderment, like Sigourney Weaver's; or the reverse, like Jessica Lange's; toughness yet sentiment, like the later Bogart's; or insolence under stress, like the young Paul Newman's or Tom Cruise's). In some ways audiences want to see performers define how they themselves might wish to be, briefly and safely, in a broad range of behavior from callous to sensitive, brassy to hesitant, enraged to serene, clownish to dignified, to live the sensations of such identities vicariously. Rarely do vulnerable or dependent men or invulnerably independent women achieve stardom, for example; in a predominantly patriarchal culture, men are expected to seem self-assured and women to seem in some sense in need of such men (Katherine Hepburn and Greta Garbo became "box office poison" despite their enormous reputations when they played completely self-sufficient women too frequently). These days men and older women (in France even younger men) need faces marked by "experience" to become stars, while younger women

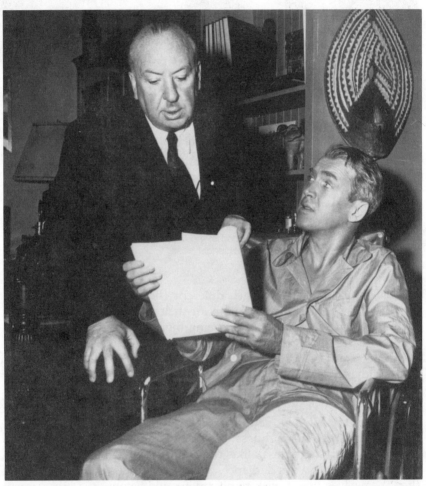

Asked if Hitchcock thought of actors as cattle, Stewart replied, "No, but he sure treated them *like* cattle." Hitchcock expected actors to do precisely what he wanted; here, wearing Jeffries' cast for *Rear Window*, Stewart asks him what he wants. Early during the shooting of *Vertigo* (1958), Stewart has said, the method-trained Kim Novak inquired intently of Hitchcock about her character's underlying motivations, the subtexts of her lines, and other intricacies, until Hitchcock finally replied, "My dear Miss Novak, it's only a movie!"

still need mainly fashionably thin waists and faces as vacant of notable characteristics as a baby's or a model's (from which world of fixed or expressionless posturing many actresses emerge, to then reveal their individuality). Through such figures of desire audiences test out their own similar capacities or live out briefly compensated fantasy lives.

The Actor as Character   Much film acting is a consequence of various techniques, but film acting and the star system especially value the actor's own ready personality put to the service of a role. "I always play myself, but with deference to the character," James Stewart once said, attributing the statement to Laurence Olivier, for whom it is much less true. In a highly external, artificial, and economical medium, each scene or gesture repeatedly reenacted, some actors always seem "natural" and unstudied, not acting at all, as if their characters were their own un-self-conscious selves; when someone once told Spencer Tracy that he too was an actor, Tracy is said to have replied, "Don't let it show." If such a character proves popular, the actor becomes a bankable commodity, and other films are written for that actor's known personality and range.

Many studio actors (Stewart, Tracy, or Bette Davis) played repeatedly with small modifications the characters audiences thought them, typecast as themselves, accumulating in their faces the implied characteristics of previous roles to bring to later roles. Bogart's Sam Spade in John Huston's *The Maltese Falcon* (1941) is a cagey private eye who plays his cards close to his buttoned vest, elbows tight to his sides, well-closed in, and so these characteristics could be assumed to be beneath the surface appearances of his Philip Marlowe in Howard Hawks's *The Big Sleep* (1946), where the character seems unbuttoned, open, and expansive in his gestures; audiences knew that nevertheless he was buttoned up, with his own purposes well-guarded. Cast against type as the timorous, polite drunkard of *The African Queen* (1951), Bogart's performance was unexpected and therefore all the more amusing. The embittered, vengeful James Stewart who appeared in Anthony Mann's Westerns was recognizably alienated from the harried but decent man of his earlier roles; audiences could expect his "true" nature to emerge by the picture's end, as it did. Sometimes actors become so indistinguishable from screen characters that audiences think they *are* that character. Sylvester Stallone and Woody Allen write and direct their own films, yet many fans imagine they are their popular screen personas, almost too muscular or incompetent to tie their own shoelaces, and it was the simpering, idiotically trustful boob Stan Laurel who off-camera conceived Laurel and Hardy's gags, not the unimaginative Oliver Hardy.

5

Genre Conventions

Customary, highly conventional, recurring combinations of plots, characters, settings, and other attributes together create familiar patterns of expectation and dramatic experience, and each film played for the audience becomes a variation of all others known. **Genres** originate in the industry's need to replicate salable commodities, films like previous box office successes yet different enough to sell again (the same need encourages the industry to remake once-popular but forgotten films or to commission sequels to recent successes). Genres also originate in the medium's need to program audience expectations selectively: A film's dramatic conventions must seem immediately familiar enough to elicit certain kinds of attention and exclude others, to concentrate the audience's mind. Moreover, some genres persist through the ages, helping to transmit and reinforce certain complex attitudes and values from generation to generation. Like the myths and legends of nonindustrial cultures, genres are means by which contradictory hopes, beliefs, and ideologies are posed, acknowledged, explored, and seemingly reconciled.

The most profound and persistent genres develop a customary cluster of surface characteristics, a set vocabulary of sounds, settings, props, costumes, and kinds of characters signifying certain coded meanings, understood by audiences as the genre's characteristic language for discussing its concerns. In the Western for example, guns visibly worn signify force frankly available to any wearer's instincts and a society based on individual intimidation or self-restraint, whereas in the crime film concealed guns imply violent purposes deceitfully hidden and a society based on institutional repression. The major genres have also evolved certain conventional structures of action, sometimes ritualistic in nature, posing key issues within the narrow range of any one genre's concerns (e.g., open violence honorably performed in public, the walk-down duel, versus hidden violence surreptitiously performed in dark alleys, murder).

The less profound and persistent genres also have similar characteristics less well codified, and these rise and fall in cycles of popular taste often coinciding with cycles of public concern, usually over a five- to eight-year period. The now-defunct natural disaster cycle followed the turbulent, seemingly apocalyptic Vietnam war period, and the currently dying mad slasher cycle may now signal among other things changing teenage attitudes toward sexual guilt and parental retribution. Sometimes lesser genres are embedded in greater, providing cyclical variations within well-fixed conventions, and following the French New Wave's example in the early 1960s, some films have deliberately mixed genres to thwart yet delight rote expectations, to flaunt their own freedom from convention, or, with certain inconsistencies, to avail themselves of the advantages of each component genre. No genres are fixed forms;

all evolve with the culture's own concerns and compulsions as these transmute themselves over time. But we are all familiar with most of them, and studios deliberately label their films by one or another genre early in the production process, for their own guidance.

Certain essential genre distinctions are known even by very small children, who can tell by the time they are four years old that different imaginative worlds are constructed by different rules and display their own different kinds of consistency. Children know for example that "people" in television dramas, commercials, news reports, or animated cartoons are not all the same order of beings as each other, the people they know in real life, or their own mirror images. That is, they know "make-believe" when they see it, though like the rest of us they spend much of their lives sorting out the illusions generated by make-believe worlds.

In the first decade after invention of the motion picture camera, two basic genres emerged: the Lumière brothers' seeming photographs of actual events (the realist tradition), and George Méliès's photographs of marvellous fantasies. Audiences enjoyed both. The pragmatic yet moralizing genius of U.S. film quickly combined them: The external world and its inhabitants are photographed as if actual, with close attention given to familiar or likely details, but the inhabitants are distinctly coded with approvable, objectionable, or incredible moral qualities, as few people ever are in life. In effect, U.S. films provide Lumière worlds populated with Méliès characters, supposedly real gardens with imaginary toads in them. Our own fantasy lives and emotional needs are nourished by this tradition. Some theorists fear that films recommend and increase antisocial behavior because they show it, that violence is condoned and encouraged in life because it is condoned and even welcomed in certain genres. But few people are fooled. We learn early to know what to expect from the various distinctive worlds we encounter in narrative films, each with its own rules. Asking and answering the question "What kind of a film is it?" is a movie goer's first essential critical act. If answered wrongly, any film will be dissatisfying, even bewildering.

The primary genres have been freely adapted from stage genres, from fiction or reportage, or from equivalent tendencies in the other arts, though with their own established cinematic conventions as well, because of the unique nature of cinema and its unique relationships with its audiences.

COMEDY

Originally any tale with a happy ending, **comedy** is one of the major persistent literary genres in our culture, definable by its appearances and its plots, by the unique ways these are arranged to affect audience attitudes, by its techniques for positioning the audience with respect to its own perceptions, and above all by its effect on audiences, its ability to generate laughter or feelings of amused congeniality. Derived from a Greek word meaning "festive song," comedy preserves from Greek times its original celebratory functions and often preserves as well a characteristic final harmonious dance, social celebration, or marriage, all conflicts reconciled. Comedy as a genre now tends to describe any dramatic event which generates a sense of well-being, or more peculiarly, which generates the spontaneous sociable noises we call laughter. A carefully constructed form of public ritual enabling us to acknowledge shameful desires, contradictory beliefs, and hopeless dilemmas in each other's presence, subverting traditionally sanctioned self-delusions, comedy is one of the most profound of all the genres while seeming to be the most trivial, the least intellectually searching. Comedy is especially effective in its filmic forms, because film techniques exclude the real while seeming to represent it; films manipulate our normal moral reactions to people who are in desperate trouble, or are confronting impossible dilemmas, by invoking and reshaping our reactions without awakening customary defense mechanisms. Comedy amuses us by portraying our own tendencies toward folly as other people's, as fully acknowledged fictions. Its ultimate pleasure is self-recognition.

Critical Terms

Terms commonly associated with comedy derive from earlier systems of psychology and other related literary forms. **Humor** refers to the medieval belief that excess of one of the four bodily fluids or "humors" causes odd behavior, blood rendering a person sanguine or cheerfully optimistic, phlegm rendering one phlegmatic or lazy, choler inducing a choleric or angry disposition, and black bile inducing melancholy. These traits persist as temperamental excesses in comic characters along with other similar moral and psychological compulsions. **Wit** in its Renaissance sense is the capacity to know quickly how things are similar ("fancy" discerns similitude) yet different ("judgment" discerns differences among similar things), the two together making up a quick-witted cleverness in a character (or by implication, in a screenwriter or director), the ability to see absurd contradictions and deftly point them out. The word was once an equivalent for our word "intelligence," and **comedy of wit** emerges from its uneven distribution among us. "Witless" or "half-witted" characters often believe themselves in full possession of their wits (as do people who have lost their wits altogether) and are all the more ridiculous for their mistaken self-perception. A humorous or witless character is a **buffoon** or **clown**. **Farce** is a generic term covering much comic merrymaking, usually displaying energetic or frantic irreverence, with whole social orders run amok. **Satire** refers to an ultimately moral purpose in certain comedies, seeking to correct human excess (especially hypocritical impercipience or self-delusion) and so to produce a more honest if not better world. Satire's traditional devices are irony, mockery, sarcasm, ridicule, or derision, all these being ways to mask or subvert the meanings of words in an invited conspiracy with the viewer, who knows that certain tones of voice will convert all apparent praise into blame and all agreement into disagreement ("Sure they will, no question about it!"). **Invective,** or direct insult, however, freely tells it like it is as we ourselves never can without risking serious repercussions. Characters who insult others such as Groucho, Hawkeye, Archie Bunker, or the standup characters played by Don Rickles or Andrew Dice Clay easily become a polite society's culture heroes.

Parody, camp (once limited to mimicry of gender mannerisms), **spoof,** or **travesty** are special kinds of comedy, ridiculing by exaggeration not aspects of human behavior but the conventions of other genres. Although

Luis Bunuel's sardonic parody of Da Vinci's *The Last Supper,* in his *Viridiana* (1961). Here thieves and degenerates have taken over a naively generous and devout young woman's estate, brutally violating her faith that souls can be redeemed through kindness, eventually raping her. Parody seems superficially to mock mannerisms or artifices in the work being parodied, but it is more concerned with our misuse of those works as imaginative constructs by which we understand and live our lives. The devout, Bunuel says, are too sentimental to comprehend real human depravity. Another more shallow allusion to the religious faith familiarly figured in Da Vinci's fresco occurs in *M*A*S*H* (1970), when the doctors assemble at a dinner to bid farewell to a would-be suicide.

parody seems to be mocking those conventions for their artificiality, it also chastens the self-indulgent imaginations of audiences enthralled by those artifices. Many comic artists such as Mel Brooks and Woody Allen began as parodists: Brooks wrote parody TV skits for Sid Caesar's *Your Show of Shows* and went on to such films as *Blazing Saddles* (1974), *Young Frankenstein* (1975), and *High Anxiety* (1977); and Allen's films before *Annie Hall* (1977) are all based on parodies of supposedly serious genres. Allen's *Bananas* (1971), for example, contains a political assassination and a honeymoon night each treated like a TV broadcast of a sporting event, complete with interviews by Howard Cosell; sports reporting is parodied along with its mind-numbing clichés, but these bits also satirize TV's and the TV audience's tendency to regard all kinds of human events as the same kind of public spectacle. Many comic performers begin their careers as impersonators "doing" other people's mannerisms.

Terms associated with comedy's subgenres and components include **burlesque,** which treats the traditionally lofty in a low vulgar manner, spiritual or intellectual attainment seen as self-serving fraud, or dignity as pretentious pomp, celebrating a world without hierarchical propriety by emphasizing the merely physical, which we all share. Burlesque's opposite is called **mock heroic,** which treats the low as if it were lofty, serious, and dignified, simultaneously confirming yet denying those solemn virtues. Other comic components are jokes, jests, quips, and wisecracks (these tending to be verbal), and gags (usually visual or physical, often wittily structured while seeming spontaneous). In general, U.S. silent comedy tends to be **gag comedy,** concerned with our physical pretenses and limitations and inclined toward humor, whereas sound comedy is satirical comedy or **comedy of manners,** more intellectually concerned with our personal and social pretenses and self-deceptions and inclined toward wit and witty observation. But the two are not mutually exclusive: Lubitsch's delicately witty *Lady Windermere's Fan* is a silent comedy, and sound comedies include witless ones such as *Porky's.*

Comic Characters

Comic characters are usually single-minded and single-traited, that trait a dominant characteristic such as gullibility, a humor such as melancholy, a shameful desire such as greed, or a vice such as gluttony or lust. But with few exceptions comic characters do not know this. They therefore seem morally and intellectually inferior: We view their grotesque behavior with condescending amusement, yet we nevertheless envy their lack of inhibition, and so, though we may take pleasure in their downfall, we also feel pleased by their success. With no inner self-perception, these characters cannot be humiliated, because they cannot know that their inadequacies are exposed. Unable to see themselves as others see them, and devoted to their folly, they never suffer psychic pain (or even severe physical pain), and so cannot grow in wisdom nor learn from experience. They persist, simultaneously their own victims and survivors.

Comic characters are usually singular figures, loners, denied membership in normative society and its rewards. Their difference is usually signalled by some singular physical attribute (owlish eyeglasses like Harold Lloyd's or Woody Allen's) or odd mannerism (a fixed melancholy expression like Buster Keaton's or Rodney Dangerfield's), or both (a tramp's castaway clothing coupled with genteel, even effeminately delicate gestures like Chaplin's). But comic characters are chiefly the creatures of their own compulsions or the overly naive victims of others'. Some, such as Buster Keaton, are the unwitting and uncomprehending causes of other people's misfortunes while they strive heroically merely to get through the day. Comic characters usually want something (if only to be left alone) and concentrate their minds on getting it. In this respect these characters serve as martyrs or scapegoats to our own similar but successfully suppressed inclinations. As heroes of our own repressed selves, they enact what we desire but dare not perform, endure and survive what we fear, carry on, and report to the rest of us what such behavior entails.

Sometimes they appear as comic pairs or triplets, contrasting foils enabling us to see as ludicrous the excesses of each (as with the timid Laurel and the blustering Hardy), or the pair may consist of an eccentric and a straight man, exaggerated traits played against steadfast normality (as with Gracie Allen and George Burns, Tommie and Dick Smothers, Jerry Lewis and Dean Martin, or Lou Costello and Bud Abbott, the zany exasperating the ostensibly sane). In a **sentimental comedy** we sympathize with the characters' feelings, identifying with them even while we are, in a kindly way, amused; everyone in such a comedy is decent at heart though perhaps misguided. In a **romantic comedy** we tend to admire both romantically involved characters, though one may seem too innocent and the other too calculating (as in Preston Sturges's comedies); we sense that each must change before a proper wedding can take place. We envy even the born losers, frequently played by Jewish comedians and called in Yiddish **schlimazls** (unlucky ones) and **schlemiels** (blunderers). Woody Allen still plays a worried combination of the two, but they remain different: Schlemiels spill their coffee, schlimazls get coffee spilled on them. Expecting the worst and never disappointed, these losers are invincible because they cannot be further de-

Laurel and Hardy not only served as foils to each other, each seeming the more excessive in the other's presence, they also resembled each other. Both characters were easily comprehended, not too bright (though Laurel's character had his moments), and blundering, mischievous, or morally self-righteous enough to devastate their surroundings once set in motion. Here in *Blockheads* (1938) they do just that.

feated. These comic characters often speak for our deepest and most ambivalent desires and therefore our darkest fears.

Comic Situations

Comic situations vary widely. All have what can be construed as happy endings, the heart's deepest needs finally met in a ceremony of social acceptance, whatever the heart may have originally imagined it wanted. All comic situations have nonconsequential actions: that is, characters may endure much and gain nothing, but neither they nor anyone else will suffer serious consequences, and so in the end all will be well, or will seem so. Comic characters feel pain but do not suffer, and like Tom the Cat in his frequent catastrophic efforts to catch Jerry the Mouse, they are never injured for long. In **black comedy** serious and irreversible

Harold Lloyd's most successful comic character, an earnest, overly eager young go-getter on the way up, has here in *Never Weaken* risen higher than he meant. The long shot reveals his full predicament while keeping us safely distanced; comedy encourages us to laugh at other people's desperate straits as a way to govern our anxieties about our own. Though Lloyd was a skilled acrobat, he had to seem even more clumsy and terrified than any of us would be, his foolish excesses punished by his terror.

consequences do occur, including irretrievable loss or physical mutilation, as in *Monty Python and the Holy Grail* (1975), *A Fish Called Wanda* (1988), or *Dr. Strangelove* (1964), which ends with the destruction of our whole planet. But such comedies outrageously distance us to feel only amusement or contempt for the victims, and so the effect is the same. Black comedy seemed bewildering when Chaplin presented it in *Monsieur Verdoux* (1947), but many comedies now belong to that subgenre, "sick jokes" abound, and our age has grown accustomed to their perversities.

Silent comedy is often structured around **sight gags**, physical predicaments confronted by coping in various ways, with a single prop (as often in Chaplin), or with ingenious role playing (again Chaplin, and occasionally Harpo Marx). These predicaments can be intricately nested so that efforts to escape one problem precipitate a worse, as in Keaton, who often concludes with an incredible burst of ingenuity resolving all the problems all at once. **Slapstick** comedy presents wanton physical buffeting, uninhibitedly aggressive behavior of one kind or another (so-called from the vaudeville slap stick hinged in the middle so as not to injure the clown when hit with it); much Three Stooges comedy is simple slapstick, rarely more. We all suffer as the price of maturity the repression of our desire to hit out, or to "make a mess." Such repression is here avenged, and our infantile desires justified.

Like Roman and Shakespearian comedy, sound comedy tends to present more elaborate plots, structured in triads. In the beginning an established social order is seen to be unsatisfactory, based perhaps on deceit, hypocrisy, injustice, suppression, unfulfilled desire, or mindless habit. There follows a radical disorder while frantic reshufflings and reperceptions take place. Finally a reintegrated social order emerges, less pretentious, cleansed and more humble, based on human needs as they are and often celebrated with a marriage (or after an earlier divorce from a couple's earlier failure to recognize their most profound individual needs, a remarriage). The **screwball** comedies of the 1930s sometimes paired a conventionally repressed person with an unconventional opposite, apparently flea-brained but in fact instinctually shrewd, who altogether overturns various solemn plans and thereby makes possible a future together laced with impulsive vitality, sportive fun; *My Man Godfrey* (1936) and *Bringing Up Baby* (1938) are such films, and *The Accidental Tourist* (1988) a recent attempt at one. What precipitates the chaos may be a scapegrace mischief-maker, a character's single-minded ambition or compulsion, overly elaborate planning, or mere misfortune.

Comedy is always wary of elaborately rational schemes, of people and their unpredictable contingencies treated like predictable mechanical contrivances; often, especially in French comedy, a single character will assert a mistaken premise and then act on it, entering a whimsically fictive world of her or his own devising though invincibly confident that he or she knows the truth of things. In Shakespeare and sometimes in dialogue films the central rearrangements occur in a "green world" such as the Forest of Arden or a seaside vacation resort, a place away from ordinary routines and habitual inhibitions, where natural inclinations may freely emerge. In both silent and sound comedy, secondary characters are revealed to be fools by the initiatives of the primary fool, or secondary characters themselves may provide the plot-advancing initiatives complicating the main comic character's original predicament. In both silent and sound films **running gags** may occur, repeating the same jokes or gestures with minor variations, providing surprise yet familiarity, sometimes amusingly tricking or violating expectation, and in its ritual patterning reminding the audience that the comedy is not a version of life but an agreeable artifice.

Comic Moral Vision

Comic moral vision celebrates liberation from repression (psychic or social), and impulse, intuition, improvisation, ingenuity, wit, imaginative role playing, and the pleasures of the flesh. Such vision tends to be against repressive authority, social respectability for its own sake, orderly arrangements, the life of the mind abstracted from experience, and belief in the sufficiency of human reason, and such vision does not suffer kindly fools committed to such restrictive vices (though it may in the end acknowledge their countervailing necessity). Above all comic moral vision acknowledges paradoxical, ambivalent, and contradictory desires and therefore holds solemnity to be pompous, either stupid or hypocritical. People convinced of their own rectitude, like prudes, are often offered up for ridicule because once in authority, they can be dangerous.

To participate in this vision an audience must be carefully distanced, responsibly disapproving clownish behavior, yet engaged, acknowledging the clown's subversive virtues as liberating and revitalizing. Audiences must believe themselves superior to the events portrayed and yet participate in them vicariously. Comedy structures its quips, gags, and situations to bring the audience back repeatedly to acknowledge recognition of this ambivalence, its own radically divided attitudes and loyalties. This recognition expresses itself as laughter, a signal inviting others to share and acknowledge our otherwise unmentionable complicity, in the face of hopeless predicaments, an accessible hedge against despair. In Aristotle's time though not often since, the comic vision was considered an alternative to the tragic vision, even a means for completing it.

TRAGEDY

Tragedy presents the serious confrontation of dilemmas, no-win situations in which loss is chosen and then endured by protagonists who thus participate in their own downfalls and acknowledge responsibility for them while others suffer undeservedly as a consequence. Derived from the Greek word meaning "goat song," tragedy has been regarded as the most noble of the dramatic genres, a saving ritual in which a scapegoat is sacrificed to propitiate a diety, forestall misfortune, or provide an awesome dramatized parable of human fate. The word is often used casually to describe any misfortune, such as the accidental death of a child, but the grandeur of tragedy lies in its moral vision, not in its unfortunate incidents or unhappy endings. Tragedy presents an image of human beings enduring the worst, including the worst perceptions of themselves imaginable, and yet not surrendering to self-protective evasions or self-destructive despair; in this respect the tragic effect is affirmative, even exhilarating in its display of human fortitude, purging unresolved pity for others and fear that we may find ourselves in such situations. Tragedies in this sense are rare in any dramatic tradition and even more rare in popular arts such as movies, where audiences do not wish to regard any situation as hopeless; yet there are some, such as John Ford's *The Informer* (1935), or Hitchcock's *Vertigo* (1958); and other films such as Fritz Lang's *M* or other genres such as gangster films can tend toward tragedy.

Tragic Characters

Tragic characters usually embody pridefully the culture's more admirable traits—ambition, patience, fortitude, self-assurance, moral consistency, intelligence, or social responsibility—but eventually find they are inadequate to their own initial high image of themselves. Their overestimation of themselves comprises the tragic flaw which defines their common humanity and ensures their complicity in their own downfall. These characters tend to believe themselves sufficiently knowledgeable and justified, then suffer from events they themselves have set in motion. They are layered, even profound, and the process of a tragic drama is usually of protagonists coming to comprehend their own essential natures and predicaments, as well as a tracing of the consequences of their initial action. The greatest suffering tragic characters endure stems not from the external situation but from comprehending how it came about (a person undeservedly or uncomprehendingly beaten down by misfortune is pathetic, not tragic). Such a character becomes in a sense the scapegoat or martyr by whom we comprehend our own condition and, with difficulty, reconcile ourselves to it.

Tragic Actions

Tragic actions like comic actions begin with a political, social, familial, or psychological order precariously founded on evasions and unacknowledged truths, then often follow with a rash but decisive action by the protagonist, from which all else results, including even the protagonist's death perhaps after some kind of moral regeneration. What follows has the shape of an unalterable destiny or fate, but it is more often the progressive revelation of a past previously ignored and now seen to be determining, the present predicament created not by "the gods" but by the protagonist's past choices and commitments. Film being a product of a secular century, with naturalistic assumptions, fate or the gods rarely enter into consideration; rather, people make choices among limited options, all known though their full nature and the eventual outcome are not known. Theology may provide a further way to comprehend such choices and consequences, and does so with facile ease in Hollywood biblical epics or with playful charm in films offering consolation of sorts during World War II, such as *Here Comes Mr. Jordan* (1941) and *It's a Wonderful Life* (1946). But rarely are movie invocations of religious truths profound, as they are in the films of Robert Bresson, which preserve an apprehension of mystery in the great religious tradition they draw on. And rarely are these movies recognized in their secular guises when they do appear: *Midnight Cowboy* (1969) and *American Gigolo* (1980) are both crucially informed by Christian views of redemption achieved through acts of sacrificial love (in its script *American Gigolo* looks back through Bresson to Dostoyevsky), though both seem utterly irreligious. Many films noir present tragic actions with mediocre protagonists too self-absorbed or petty in their vices to serve as tragic heroes.

Tragic Moral Vision

Tragic moral vision stresses the inevitability of death, loss, and pain, the unpredictability of the consequences of our actions and their irremediable irreversibility, and the confronting of hopeless dilemmas. At the same time tragic moral vision provides a way to comprehend, even to reconcile one's self to such catastrophic events without diminution or denial of our moral dignity, counseling cautious restraint, stoic acceptance, respect for human limitation, humility before events and powers beyond our control, and above all self-knowledge. Superficially tragedy seems gloomy, even pessimistic, because it confirms difficult or inevitable truths customarily evaded, and things never work out well for its main characters; but more profoundly, a tragedy can leave its audiences in a state of awed exaltation, "calm of mind, all passion spent."

MELODRAMA

Melodrama is a broad term applicable to most movies, stressing strong emotion, high adventure, and frequently, suffering or self-sacrifice in service to some noble, presumably deserving cause, or difficult passages of life recast as dramatic action. Melodrama is a modern form of the old morality play in which long-tried virtue eventually subdues vice at great cost or is rescued from its helplessness before vice. The characters are all definable by their moral or social commitments even when these are mixed or ambivalent. The term originates in Victorian theatrical practice, when drama was accompanied by orchestral music to intensify the feelings appropriate to each scene, as still in many films since D. W. Griffith's (a sweetly sorrowful violin playing "Hearts and Flowers" accompanied an impoverished mother's pleading with her heartless landlord then as now, and stock orchestral music still accompanies stock chase scenes). Now the term "melodrama" is applied more properly to films designed to arouse feelings indulged for their own sake—anxiety, fear, hatred, indignation, apprehension, sympathy, or joy. Melodrama is expected to provide audiences with vicarious emotional experiences enriching uneventful lives (compensation fantasies) or to provide shape and occasion for fantasy enactment of real but repressed inner turmoil. What a melodrama says about its situations is usually banal and reassuring—virtue will triumph over evil, love can defeat all obstacles, great courage has supreme rewards, suffering ennobles the spirit. Melodramas need not be profound, though some studies find some of them indecisive or conflicted.

But what these feasts of feeling reveal about our own unacknowledged predicaments can be quite profound, carefully analyzed. Recently much attention has been given to **domestic melodrama,** "soap operas" such as *Stella Dallas* (1937) or *Magnificent Obsession* (1954), a form of the genre designed to appeal especially to women by displaying their real anxieties as the dominated gender in a patriarchal culture and their real power among themselves within a narrow sphere of courtship, marriage, childrearing, and household obligations. These middle-class dramas, once examining adulterous desire or maternal sacrifice but more recently, like *Terms of Endearment* (1983) concerned with mother-daughter relationships, tend to divide people into the saintly and the selfish, the noble and the bitchy, victims and schemers; many tend toward the sentimental convention that unmerited suffering can convert villainy into something else, since people are essentially good at heart though misguided (in this tradition a steadfast scheming scoundrel like *Dallas*'s J.R. seems unaccountably evil). The term "melodrama" now refers primarily to these kinds of films, though its range extends even to *E.T.*

ADVENTURE

Adventure films are often also melodramatic and include several highly codified subgenres. What they have in common is action, the promise and eventual display of physical conflict, masterful confrontations in which honest decency, aided by ability, shrewdness, experience, and persistence, wins out over chance or the intrusive schemes of opportunists and sadists. These films may have classic fairy tale structures, such as a journey through successive ordeals into maturity [*Star Wars* (1977) is a recent example], or they may follow a traditional revenge plot, in which an originally helpless hero finally locates and destroys the perpetrators of an earlier outrageous injustice, cleansing the world of such villains and therefore of such injustice. The heroes are bundles of traits we tend to admire—resourcefulness, toughness, suavity, elegance, above all imperturbability—never of traits we cannot approve. The action usually takes place in an exotic setting, such as jungles or foreign fleshpots; if familiarly urban, scenes take place in parts of the city unfamiliar or inaccessible to most audiences—expensive penthouses or back alley slums. A **thriller** is strictly speaking not a genre but a characteristic of many adventure films and other kinds as well, placing heavy weight on suspense and fearful anticipation, and, as Hitchcock observed when discriminating thrillers from mere shockers, exploiting the audience's prior knowledge of dangers unknown to the characters.

Swashbucklers

Swashbucklers, and sword and sorcery films, derive from older historical novels, medieval chivalric romances, primitive Germanic myths laced at times with Renaissance court etiquette, and modern imitations of all these. These films are aristocratic in their social vision, depicting the exploits of some vigorous and resourceful individual. This person, if not nobly born then "naturally" noble, confronts enemies at sword's point and eventually earns high place in an established hierarchy of otherwise hereditary privilege. Films seemingly of other genres, such as the *Star Wars* trilogy, derive heavily from these. Swashbucklers—a "swash" is leg armor, incidentally—were especially popular before World War II, when they provided various political analogies for the affirmation of freedom against tyranny, the threatened Nazi domination of Europe figured by Spain of the Armada in Elizabethan times. Films were often about pirates or Imperial Rome, occasionally films on the discovery of the Western Hemisphere, and sometimes films of colonial conquest. The male hero was often a gallant, self-sufficient individualist and natural leader by virtue of his superior duelling skills, cleverness, and good manners, nearly unflappable whatever the situation, at all times debonair. His honor is defended by his sword, deftly wielded to aid comrades or country against the snobbish tyrants threatening either. As played by Douglas Fairbanks, Douglas Fairbanks, Jr., Errol Flynn, or Tyrone Power, in films such as *The Adventures of Robin Hood*

(1938), *The Sea Hawk* (1940), or *The Captain from Castile* (1947), later parodied by Gene Kelly in the musical *The Pirate* (1948), the hero is a free-
spirited cavalier, perhaps a dispossessed nobleman outside the law but
nevertheless accustomed to the prerogatives of his former rank, a free-
booter enlisted in the service of socially responsible ends who cannot
be out-faced. His agile skill with a sword ensures effortless superiority.
His rewards are wealth, honor, and usually the love of a "proud
beauty"—a woman of high social rank who disdains his advances at
first but is finally brought to submission by his courtesy and masterly
courage (Maureen O'Hara specialized in this role for a time). Other
films borrow its characteristics from time to time, from *Gunga Din* (1939)
and other films set in British India to *Raiders of the Lost Ark* and other
films similarly set in colonized third-world countries. **Sword and sorcery**
films vary from versions of the Arthurian legends to barbaric pre-Chris-
tian inventions set in arid landscapes and often present a series of
ordeals constituting a young man's rites-of-passage or the creation of
kingdoms. Magicians, occult manifestations, and savage brutality are
among the commonplaces one must confront and overcome.

Westerns

The **Western** is by now classical, a native U.S. genre based on the
country's unique possession of a western frontier until the end of the
nineteenth century, when movies were invented and myths of the West
could move from dime novels to the screen. Westerns are concerned
with justice in an open world, an empty landscape populated by exter-
nally unrestrained individuals, and especially with the traits of character
and behavior supposedly essential to nation building; in fact, the Western
constitutes a language Americans have used for a century to critically
examine their identity as Americans. Until the post-Vietnam period,
when faith in the U.S. character and mission which is its subject finally
dissipated, Westerns were a staple product of all U.S. film studios.

The Western was preceded by James Fenimore Cooper's novels following the frontier from upstate New York to the western prairies, by
decades of pulp fiction, and finally by Owen Wister's turn-of-the-century
novel *The Virginian*. The first edited narrative film was also the first
Western, Porter's *The Great Train Robbery* (1903), shot near the Edison
Studios in East Orange, New Jersey. Screen Westerns are usually set
in a barren wild locale, "God's country" but not yet "tamed," needing
to be dominated. Westerns developed their legends and conventions
in filmic terms during the 1920s and were periodically adjusted to address
new public concerns until the 1970s. Pacifism was an issue before World
War II, as in *Destry Rides Again* (1939), psychological obsessions during

the fifties and sixties, as in *The Left Handed Gun* (1958), and finally the individual's helplessness before corporate power. Westerns' primary concerns were always with values dating back to medieval chivalric tales, especially with concepts of manhood committed to a code of honor and defended by duelling. What Westerns query can be summed up by the Preamble to the U.S. Constitution restated as a question: can "we the people" in fact form a more perfect union, establish justice, ensure domestic tranquillity, provide for the common defense, and promote the welfare of all citizens, securing for future generations the blessings of liberty yet civil order? If so, how? In the Puritans' language, from a new beginning can we build God's city on a hill? Western films like the cheap novels before them proposed answers in terms of deep-set U.S. desires and doubts, not always affirmatively.

Iconography   Westerns have a distinctive look. There are broad-hatted men on horseback wearing gunbelts, the good guys clean-shaven or full-mustached in token of respect for the social propriety they serve, the bad guys unshaven (or trim-mustached if propertied and vain); both kinds are militantly self-reliant, and their horses and guns are extensions of their individual instincts. The setting is a desert landscape, often identified as "good grazing land" though we see only its bare inhospitality; if it is to yield abundance it will be because of what people bring to it, not what it is. There are isolated cattle ranches providing microcosms of family life and often of capitalist enterprise, sometimes with a tyrannical "cattle baron" patriarch enthroned there. Occasionally there are "Injuns," until the 1960s Civil Rights movement treated as lesser breeds or else as antagonistic forces of nature to be overcome, like bad weather, but since then treated as victims of our racism, greed, and political hypocrisy. Some are "cavalry Westerns" stressing order, discipline, and obedience within command structures, military virtues rather than the individualistic creeds of most Westerns (though even the cavalry Western examines the conflicting claims of anarchic self-gratification and the obligation to maintain social order). There are stage-coaches for the gentry, women, and others who lack the manly strength to ride their own horses, a rolling social microcosm in *Stagecoach* (1939), with briefly enforced social democracy among its passengers. All Westerns present false-facaded, dusty towns on the edge of nowhere, each with a livery stable, general store, saloon, church, and jail, each of these a center of the different values implicated in the town's future. Always the railroad lurks in the outskirts, the harbinger of the industrialized future, which will destroy the nobility of individual self-reliance altogether, and the established link with other towns and "the East," that effete terminal condition the town tends toward. Women have little to do in this genre, except to offer the promise of domesticity if they are "good" women or alluring companionship if they are "bad" women, saloon prostitutes usually called "dance hall hostesses," invariably more liberated and understanding of male necessities than the conventionally good women.

These elements are arrayed in a mythical West of the imagination. The real western frontier crossed the prairies and the Mississippi as farmland preceded only briefly by range cattle and developed alongside mines and railroads. There was no single "West." The weather, topography, and ways of living in various parts of the western territories varied enormously, as they still do. The West was as often cold and muddy as hot and dusty and populated by immigrants of different ethnic and national backgrounds as well as by miners, land speculators, farmers, peddlers and storekeepers, and some cattle barons. At the bottom of the social scale, like hired hands anywhere, were the cowboys or ranch hands. These were often newly freed blacks, Hispanics, and rough-trade semioutcasts, people willing to work long hours in bad weather for low pay, with little chance for advancement or eventually a family life of one's own. The isolated, frugal, hard-scrabble, family-driven cattle farm depicted in *Heartland* (1979) or the human alienation of *The New Land* (1973) were probably more typical of the West than the forts and ranches of John Ford's Monument Valley sagas. Then as now the myth of the West provided easterners and westerners alike with a dream more satisfying than the reality they inhabited; as two of Ford's Westerns put it, when fact and legend conflict there is never any question which to present as fact.

A Western's historical period is almost always that brief period after the U.S. Civil War, when the frontier was no longer located in a forested wilderness and the slavery issue was presumably settled and forgotten, yet before urban industrialism had overwhelmed the heroic myth altogether. The behind-the-credit music is unmistakable throughout the genre, folk songs or imitations of them set to loping equestrian rhythms, elegaic or nostalgic, celebrating yet mourning a past now irretrievable.

Plot Issues   Westerns tend to cluster in three kinds:

1 Beginning-of-the-West Westerns are epics concerned with the settling of the land, the antagonists being the weather, the terrain, Indians, or renegades; the protagonist is usually a powerful and self-determined loner whose force of will creates the town or ranch—that is, the new community. As in *Red River* (1948), the dominant issue has to do with reconciling the despotic rule necessary for carving civilization out of wilderness with the democratic humanism justifying that great enterprise—the politics of authoritarianism versus those of group participation (the analogues with U.S. industrial tycoons, with any paternal authorities, or with the issues of World War II just ended, are obvious). Cavalry

John Ford's Monument Valley, magnificent, austere, and barren, land well worth fighting over, as in nearly all his Westerns, but land which gives no more back than men and women happen to bring to it. Though the real West developed on good soil near water, mineral deposits, railroads, and relatives who had gone before, this kind of empty place became the West of our imagination. It is a fit site for the genre's morality tales of people tested by adversity and challenged to convert deserts into gardens and savagery into civilization.

Westerns with their built-in chains of command seem more comfortable with these concerns than most other Westerns.

2 Middle-of-the-West Westerns are morality tales set in small towns perched precariously on the edge of the desert, testing whether they can grow or will return to dust, exploring traits necessary for good (family virtues and civil order) to overcome evil (male violence and self-indulgence) to liberate the community from such threats and so ensure a peaceful bourgeois prosperity. Most Westerns are of this kind, ritually exorcising the snake of selfish individualism from the garden of a law-abiding community, so the desert may one day bloom into God's country and the country's destiny among the nations be fulfilled.

Whatever the town's past, a stranger rides into town and a period of testing begins. In *Destry Rides Again* (1939) the town meets its challenge, led at the last minute by militant townswomen; in *Gunfight at the OK Corral* (1957) and *My Darling Clementine* (1946), both dealing heroically with the same in fact trivial historical event, heroes are found; in *High Noon* (1952) the town fails, though a heroine is found to support the hero. A dominant issue rests in the paradox that violence is necessary to protect the peaceable against violence, tainting with moral isolation the champion who rescues the society at cost of his own exclusion from it—see *The Gunfighter* (1950). Taciturn and self-sufficient, the hero is by nature and calling a stoic, melancholy loner, in the end honored, but necessarily heading further west away from encroaching civilization, into the setting sun which is his archetypal destiny. These morality Westerns explore other issues as well: the viability of codes of manly honor mandating all male behavior; the perils of success in a competitive society (the "top-gun" theme, as in *The Fastest Gun Alive* (1956), where a superior fast draw can condemn one to kill young challengers repeatedly until one day . . .); and the costs of vengeance, especially of avenging violations of family, honor, or property.

3 End-of-the-West Westerns are ironic essays on the nature of the myth itself as well as elegies on its loss. These films are set around the turn of the century, when the corporate state has presumably fenced and suppressed free-spirited individualism, the railroads and banks with their massive industrial power and impersonal employees govern, cars are replacing horses, law is enforced by professionals merely doing their job, and there is no room for free spirits unwilling to become managerial functionaries. Old-style heroism and villainy are alike irrelevant, and the frontier has closed. Though some, such as *The Man Who Shot Liberty Valance* (1962) or *Lonely Are the Brave* (1962) are earlier, most date from the Vietnam war period's reexamination of our faith in the sufficient innocence of the U.S. mission, with bitter side-observations on the fate of individual self-reliance. *Butch Cassidy and the Sundance Kid* (1969), *Little Big Man* (1970), *McCabe and Mrs. Miller* (1971), and *Buffalo Bill and the Indians* (1976) all find that the values associated with the West have died and may always have been delusions (*McCabe* in fact can be read as a brief history of the American dream from its beginning, the founding of the town of Presbyterian Church, to its final surrender to drugs).

Along with this questioning of fundamentals in the end-of-the-West films came Sergio Leone's sardonic tales of sadistic viciousness in **spaghetti westerns** such as *The Good, the Bad, and the Ugly* (1968), made in Italy a long way from the Western's rough-hewn optimism. The whole genre then disappeared. Its language reared issues we no longer wished to hear about. Wilderness films such as *Jeremiah Johnson* (1972) provided a substitute for Westerns, but the West now appears mainly in films about our commercial exploitation of the myth, such as *Westworld* (1973), *The Electric Horseman* (1979), or *City Slickers* (1991). Some Australian directors still feel drawn to make them, some features of Westerns are celebrated in mock-swashbucklers like the Indiana Jones sagas, and certain of their concerns have migrated like the actor Clint Eastwood, the slit-eyed "man with no name" of spaghetti western fame, into crime films.

Crime Films

The **crime film** presents the problem of justice in a closed urban world, meaner and more cerebral than the Western because its evil is more hidden, often more unapproachable, devious, and irremediable, and only the law, or superior determination and cunning, can offer protection from it. The world being corrupt, innocence cannot survive unaided, nor can we return to innocence by catching the criminal (there are always many more). But ordinary people can be protected by professionals who track down those criminals who threaten too obtrusively. Though in life most crimes are unsolved, and it is often impossible to identify a "bad guy" with moral or legal certainty or to find an appropriate punishment, in crime films criminals are clearly guilty, caught, and punished. This implies that crime films are not social exposés nor meditations on justice but public rituals, affirming despite the evidence to the contrary that honesty is the best policy, that justice is adequately served by our criminal justice system, and that we are not helpless before urban criminals and hoodlums or the figments of our suppressed fears of them. The category of crime films includes several distinct, fully formed genres, each remarkably persistent in film history.

Gangster Films   Gangster films mirror in the underworld the ambitions, anxieties, and difficulties of achieving personal success in the legitimate upper world of competitive capitalism, with its concomitant rewards of power, wealth, and prestige, and its risks of going under. From thirties tales of the rise and fall of individual entrepreneurs such as *Little Caesar* (1930) or *Public Enemy* (1931), through recent tales of corporate conglomerates eliminating disloyalty and competitors alike, as in the *Godfather* films (1972, 1974, 1990), the camped *Prizzi's Honor* (1985), *Miller's Crossing* (1990), and many others, these films raise distinct ambivalence in their audiences. Viewers are appalled by the violence gangs employ to enforce or calculatedly breach agreements, yet they admire the shrewd determination exhibited by mobsters in their attempts to get ahead and stay there. Even among the low-level hoods of *Goodfellas* (1990), success carries its own justification. Thus the chief character in a gangster film may resemble a tragic hero, awesome yet deplorable, sympathetic though ruthless, in the end victimized and doomed by his humanity or his ruthlessness. Nowadays, without the Production Code's requirement that crime never pay, a gangster's superior scheming may earn him the power and respect he seeks. Little Caesar was de-

Near the summit of his power, Little Caesar stands tall to model his fancy duds, his grandeur evident in the admiring face of a small time punk and framed by a mirror, the two reflections suggesting what this essentially naive gangster has actually accomplished.

stroyed by choosing loyalty to a friend over the need to keep "dishing it out," losing all but maintaining that shred of humane decency; *The Godfather, Part II* (1974) shows a man successfully suppressing family feeling to consolidate his personal power, gaining all at the cost finally of his ability to feel anything.

A small group variant of the gangster film is the **big heist** or **big caper** film. Perhaps derived from the wartime single-mission film, which itself may be indebted to the thirties "let's put on a show" backstage musical, these films show highly skilled and daring professional criminals brought together to perform a single fabulously remunerative crime, a "killing" which will enable them to retire in luxury. Older films such as *The Asphalt Jungle* (1950), Kubrick's early *The Killing* (1956), or *Topkapi* (1964) show something finally going wrong; recent versions may show complete success, the team's extraordinary cunning and courage well-rewarded.

In most gangster films law enforcement officers are corrupt and hypocritical (especially if local), or else bloodless bureaucrats or technocrats (especially if F.B.I.). Some gangsters may be cold sadists, but those who matter are ambitious, tough, courageous, resourceful, or harmlessly amusing figments of our own desires portrayed dramatically as theirs. Our admiration for them is sustained as long as we never actually see them injure the innocent nor extort money from the vulnerable.

A seeming variant, probably not a crime film at all, is the **prison film**. The prison may be a major penitentiary or "big house" as in *San Quentin* (1937), a chain gang's barracks as in *Cool Hand Luke* (1967), or a local jail as in *Rambo: First Blood* (1982). These films are metaphors concerned with our own subjection to restrictions of all kinds, physical, psychological, social, or institutional, mandated or arbitrary, and with modes of resistance, how to find free space within these constraints, or how to escape altogether. Prison films can be nightmares of adolescent guilt punished extravagantly by corrupt established power, such as *Midnight Express* (1978), essays on the function of private fantasy in a politically repressive age, such as *Brazil* (1985) or *Kiss of the Spider Woman* (1985), or other such explorations of anxieties over loss of control over our own lives. But their steadfast popularity reflects our repressed acculturation, in no way implying a lively public interest in criminal or prison reform.

Crime Detection   **Crime detection** films are concerned with processes rather than results, with comprehending events more than with catching criminals (though that too, if the challenge seems worthy). Ultimately the drama of detection gratifies our desire to see intelligible explanations achieved, while assuring us that those who wander outside the law will surely be caught (as in fact few are), and punished (an issue usually side-stepped or else settled immediately by having the criminals defiantly declare their guilt and then die trying to escape). The crime—often the murder of someone we care little about, often not even known until some lesser investigative process reveals it—provides the excuse for detectives to do their work. Then, their manner of procedure, their style, dominate our attention; famously, Bogart and Bacall's relationship with each other in *The Big Sleep* (1946) so overwhelms the plotting that few notice and even fewer care who killed Geiger.

Private-eye films confirm our faith in the efficacy of the lone individual unhampered by due process. Their heros may be amateur sleuths such as Sherlock Holmes, Miss Marple, or the Thin Man, or they may be street-smart professionals such as Sam Spade in *The Maltese Falcon* (1941) or the many Philip Marlowes of many films based on Raymond Chandler stories. The knowledgeable amateurs proceed intellectually, by deduction (they originated during the late nineteenth century's fascination with scientific procedure), and the plot often ends with all suspects assembled and the sleuth's ratiocinative processes revealed while identifying the culprit. The professional private detective testifies to our faith in individuals, especially in self-employed loners who can maneuver knowledgeably through the city's jungles, improvising and calculating as they go, sometimes treating legal due process as a minor inconvenience. A private eye's motives may vary—the pleasures of the chase, professional obligation, service for fee (though when the case is under way money rarely seems to matter), chivalric feelings for a victimized woman of recent intimate acquaintance, loyalty to a buddy, or personal revenge—but the film's techniques closely identify the audience with the detective, whose exceptional toughness, shrewdness, or dedication become their own attributes vicariously enjoyed, often pointed up dramatically by the bumbling sidekicks or cops serving as foil characters.

Police procedure films confirm faith in the system and in due process rather than in exceptional individuals. These films show us cops doing the job more or less as a job, though one requiring skilled professionalism. A "procedural" tends to stress hierarchy, teamwork, experience, and laboratory analyses rather than instinctual resourcefulness, and it affirms the efficacy of patient plodding and careful searching through official records, rather than access to a network of friends on the street (a private eye may ask a "friend" on the force to look up records as a favor). Occasionally a personally motivated maverick within the system but outside the law like "Dirty Harry" simultaneously gratifies our contradictory faith in the efficacy of individuals yet institutions, our need for utterly dedicated loner heroes yet capable hired functionaries. This ideological contradiction originates in our mistrust of the State yet dependence on it, and is certainly implicated in the upsurge of such films during the 1980s. Recently pairs of investigators, differing in race, temperament, or gender, have been teamed to solve crimes while exploring our different class or feminist concerns, showing how such differences can be respected yet subsumed by commitment to a common goal. The supervising officers sending the mavericks on their missions and later disciplining their zeal are almost always black, in films though not in life, possibly to overly reassure skittish white audiences that blacks are found on both sides of the law.

Courtroom scenes occur frequently in crime films (as in other kinds as well), for their dramas of dark schemes brought to light by orderly procedures, dedicated attorneys fictive or real, such as those in *The Verdict* (1982) or in *Reversal of Fortune* (1990), ensuring that justice can prevail. Such courtroom dramas or concluding segments of crime films, finally bringing private entangled plotting into the public sector for orderly adjudication, have been common in drama since the Renaissance;

Shakespeare's happy endings as well as *L.A. Law*'s often emerge from courtrooms. But most often the subject of these films is the affirmation of innocence, not the revelation of guilt, release from fear that we have been found out or may be unjustly accused rather than release from our fear of lawlessness.

HORROR FILMS

Horror films horrify by invoking uncanny experiences, the unfamiliar encountered amidst the familiar, threatening with the unknown and destabilizing the security of the known. Horror films provide occasions, or objective correlatives, for reworking especially the anxieties of childhood, with its nameless fears and guilty apprehensions, and others as well carried on into adolescence and afterward. Their surface characteristics are familiar enough: They use low-key lighting to intensify the contrast between the visible and known and the dark—or startlingly revealed—unknown. Behind the titles we hear dissonant music implying a perverse disharmony below placid surfaces. Opening events display a normality almost stereotypical in their reassuring detail followed by hints of something awry, loomings and lurkings beyond the ordinary, then incursion or outright invasion by some grotesque destructive force, its perversion of purpose figured in its physical monstrosity, often in its mutilation of others. Next is a period of helpless terror or variegated forms of futile resistance while the countervailing force gathers knowledge and will (and if there is a political dimension to the film, overcomes popular or official skepticism). Finally comes liberation and comprehension, the awakening from nightmare back to a normal world, all survivors chastened but some also now tested and found heroic. DePalma's *Carrie* (1976) shockingly violated the convention that the final sequence clears the air and returns characters and the audience to a wholesome and secure world, and other films have since followed *Carrie*'s example.

To read the subtexts of these fables, one can ask "What is the customary condition which proves so vulnerable, what is the nature of the threat, and what can save us?" The answers vary from decade to decade (the military, or a fatherly scientist or detective, or a youthful maverick despite the military, will save us), but the conventions persist along with our need to reimagine and so dominate whatever haunts us. Usually whatever the monster or psychopath, he, she, or it is immune to ordinary human compassion and keeps coming at the victim despite all pleas; the sense that we may be helpless before impersonal forces insensible to our desires is part of the horror. Usually the monster is frankly malevolent, but sometimes the monster turns pitiable (like the Frankenstein monster), allowing audience acknowledgment of the monstrous

Probably the best-known sympathetic monster in film, Boris Karloff, is about to incur the village's rage and his own destruction by unwittingly drowning the little girl, throwing her in the water in the belief that like the flowers they are plucking, she will float.

in ourselves or of its isolating consequences. Many subgenres persist with the genre: mad scientist films, from *Metropolis* (1926) and *Franken-stein* (1931) through the older and more recent versions of *The Fly* (1958 and 1986), display our persistent mistrust of rationality divorced from its human contingencies (as the painter Goya put it with precise ambiguity "the dream of reason creates monsters"); living dead films from *Dracula* (1931) to George Romero's zombie series spawn generations of walking corpses who visit upon us our own fear of the dead and of dying, of our failed obligations to the memory of the dead, and of creatures who threaten us implacably; conversion films such as *The Fly* again, or *Dracula* again, or *Invasion of the Body Snatchers* (1956 or 1978), are a kind of minor form of pornography playing on our fear, sometimes laced with unacknowledged desire, of becoming what we are not, of losing our sense of self in submission to some overwhelming compulsion; and mad slasher films such as the *Friday the Thirteenth* (1980 and after), *Halloween* (1978 and after), or *A Nightmare on Elm Street*

(1984 and after) series invoke fears of horrible mutilation, especially in retribution for being young and sexually active. Horror films sometimes blend comedy or parody into their formulas, the comic vision conferring on us yet one more way to govern our anxieties, and the successful series end by becoming parodies of themselves (Freddie, the horror of the *Nightmare* films, is now an accustomed and amusing clown).

SCIENCE FICTION

Science fiction films offer yet another form of uncanny experience, sometimes as a subgenre of horror films, sometimes with their own unique agendas. Science fiction's cardinal fictive convention is time displacement into a technological future where some current tendencies of our culture have become dominant and can be examined in a relatively disengaged manner, free from contemporary assumptions about them. Sometimes, as in fifties films such as *The Day the Earth Stood Still* (1951) or *It Came from Outer Space* (1953), some technologically advanced culture invades our own, which then reveals its underlying strengths and limits by the way it attempts to cope. Though time displacement opens the setting to **utopian** social speculation, most science fiction is **dystopian** in nature, pessimistic in its vision of the way further scientific achievement will affect social progress or individual happiness. Young males especially in our culture tend to eroticize technology and find the sets' futuristic geometries exciting and satisfying even when the plots counsel otherwise. *Close Encounters of the Third Kind* (1977) shares this heartening vision without taking note of its own poignant implications, and many viewers fail to notice that the clean technological world of *2001: a Space Odyssey* (1968) is sterile, and even birthdays are rote.

Many ostensibly "sci-fi" films are little more than traditional action genres disguised by their setting. "Horse operas" such as *High Noon* (1952) easily translate to "space operas" such as *Outland* (1981), and *Star Wars* (1977) derives heavily from World War II combat films as well as prewar swashbucklers; some apocalyptic films—postnuclear like *A Boy and His Dog* (1977) or *Mad Max* (1979), for example—use their futuristic situations to warrant old-fashioned preindustrial derring-do. Even so, science fiction is readily discriminated from **fantasy,** sorcery, or other films invested in magic, by its strict assumption that we inhabit a universe of predictable physical laws, though new "laws" for apparent marvels may become known, as in the horror sci-fi film *Alien*, by their unforeseen consequences.

MUSICALS

Musicals are on their surfaces entertainments displaying their performers' and composers' talents and expressivity, satisfying for what they evidence of both. Singing, dancing, and making music are themselves as satisfying to witness as the songs, dances, and production numbers themselves, since all display rare gifts in apparently easy and effortless performance, as if anyone could do it. But, more subtly, musicals affirm the power of grace, skill, energy, and optimism to overcome obstacles, shape conflict into harmony, and lead desire into the forms of its own gratification. Ultimately these films affirm that readiness to use one's abilities to please others is a virtue others will certainly appreciate and a saving power in itself.

Musical films originated in stage musicals, varieties, revues, and musical dramas, shows consisting of bundled but separate musical numbers as well as numbers strung into a thin dramatic plot ostensibly providing occasion for their performance within a set action; they are distantly related to high culture's operas as well as more popular "operettas." Musicals did not form a film genre until the late twenties, when synchronized sound made it possible for the screen to reproduce both essential elements of stage performance, sound as well as sight (though not of course the marvel of a performer's physical presence). In fact, it was studio desire to bring segments of stage musicals to larger film audiences that brought cinematic sound from its twenties status as a mere technological novelty to images synchronized with phonograph records, finally to optical sound tracks fixed on the film itself. The "talkies" were originally only an astonishingly popular by-product of filmed vaudeville shows.

A staple especially in the 1930s through the 1950s, when major studios put considerable money and effort into them, the musical as such changed during the 1960s along with popular music itself. Unsourced musical numbers increasingly accompanied straight dramatic action, as in *The Graduate* (1967), and concert films emerged documenting known performers and groups on actual stages; even the Beatles' *A Hard Day's Night* (1964) is more a concert film than a musical narrative. Nowadays rock video provides images synchronized to preexisting music, sometimes of performances, sometimes as expressionistic or surreal commentary, often as both.

Unintegrated Musicals

Unintegrated musicals are essentially variety shows (as were the earliest Hollywood musicals), or narrative films punctuated by musical numbers cued by the story but not essential to it. In such musicals a performer pauses to sing, perhaps in the theater or night club where others may watch, while plot development hangs suspended (even the romance/ thriller *Casablanca* contains such a moment). *The Rocky Horror Picture Show* (1975) parodies this old device as well as many others. The main characters may be identified as professional performers, as in some Astaire or Presley films, but their occasional performances do not advance the action. Full choral numbers with ensemble dancing may be justified within the film's dramatic frame, as a character's dream in *Lady in the Dark* (1944) or as a reverie as in the final number of *An American in Paris* (1951); in a **backstage musical** choral numbers result from many characters' efforts to put on a show, as in *42nd Street* (1933), *Babes on Broadway* (1941), or recently *A Chorus Line* (1985). But essentially an unintegrated narrative musical stripped of its songs and production numbers would make an understandable if brief and perhaps dull drama.

Performances in such musicals are frankly directed toward the camera wherever their ostensible audiences may be located, and unsourced orchestral accompaniment is customary even in intimate love duets. Such films may be designed to exhibit the performer's abilities in a mixed or **medley** entertainment, with the plot a minimal excuse for the performances but provided for those who would also enjoy it. Even so, whatever the issue at stake, all musicals speak implicitly of the performer's pleasure in performing. The singing may be dubbed, as in *My Fair Lady* (1964), or the dancing, as in *Flashdance* (1983), with the performer we see someone else, but the spectacle is the same. Often musicals underscore the audience's enjoyment of such performances as well, with inserted reaction shots, and so carry other implicit meanings as well. The backstage musical, for example, usually affirms Yeats's observation "that we must labor to be beautiful" yet make performing seem spontaneous, a natural mode of expression. Financial success and popular admiration are among the other rewards.

Integrated Musicals

Integrated musicals are narrative films in which the musical or choreographic numbers not only augment but advance the action, providing key moments of revelation and transformation as well as enlarging on dramatic points established elsewhere. The characters need not be identified as professional performers, but in moments of joy, adversity, understanding, or bewilderment, they turn nevertheless to the range of vocal and physical expressivity available in song and dance. Such performing reveals otherwise inexpressible conflicts and reactions and further develops the action. Watching an integrated musical, an audience's double

James Cagney shows the dance coach how he wants the choreography danced, one foot turned out, while supposedly the chorus line is rehearsing a number in the backstage musical *Footlight Parade* (1933), through hard work creating what will finally seem spontaneously beautiful. Cagney's compact body and tight, precise movements helped his gangsters seem menacing and his dancers seem entertainingly eccentric.

vision of a performer performing a character fuses, creating a heightened experience of life fulfilled as art, of life lived artfully. Many originate in stage musicals, though some (e.g. Busby Berkeley's musical numbers, or Bob Fosse's) were conceived for the screen. Ostensibly the first such stage musical was the 1943 Rodgers and Hammerstein *Oklahoma!* In fact some Astaire films of the thirties were integrated, as was *The Wizard of Oz* (1939), and as some musicals have been since including *Carousel* (1956), *The Music Man* (1962), *Hair* (1979), and *Tommy* (1975), and the exuberant and expansive songs and production numbers of *Oklahoma!* are not as tightly integrated with the plot as some of these. The form is more difficult to create than the unintegrated musical, and if done well the songs may not stand alone well enough to sell widely. But a great integrated musical is almost a condition of consciousness, a vision of an energetic and gracious world audiences can aspire to enter.

DOCUMENTARIES

Documentary or nonfiction films differ from narrative films chiefly in their requiring an audience's belief that what is seen actually occurred, that is, that their images and sounds record the continuous "reality" inhabited by the viewer rather than some fictional semblance of it. The term was given these films in the 1920s, implying that the film provides as neutral a "document" or record as any of the other documents by which we trace past events. As reality recorded for later observation, documentaries seem to be a window on the world, the frame a surrogate for the viewer's eyes.

So the viewer is invited to believe. Documentaries and documentarists will sometimes claim objectivity, implying that complex events are being totally photographed and reported, presented from no point of view, or from all possible points of view simultaneously, and implying perhaps that the object itself is being shown (which is equally impossible). Journalists often confuse objective reporting with impartial reporting, a different reportorial mandate requiring equal treatment of "both sides" as if they were of equal merit or credibility, and as if there were no other "sides" as well; sometimes journalists mean "disinterested" reporting, meaning without a self-serving, self-interested bias, lacking even the cultural and professional biases that dictate what shall be reported and what not.

But documentary films such as fiction films always display a limiting point of view. They are shaped by a filmmaker's decisions about what should be photographed, from where, and what not, and by selective editing, showing what, in what order, cutting out what else altogether. Though they are not usually narratives, they may nevertheless follow a chronology of some kind, and they are always arranged to present some summary revelation in the classic climactic position, near the end, imposing significance by placement. Some of the events recorded are in fact created in order to be recorded, or altered by the camera's presence as part of the event recorded.

Though most documentaries are ephemeral, presenting topical events for informational or entertainment purposes, and some are polemical, arguing a cause or supporting some specific set of beliefs, a few achieve a visual style or profundity outlasting public concern with the events they portray, satisfying in themselves as **art documentaries** and occasionally rescreened as such. The best of these (Robert Flaherty's, or Pare Lorentz's in the 1930s, or Marcel Ophuls's more recently) are usually distinctive in their cinematic styles and strategies. Though there are as many uses for documentaries as there are for an audience's credulity, we can discriminate the primary kinds by their primary presentational strategies.

Direct Documentary

Direct documentary presents the event under surveillance as if the process of recording it were not taking place, avoids mediating explanatory voice-overs and illustrations intercut with the images, edits sparingly, and even avoids interviews, since these implicate an interviewer in the event and therefore invoke the process of filmmaking as part of the film. The result is an apparently uninflected view of the material being photographed, with viewers seemingly allowed privileged witness and left to formulate its significance on their own. Presumably this view cannot lie, and when light equipment and unobtrusive crews conspire to record whatever they confront, undistracted, it is sometimes called **cinema verité** (cinema truth). Yet, as in Frederick Wiseman's institutional studies such as *High School* (1968), the selection, arrangement, and even the persistence of certain shots imposes on the audience the filmmaker's own range of interpretation, even the filmmaker's specific attitudes—admiration or contempt, concern or amusement. The filmmaker's point may emerge only near the end, like Wiseman's in *Canal Zone,* where Hispanic vitality finally contrasts with the sterile middle-American propriety we have been watching all along. Elliot Erwitt's *Beauty Knows No Pain* subtly mocks its subject (how Kilgore College "Rangerettes" are trained) even while its spokespeople present themselves admiringly, by letting certain shots run on a bit too long. Leni Riefenstahl's superb *Triumph of the Will* (1935), once powerful propaganda, now an art documentary, is the more powerful for allowing martial music and photographed images, not voice-over commentaries, to present Hitler's Nazi Party Congress as a massive, even mythic celebration of Nazi dedication regenerating the nation.

Direct documentary only seems uninflected. All films present their narrators to the audience by implication, in the way the subject matter is treated, whether or not that ultimate narrator is masked by a voiceover interpreter.

News

Newsreel stories and features seem to be a form of public interest documentary and are in fact the main source of most people's knowledge of the world and its problems. News stories almost always guide the viewer through an understanding of their images. Traditional "news" favors the bad over the good, the extraordinary over the commonplace, that which achieves immediate viewer identification over that which bores with impersonal facts. Newsreels favor the spectacularly visual, fires and car wrecks over changes in interest rates or in military strategies, and brief quotable "sound bites" over extensive talking, whatever the

In *Medium Cool* (1969), directed by the cinematographer Haskell Wexler, a news
photographer first photographs the victim of a car wreck, then radios for a motorcycle to
deliver his footage, and only then calls for an ambulance. The film explores the objectivity
of those who report news, their responsibilities to the events they report, and the extent to
which they are responsible for those events. Much of Wexler's fictional story uses footage
shot in Chicago during the actual 1968 Democratic National Convention, with its major
antiwar demonstrations and its police riots against protesters chanting "The Whole World
Is Watching!" At one point, National Guard soldiers playing hippies are restrained by National
Guard soldiers playing themselves, tear gas rolls in, and a voice can be heard shouting
"Look out, Haskell, this is real!"

relative importance of these kinds of events. "Stories" present the day's
or the week's selected occurrences, and "features" attempt longer-range
concentration on the more complex components of a single topic, though
always for the layperson, never for the specialist. Often news stories
present press conferences, interviews, and demonstrations as if merely
recording them, though such events are usually staged *in order* to be
reported (in a democracy those with causes to propagate or issues to
be understood their way will always seek out free media exposure).

   Such news and news features may be impartial or disinterested, but
they always carry their makers' beliefs or ideologies with them. The
best do so frankly. John Huston's wartime account of *The Battle of San*

Pietro (1945) uses actual combat footage to show how a single engagement in Italy during World War II destroyed the town it liberated and many of the liberating soldiers as well. Supposedly a news feature to inform and inspire the folks back home, it resembles his fiction films such as *The Maltese Falcon* (1941) or *Treasure of the Sierra Madre* (1948) in that it admires great effort and affirms courage and endurance whether or not they are eventually defeated.

Originally pictorial news was presented in newspapers and in movie theaters, and black and white, grainy, and shaky photography testified to its authenticity—neorealism after World War II took advantage of this coding. Now most news is prepared for color television, and open frame photography, intercut talking head interviews, and a trusted anchor person introducing such footage supposedly authenticate its nonfictional origins.

Theatrical and sporting events such as rock concerts or football games are forms of news features (though photographed stage plays are rarely so-considered), often highly sophisticated in their multiple-camera techniques. *Woodstock* (1970) is a multivalent documentary account of an extraordinary outdoor concert climaxing a turbulent decade, as concerned with the audience as with the performers, its editing overseen by the then-young Martin Scorsese; and *Visions of Eight* (1973) provides eight different international filmmakers' treatments of selected events occurring during the Tokyo Olympics, the repetitive nature of sports competitions transformed by differing personal approaches.

Some **avant-garde** films begin with documentary footage but transform it into art, with mind-staggering literalness (as in early Andy Warhol films such as *Sleep*), by editing according to private moods and meanings (as in Stan Brakhage's *Window Water Baby Moving*), or by isolating it as found footage recontextualized (as in Bruce Connor's work).

Hard-core pornography (in contrast with "soft-core" or simulated pornography) is not commonly regarded as documentary reportage, but it is, of a peculiar kind. It presents actual sexual acts as such, to appeal to a viewer's voyeuristic eroticism. The cast (or their body doubles) perform for the camera as if they were characters in a fictional tale, a minimal narrative providing for six or eight physical encounters of various kinds to gratify various tastes. Though simulated sex also serves this specialized audience's needs, almost always male and more often than not middle-aged, the real thing documented unambiguously on film offers what is most wanted, feelings of privilege, gratified curiosity, and arousal. So-called **snuff films** supposedly showing actual murders would seem even more sensational for their documentary authenticity, but laws against profiting from felonies keep any real snuff films from being exhibited, if any in fact exist apart from wartime newsreels. The

A

B

fake ones fool only those who cannot see separate spliced-in cutaway shots.

Educational and Industrial Films

Educational and industrial films are features made to meet specific needs, imparting information, argument, or propaganda about a political issue, state of mind, topic, product, process, or corporation or sometimes merely conferring prestige or celebrity on the client or product. These films freely use voice-over narration in an attempt to guide or create a viewer's understanding of things seen, and they freely use animations, charts, graphs, lecturers' faces, and model demonstrations to make complex events and ideas clearer. No student, and no viewer of public television, reaches maturity without viewing hundreds of these. Audiences understand that their purposes are informational or propagandistic, and the films are rarely more than this. Yet Frank Capra's *Why We Fight* series of documentaries (1943), made as propaganda for the troops during World War II, are such masterly assemblages of images, with voice-over narration of such intense sincerity, that its propagandistic heaviness is easily forgiven. Some of the PBS "Nova" series contain astonishing photography. Alain Resnais' early *Night and Fog* (1956) compiles stock black-and-white images of the Nazi death camps with "present-day" color images shot with a camera always moving closer in or in one direction only (to the right), to achieve the most devastating of the many films that have attempted to deal with the Holocaust. However effective or persuasive films may be as information or argument, they are memorable only when well-conceived as films.

Docudrama

"Mock-Doc" or **docudrama** freely recreates, reenacts, or fictionalizes actual events, sometimes intercutting created footage with "authentic" documentary footage, sometimes using a documentary style but some-

---

The picturesque beauty of the images in Robert Flaherty's *Moana* (1925) (A), his art documentary on Samoan folkways, has far outlasted interest in the folkways which are its subject, though it was this film's apparent ethnographic authenticity that first gave rise to the term "documentary." The standard Flaherty set for such films prevailed into the thirties, and the work of Pare Lorentz, whose *The Plow That Broke the Plains* (1936) (B), like his *The River* (1937), were federally funded projects of strong enough appeal to be booked into commercial theaters. The plow lying diagonally across the spent earth it has turned into a dust bowl, while a baby attempts the same passage, provides a strong esthetic image as well as a strong message. With musical scores by the contemporary composer Virgil Thomson, Lorentz's documentaries were born into high art as then understood.

An apparently spontaneous scene from John Schlesinger's 1990 fictional reworking of William Wyler's 1943 documentary of a B-17 mission over Germany, *Memphis Belle*. In Wyler's assemblage of authentic footage, much of it shot for the purpose and much of it compiled as if shot for the purpose, the aircraft on its final mission is the main character. In Schlesinger's mock-doc the crew is the main character, and each individual is a variation on the older characters found in many fictional war films. They seem authentic compared with the obvious phony among them, an exploitative public relations man.

times using standard narrative conventions. Peter Watkins' *The War Game* (1965) portrays behavior after an A-bomb attack on Britain, using supposed newsreel and interview footage, interspersed with informational commentary; the result was so shaking that after commissioning it, the BBC decided it should not be broadcast. Yvonne Rainer's *Privilege* (1990) is a melange of supposed interviews and memories concerned with menopause and sexual abuse, all enacted (except for brief footage of the cast shot at a "wrap party," a vision of some "future" joyous mingling of ages and genders in fact actually occurring). The film deliberately disrupts its own documentary verisimilitude: at one point it replicates a memory of a threatened rape by splicing together a number of its outtakes; at another point an older woman being interviewed enacts herself when younger though unchanged in appearance. Even so, the film needs to seem authentic in order to fulfill its social objectives.

These films openly declare what they are by their subject or method. Other common docudramas such as biographical films portray supposedly real events with the selectivity and dramatic heightening of fiction, confusing utterly their claims to credibility. William Wyler's wartime documentary *The Memphis Belle* (1943), like some of Flaherty's or Grierson's earlier documentaries, conflates real footage from various sources, some reenactments by the real participants, and a sound track dubbed later, into an ostensible account of one bomber's final combat mission. The entirely acted 1990 fiction film with the same name is more honest if less truthful. But a large public prefers history to fiction, believing mistakenly that real events have more to tell us about ourselves (that judgment depends on whether the historian has more to tell us). This public often prefers entertainingly fictive versions to documentary compilations of actual footage. TV frequently obliges, and, as with *The Right Stuff* (1983) or *Reversal of Fortune* (1990), theatrical films oblige as well.

AVANT-GARDE FILMS

Avant-garde, experimental, independent, or art films employ, transmute, transgress, violate, or willfully evade the whole range of cinematic conventions in order to foreground or use them to create personal revelations or commentaries or filmic experiences for their own sake. The "avant-garde" or advance guard in the onward march of artistic refinement was once thought to be a rare group of heroic artists at the edge of the unknown, whose visions were unique and so required unique expression, comprehended by few at first, until eventually their subjects and techniques were absorbed into the general audience's cultural consciousness, to become part of later generations' inheritance. This supposed historical process explained why the most original of contemporary artists seem obscure, unconventional "Bohemians" in their own time and understood and celebrated afterward. With the collapse of the nineteenth century's faith in progress as accumulation, the term "avant-garde" ceased to be meaningful, though it is still used when art bewilders the eye or mind.

Novel or original use of film conventions is also called "experimental," because like an experiment it tries to do something for the first time. Yet an achieved work is never an experiment, a tentative testing of an idea, but an accomplishment (though sketches for it may be experimental). The modernist movement of this century required that each work of art proclaim itself to be unique, supposedly a successful experiment, but such works are more accurately described as unfamiliar or unconventional. Thus "experimental" is also a misleading term for such art (neither Rembrandt nor Van Gogh are called avant-garde or experimental painters, just different). Film artists prefer the term "independent" to describe themselves, since they have little in common with highly conventional commercial filmmakers. But since the collapse of studio production, independently produced though formally conventional narrative films have become commonplace, and so the term does not discriminate.

Despite other terms also employed ("visionary" or "concrete" film), we have no fit way to refer to these films. They are usually short (because low-budget or rigorously restricted in conception), odd and challenging (because each, or each artist, establishes and uses certain filmic codes with a high degree of self-consciousness and few or no concessions to their traditional uses), rarely narrative (though their temporal element may be structured by narrative as well as other means), and made primarily to satisfy the artist and perhaps a growing coterie, as paintings, sculptures, and most poems are made these days. Yet each film may well add to the range of significant visual and auditory experiences by which each generation can come aware of its own character and predicaments. If art does not "progress," it nevertheless responds subtly to its own age's ways of seeing, helping to characterize that age and providing options for later artists to appropriate, borrow, transgress, or deliberately ignore in their own work. Like other such works of art, these films are usually exhibited in museums and universities, rarely or never commercially, and are appreciated mainly by young people, other artists, and a segment of the educated elite. In Cocteau's *Orpheus* (1949), a poet gone conventional asks a dissatisfied critic what he should do and is told "Astonish us!"; when the poet protests that the public is satisfied with him, the critic replies, "The public is alone in that."

The categories of avant-garde films vary along with other movements in the other arts, and any one film or filmmaker resists classification. Major artists are often masters of the traditional art of their time but often subversives antagonized by that tradition, who never appreciate being pigeonholed. Even so, a few subdivisions may help orient viewers to what can be expected, and what not, so films of these kinds can be seen more immediately as what they are.

Minimalist Films   Minimalist films usually present a single filmic experience isolated for separate contemplation. They may present a succession of white or black screens flickering in different rhythms (as with Peter Kubelka's *Schwechater*) or short fragments of image and sound repeated, as in Paul Sharits's *T,O,U,C,H,I,N,G* (1968), or Gunvor Nelson's *My Name Is Oona* (1969), which finds implied in its fragmentation a girl's growing identity. Minimalist films may present the explicit image of sprocket holes or surface scratches, or one image in slowly changing light such as Hollis Frampton's *Lemon* (1969), or "found" footage shot by others for other purposes but appropriated as art for its own sake and transformed by its contexts (Bruce Conner's work). Stan Brakhage's *Mothlight* (1963) is a kind of ultimate minimalist film, consisting as it does of leaves, grass, moth wings, and other natural detritus placed on clear film and rephotographed; the result is a flashing stream of

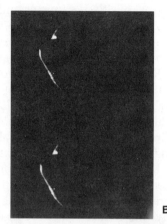

Varieties of the U.S. avant-garde: (A) one frame of Brakhage's *Mothlight* (1963), not a representation but the thing itself (though a photographed thing), the leaf continuing on adjacent frames; (B) two frames of Hollis Frampton's *Lemon* (1969), its backlighting suddenly turning the image sensuous; (C) a frame within the frames of Gary Beydler's *Pasadena Freeway Stills* (1974), cars which begin to move as the photographs are changed with increasing rapidity, the hands which hold them meanwhile growing staccato; and (D) a young girl's face is dissolved in a snow scene, also part of her consciousness, while the soundtrack chants her voice exploring the sound of her own identity, in Gunvor Nelson's *My Name Is Oona* (1969).

textures, some items recognizable during their single-frame appearance on the screen, most not quite.

Structuralist Films Structuralist films foreground temporal sequence, differences in the ways we experience time and duration by careful juxtaposition of images and spatial relationships, often with clo-sures symmetrically returning to their openings, so the audience may become ironically aware of changes in perception induced by the entire film, and become sensitive to, even absorbed by, small differences. These films may be fixed in rigorous sequential logic, like Takashi Ito's *Spacy* (1980) and many other films of the Japanese *avant-garde* or Gary Beydler's *Pasadena Freeway Stills* (1974), or they may willfully court ambiguity, like Robert Nelson's *Bleu Shut* (1970), with even the title ambiguous. Structuralist films may be aleatory, ordered by chance, like the rearrangements of shots and statements in Skip Battaglia's *Parataxis* (1980). Michael Snow's *Wavelength* (1967) is minimalist, basically a very slow zoom toward a picture on the far wall of an artist's studio, with some in-line repositionings of the camera and changes of filters along the way; the film is also structuralist in that it provides a distinctively clear mapping of its own temporal processes; its other features, like a brief acted sequence populating its offscreen space, are subordinated to those temporal processes.

Surrealist Films Surrealist films place familiar and recognizable elements of the world into disturbing or amusing juxtaposition, willfully violating custom and logic in favor of the mind's phantasmagoria. Surrealist films may present dream states transforming reality under pressure of unconscious desires, as with Maya Deren's *Meshes of the Afternoon* (1943), or they may make sardonic satirical comment on the repressions, hypocrisies, and material immobility of bourgeois reality, as does Luis Bunuel and Salvador Dali's *Andalusian Dog* (1928). The films may discuss the relationships between life and art with visual puns and other images of equivalence which seem, at first, absurd, as in Jean Cocteau's *Blood of a Poet* (1930). Surreal films have in common the revelation of repressed, conventionally unacceptable truths. Originally, surrealism looked to generate new revolutionary conditions of consciousness and eventually transform society or at the least to reveal its restrictive conventionality. The early Marx Brothers films hypothesize surreal worlds, where Groucho can actually be a college president or prime minister who acts on impulse while the dull world looks on as if nothing were wrong. Now surrealism mainly provides kitsch, or merely novel combinations of images, for record-jackets or music videos, the language of social and psychological revolution become a countercultural code for imaging adolescent turbulence or rebelliousness. Even so, surrealist films still provide us access to our own unconscious processes and compulsions, and they reappear sometimes in drug trip or horror films.

Other Films Other such films utilize a wide range of techniques and purposes, usually centering on one predominant technique which becomes the virtual subject matter being explored—looping, flash-cutting, slow-zooming, tinting, panning through off-screen space, or in "postmodern" manner posing unstable and ambiguous problems of redefined relationships between the images and their viewers. The border between avant-garde films and participatory cult films like *Rocky Horror* can disappear altogether when audiences are invited to help violate traditional taboos.

BIOGRAPHY

Biographical pictures, or "bio-pics," carry on the Victorian tradition of presenting the shapes of whole lives struggling toward great achievement and, inspirationally, succeeding. More recently these films have shown their subjects achieving only existential success, like *Lawrence of Arabia* (1962), or, if they are talented young musicians, finally overcome, by accident in *The Buddy Holly Story* (1978), by an older venal establishment in *The Harder They Come* (1973), or by drugs in *Bird* (1988). These films nevertheless provide ready confirmation to present-day young audiences that it could be worth it even though they get you in the end. In studio days real lives were freely fictionalized to provide examples of spunk and saintly devotion perhaps briefly dispirited or misled but finally rewarded with fame, material prosperity, happy marriages, and honored old age. Such films were deemed prestigious, as they still are, and audiences could feel privileged intimacy with famous people figured in their adversities and eventual triumphs. Madame Curie, Louis Pasteur, Emile Zola, Thomas Alva Edison, Charles Lindbergh, Glenn Miller, Lou Gehrig, Gandhi, and various self-destructive or self-reclaimed alcoholic or drug-ridden performers have since been some of hundreds of such inspiring subjects. Pure fiction about unsung heroes, such as *Goodbye, Mr. Chips* (1939, remade 1969), could follow the same formula and provide the same satisfactions.

Often a flashback structure ensures that whatever the early difficulties, the story will end up well. Segmented flashbacks, with occasional returning to a frame story where someone is searching for meaning in the past, opened this genre to exploration of serious issues, such as the relative roles of chance, fate, and self-determination in the forming of character, the locating of a loving spouse, the determining of a career, and the eventual meaning of it all. The crowning achievement of this kind, *Citizen Kane* (a film cast ironically against the genre's conventions), was followed by lesser grandiose attempts such as *Mrs. Parkington*. Eventually the genre blended into anxious film noir mysteries such as *Mildred Pierce*, where the flashback structure reassures us that things will end as badly as we saw when the film began.

6

Historical Contexts and Why People Go to the Movies

HISTORICAL TERMS AND CONTEXTS

No film is ever an isolated event. We see, discriminate, and judge every film as part of our larger knowledge, including our knowledge of other films. We see any film as one of many similar films, carrying our past and present expectations into the theater, then determining which of many ways to view a film are the most appropriate, cued by its opening moments. A film may be viewed for example as a creation of a particular auteur, as a star vehicle, as an instance of a particular genre, as a revelation of a particular ideology or political commitment, as a lively dramatic entertainment, or as combinations of these and other things. These frames of reference determine what we then notice or ignore as the film proceeds. We all know that the stars in the night sky are in fact randomly scattered, but that once we have learned to see them in "constellations," we can only see them in constellations. In the same way, what we "see" in a film is in many ways imposed by what we expect to see. We create much of it while looking.

Moreover, no film can ever be seen in historical isolation, as a unique product of no person unaffected by the particular historical conditions prevailing when it was made. Filmmakers and their audiences exist in time, and the times are always changing. A contemporary film may seem a slice of life itself when first seen, its period characteristics invisible for many years. But eventually, when the world and its generations have changed sufficiently, the film will be seen to have been shaped by times and circumstances long gone by, datable, even dated. All films display the methods and concerns prevailing when they were made, whatever the supposed pasts or futures they are set in. Film historians and critics, like other cultural historians and critics, use various terms for categorizing and understanding films as artifacts of their own time. These provide still other contexts for seeing films, still other guiding assumptions. Then, since what we see is what we get, we get still more.

Style

Style is the combination of visual, auditory, and dramatic characteristics expressing the values and concerns of an auteur, crew, or studio, sometimes of a genre, ultimately of an age, making up the characteristic integral look and feel of a film, elegant, gentle, whimsical, hard-bitten, decadent, or savage. Like an abrupt or a graceful gesture, a style provides certain principles of inclusion and exclusion, and certain other characteristics making up a particular coherent world of possible emotions and actions, implying certain assumptions about that world.

A style is sometimes confused with a fad or a fashion. Fads and fashions briefly meet a culture's ephemeral needs, if only for novelty or difference from whatever has gone before, then disappear when audiences grow weary of them. Some films may attract "cult" or fad followings for a time, for example, especially if they violate or transgress established adult concepts of moral and social propriety, as most cult films do. Later when the fad passes the films seem merely amusing, ludicrous, or peculiarly odd for their relentless reliance on certain techniques to the exclusion of all others, or for their exaggerated overdetermination of certain visual or plot elements. A fashion may last longer, and may even influence the evolution of a style, but it too passes.

For example, along with a sense of iconoclastic liberation there were feelings of helpless entrapment, of eventual defeat and the desire to drop or cop out, during much of the sixties Civil Rights and Vietnam war period. This encouraged production of "downer" films such as *Easy Rider* (1969) and "doomed youth" films such as *Bonnie and Clyde* (1967) and *Elvira Madigan* (1967), or the films magnifying James Dean to cult status especially after his death. These were fashionable for a time, and helpful to that generation's peculiar sense of its isolation, but the films founded no new filmic style exploring an essentially new sensibility. The fashion passed along with the national mood generating it. Now dark or bitter visions of whatever profundity do poorly at the box office: Films must end with some kind of affirmation, no matter how far fetched, or they will fail to satisfy.

A style tends to outlive its origins, expressing more lasting changes within the culture. A particular style can appear across many kinds of genre or auteur films for a time, characterizing a whole age. The clean geometric curves of the art deco or art moderne style dominated many films during the thirties as well as much architecture. After a century of Victorian accumulated domestic clutter, the new style promised and defined modernity as a clean, graceful new world created by rational technology. The art deco style provided principles of design for many movie houses including Rockefeller Center's Radio City Music Hall, and the style entered films themselves in places as diverse as Busby Berkeley's choreographies, the sets for the musical *Top Hat* (1935), and even the arrays of massed uniformed men seen in the Nazi documentary *Triumph of the Will* (1935). Similarly the film noir style dominated crime films during the forties and early fifties, with their night settings, wet streets, low-key lighting, flashback narrators, and concern with ordinary people helplessly entrapped or betrayed by their own past actions, with no way out. Film noir had its equivalents in the politics of the time, the McCarthy period also fearful of subversion, betrayal, or exposure. But film noir's mood with some of its stylistic characteristics entered even into ostensibly cheerful musicals such as *The Band Wagon* (1953) and *Lady in the Dark* (1944), and it is still revived from time to time, the classic *Double Indemnity* (1944) reconceived and remade as *Body Heat* (1981). A style may permeate several genres, and certain genres such as the Western may even have characteristic styles especially well-suited to them, visible as such when abstracted from their origins and employed elsewhere.

Movements

A **movement** is the shared tendencies of particular filmmakers and their followers who commit themselves to the same political or artistic ends and many of the same subjects or techniques, sometimes by deliberate intention, sometimes with each member subscribing to a common manifesto, but sometimes out of admiration for the example set by one of them. As a form of commercial art, films rarely fulfill programmatic objectives (except perhaps to make money). Yet some movements with distinctive concerns and styles, dedicated to other purposes, emerge from time to time even within commercial filmmaking. Surrealism and Dada were for a time movements in many of the arts after the first World War, including film. Italian neorealism after the second World War emerged in Italy out of the earlier documentary traditions and postwar economic necessities dictating its style, and it was never popular in Italy. Yet its approach to filmmaking, using nonprofessional actors and nontheatrical settings, portraying ordinary poor people in simple dignity confronting some overwhelming common human predicament, supported a politics many filmmakers could promulgate or explore with integrity. Guided by each other's example, Rossellini's, DeSica's, Visconti's, early Fellini's, and early Antonioni's films constituted a loose movement with worldwide influence before it faded during the fifties.

The French New Wave was a manifestation of relatively new filmmakers—their core being the *Cahier du Cinema* film critics Truffaut, Godard, Chabrol, and others—who stressed realism in its many forms, the *politique des auteurs* or mandate that filmmakers adopt distinctive personal styles, and exploration of the qualities and ironies of life in an existential pop world, including the world of film culture. In some ways their breaches of classical filmmaking encouraged a similar German New Cinema movement during the sixties and seventies, younger German filmmakers such as Fassbinder, Herzog, or Wenders who found their subjects and techniques in postwar German consumerism, self-indulgence, and amnesia about the immediate national past. In Britain the Free Cinema movement was created by filmmakers such as Lindsay Anderson and Tony Richardson to examine the predicaments especially of deracinated working class "angry young men," using an uncompro-

In Tony Richardson's Free Cinema *The Loneliness of the Long Distance Runner* (1962), a bright young working-class malcontent, unwilling to lead his parents' limited lives but unable to conceive another, ends up in a "Borstal" or reform school, where he finally sees his expected role in Britain's system of class privilege and defiantly refuses to cooperate further. Actual locations and local dialects authenticate the neorealist documentary style.

mising neorealist style. In each case these movements defined themselves in opposition to a dominant national film tradition that seemed to have gone merely mannerist, even trivial, its vitality spent, and each movement revivified that tradition while greatly extending its range and accommodating it to a new generation's unique experiences.

Schools

A term commonly used in art history (e.g. the Dutch school or Siennese school of painting), though rarely in film history, **schools** refer to local or national traits, styles, and concerns, the distinctive mix of practices making up the distinctive subject matter and look of the art of a single culture over time. It originates in the teachings of certain artists, academies, and cultures seeking to propagate their kind. Films rarely can

During the brief midsixties "Prague Spring" several Czech filmmakers made films indirectly satirical of life under the communist regime. Many, like Milos Forman and Jan Kadar, came West when the Warsaw Pact armies cracked down on such liberalism; their movement ended, and they made fine films elsewhere on other subjects. Vera Chytlova stayed and was forbidden the right to make any films for a time. Here in her semisurreal *Daisies* (1966) two bored girls decide to assert their existential being, have a food fight, and make a mess of various kinds of hierarchical and patriarchal privilege. When finally a falling chandelier makes a mushroom-shaped explosion, Chytlova dedicates the film "To all those whose indignation is limited to a smashed-up salad."

afford to separate themselves from the ideologies of the marketplaces they need for survival. The term, however, is potentially valuable for examining what may be recurrent or unique in a national or regional cinematic tradition, French, Italian, Brazilian, or Japanese, from California or New York—what persists or only slowly evolves through individual styles and occasional movements, expressing finally the genius of that national culture or regional community.

With all due care to avoid national caricaturing or stereotyping, films of some countries do resemble each other in certain ways more than they resemble similar films of other countries, subtly but persistently. In France, ironic, well-made plots persist, apparent chance weaving an artfully determined dénoument, fate observed with rueful sadness or amusement, in Carné's and Pagnol's thirties and forties melodramas and in Rohmer's later New Wave ironic comedies. From the beginning French comedies—unlike U.S. comedies, for example—have especially focused on characters with exaggerated confidence in their own rational processes. Even Truffaut's imitation U.S. films such as *Shoot the Piano Player* (1962) remain variously Truffaut auteurist films, New Wave movement films, and charming French school films. For decades U.S. films confirmed the sufficient virtue of innocent intentions whatever the consequences, in vigorously plotted morality tales opposing villainy with that virtue, and they still struggle to do so. British films frequently caricature their governing classes and repeatedly admire the eccentricity of any individual maintaining conscientious moral "decency" under stress. German films are not known for comic wit or wry humor nor for deft shot strategies, but they are frequently absorbed with exploring the consequences of self-absorption.

One of the pleasures of coming to know a new cinematic school is attuning to the unique kinds of experience its films make available, however bewildering they may be at first. Movies tend to be international in their primary cinematic language, but they are invariably national in their use of it.

Period

A **period** represents a length of years when national or international films seem to contain certain distinctive characteristics or tendencies. This concept is especially useful when we examine the process of accommodation and absorption following some artistic, technological, or industrial innovation, or some historical crisis preoccupying the culture for which the films were made. Historical periods, such as the Great Depression of the thirties or the Viet Nam war period, are usually self-defining, whereas periods in the evolution of film are more often superimposed upon the turbulent flow of film history in retrospect. Filmmakers who make cinematic history are rarely concerned to take the broad view; more often they do what they can as they can, unconcerned that what they do may eventually seem dated. As with politicians who attempt to define their own place in history, filmmakers who conceive their work for the ages are as often as not self-deceived; such films date quickly, such as *Winterset* (1936), their pretensions alone marking them very much of their own time. Each generation has its own uses for the past, revises or ignores those defined by its immediate predecessors, and treats the record of its inheritance as it will and must. Just as the Renaissance was a creation of nineteenth-century historiography (to eighteenth-century historians of the self-proclaimed Enlightenment, nearly everything from the fall of Rome to themselves was barbaric or "gothic," the opposite of themselves), so periods of film history are imposed by historians on particular episodes in social and economic history, technological history, the history of popular culture (a relatively new subject for study even now), and the history of a new art form. Moreover, what we call "history" is famously ethnocentric, different according to the nationality, class, and ideological commitments of the historian. The past always provides more to choose than can be chosen.

Thus periods of film history are never fixed stretches of time, and the core events of each period can seem to vary. We nevertheless discriminate periods to generalize, and concentrate analysis, on certain characteristics of films of certain times and places, when for whatever reasons they seemed different from films made previously or since. As an example, the following is a traditional periodization of film history, stressing U.S. mainstream film production. It leaves out much (third-world films, the development of alternative, independent, and countercultural films, and mainstream genre transformations among other things), and it avoids superimposing developmental teleologies on the flow of events (that is, assuming that whatever comes later is not merely different but better, because more inclusive). But like do-it-yourself connect-a-dot constellations of stars these classifications help us to see patterns and provide benchmarks for relating film history to other historical events:

Prehistory to 1894 The first period covered the effort to place images of the world on two-dimensional surfaces such as the table of a "camera obscura" (a darkroom with a pinhole, later a lens, admitting light), followed by the development of still photography with photosensitive chemicals on portable surfaces, experimentation with different "persistence of vision" toys and displays, and finally, the invention of a mechanical device able to photograph successions of images on flexible flat strips covered with photosensitive emulsions and then project them onto large, flat surfaces, a persistence-of-vision machine which could record and later display seemingly moving images to the public at large. This mechanical device required no new basic science and employed largely extant technology, and several were designed almost independently, within a few years of each other, by dedicated inventors in the United States, England, and France. Thomas Edison at first believed the device a mere novelty, and so film history begins in France with the Lumière brothers' unedited presentations of events from daily life, some created for the camera, and with Georges Méliès' magical theatrical marvels, all created by or for the camera. Such films evolved as a branch of theatrical and carnival history.

Early Film, 1895 to 1914 In the early period we see the rise of store-front nickelodeons for display of brief moving vignettes, some recorded from daily life, some created or enacted, and the building of early motion picture fantasy "palaces" in fancifully luxurious architectural styles. Recent immigrant entrepreneurs start out as exhibitors and then begin manufacturing films for these theaters, and the studio production system begins, along with the star system, to attract audiences; film product is tailored to consumer tastes but is already considered by some a dramatic art form as well as an entertainment. The main principles of continuity editing are discovered, lengthening narratives to ten minutes, eventually to seventy or more, and a manipulated, heavily stylized realism becomes the dominant manner. The dispersed industry gradually concentrates itself in southern California to evade Patents Trust monopoly restrictions back east and to take advantage of the sunshine. Since language offers no barrier, films are genuinely international, but when World War I inhibits European competition, U.S. production begins its long domination of world markets.

Classical Silent Film, 1915 to 1927 In the classical silent period, the Supreme Court decrees that films are a commodity, not protected artistic expression. Larger studios establish their hegemony and pour forth films for exhibition in their own or contracted chains of theaters, in screenings accompanied by large seventy-piece or small twenty- or ten-piece theater orchestras, or in "last run" theaters by single organists or pianists. Russian montage develops in revolutionary Russia ostensibly as a method of transforming audiences' minds to hold new concepts and is adapted to special-effects narrative purposes in the United States. Similarly German expressionism evolves in Germany after WWI as a method of dramatizing and eliciting unconscious fears and desires, and many of its artists and technicians are soon hired to make horror films and melodramas for the U.S. entertainment industry. Early experiments with color appear in some films, and projection time for narrative films standardizes at somewhat less than two hours. Comedy and melodrama in the United States establishes and extends its genre conventions; in Europe and the United States, especially during the last three years of this period, most of the great silent films are made. This brilliant flowering of film as an exuberant and powerful art form ends when experiments with synchronized sound, spurred by efforts to bring vaudeville to smaller cities cheaply, produce the talkies, synchronized dramatic dialogue. Audiences demand more of it. The end of the silent era coincides with the spread of domestic radio, and a two- to three-year transition to sound movies begins everywhere, completed in the United States by 1929. Thereafter foreign language films find only limited release in

An extraordinary moment in motion picture history, the silent era unwittingly destroying itself. Alan Crosland is directing one of Al Jolson's performances in *The Jazz Singer* (1927), using a silent film camera for the shot (it is not "blimped," covered with heavy soundproofing). The orchestra visible below probably served as performers, the scene's "theater orchestra," but may also have played to help Jolson perform. Most of the film was silent, but audiences were electrified by a few reels of Jolson singing on synchronized Vitaphone sound recordings, with interspersed dialogue. Those few were enough.

the United States, though U.S. films—dubbed or subtitled—continue to dominate European markets. Only Japanese and Indian films preserve primacy in their own countries, as they still do.

Classical Sound Film, 1928 to 1955   In the classical sound period, the studio factory system with its contracted retinues of writers, directors, technicians, and actors prevails, sustained by careful development and exploitation of certain stars and genres as known marketable commodities. The predominant mode is realistic, but the realism is an obvious superficial convention used to dramatize morality tales or gratifying or amusing fantasies, the realistic films in fact serving as troubling or inspirational adult bed-time stories fooling few people old enough to purchase a ticket. The realist esthetic nevertheless dictates the principles of continuity editing, with narrative time and space persistent and ostensibly seamless. Narrative conventions are standardized and cinematic techniques extended, as long as they never call attention to themselves. The Hays office Production Code is adopted to forestall vigilante actions closing out exhibition in various cities, its voluntary preproduction censorship ensuring that family values will be promulgated in all films. With the Great Depression films occasionally take on social themes, characteristically disturbing yet reassuring, or they altogether avoid direct reference to economic distress, concentrating on optimistic, ambitious, or very wealthy characters. The continuously playing double feature (a high-budget and a low-budget narrative film on the same bill, with selected short subjects) becomes standard for screenings in neighborhood theaters. The first full three-strip Technicolor films appear in the mid-thirties and offer an optional way to shoot high-budget historical or musical spectacles.

With World War II, films take on morale boosting as well as patriotic functions, sometimes also racist and sexist functions, serving the home front as well as "our boys overseas." The postwar period is troubled: Some films seriously address social questions concerning minorities (usually expressing optimistic liberal sentiments and evasions), film noir conventions express vague but real anxieties, screen women are repressed into domesticity as rarely earlier, and the reabsorption of millions of military men into civilian life—marriage, a suburban house, and children the preferred norm specially after the Depression's uncertainties—redirects family entertainment budgets away from downtown movie going. When New York bans Rossellini's *The Miracle* (1948) as sacreligious, the Supreme Court decides that films are speech protected by the first amendment. But with the *Paramount* decree the Supreme Court ends the studios' vertical monopoly over film production, distribution, and exhibition; they sell their theaters, and the factory production system becomes precarious. Simultaneously, TV in the home, especially with small children and movement to new suburbs limiting access to theaters, forces the closing of neighborhood cinemas; despite widescreen, 3-D spectacles with casts of thousands, production for urban-fringe drive-in movies, and other innovations, box office receipts decline. These problems continue into the sixties, the decline apparently irreversible. Studios rescind their contracts with stars, and some close or concentrate on TV production, especially when nationwide coaxial cable allows national TV entertainment broadcasting to relocate itself especially on the West coast, where the stars and technicians are concentrated. Many studios are bought out by larger communications conglomerates.

Independent Production, 1956 to 1975   In this period, motion picture production increasingly depends on the venture-capital skills of independent producers (more recently of talent agents creating work for their clients and percentages for themselves), who put together bankable packages of stars, artists, and technicians for individual films, the residual studios sometimes contracting partial financing or distribution for several films in return for a share in the profits if any. Occasionally small films are made to attract adult audiences away from TV, but the predominant audience lowers in age, centered in a hard core of teenagers needing to go somewhere out of the house. The Code collapses, and new subjects such as drug addiction, divorce, and sexuality as such are broached in films, while displays of sex and violence denied to domestic TV grow bolder, culminating in frequent unsuccessful prosecutions for pornography into the early seventies. By the mid-sixties color TV sales dictate that all films must be shot in color, especially with the Technicolor process's monopoly broken by Eastmancolor and other cheaper processes. The sixties Civil Rights movement and the anti–Vietnam war movement further extends narrative subjects into new areas, the traditional studio genres reach to redefine themselves in unaccustomed ways, and the French New Wave's influence revitalizes many cinematic conventions (though few people see foreign films, thought of as art films, because with U.S. entertainment products dominating, imported foreign films are usually auteur films, substantial cinematic statements). The Steadicam and new cranes make camera movement easier if not cheaper, and more sensitive fine-grain color film stocks also reduce the effort of shooting if not the costs. TV and film school artists and technicians replace their studio-trained forebears; often ingrained film buffs, they are familiar with film history and ingenious in adapting older conventions for new audiences. Meanwhile audiences grow more sophisticated, aided by fan magazines providing production gossip, TV behind-the-scenes features, and college courses in film rising from the collapsed boundaries between the traditional "high" arts and the popular arts.

Current Production, 1976 to Present   During the seventies the box office decline bottoms out, the nation's average film-going age begins to grow older, and suburban shopping mall multiplexes begin to be built, small, highly cost-effective exhibition halls serving many variegated tastes simultaneously, their screens also relatively small though large in comparison with TV. TV, cable, and VCR subsidiary sales (along with film-related records and toys) outstrip box office receipts by the mid-eighties, and the numbers of theatrical films produced annually begins once again to edge upward. There is little innovation in plot construction or subject, in noticeable technology (except for improved special effects and theatrical sound systems), in personal vision, or in cinematic mission in this period, no more than in the politics of the period, which themselves rework the old sustaining conventional assurances. But the multiplexes' increased demand for product, TV resale income, and the proven bankability of actors and personalities well-known from TV again justify heavy risk-capital investment; cable companies begin to produce films for their own use, and studios again begin to own or control theaters. This reversal in the industry's fortunes, wider adaptation to theatrical films of the story conventions and technologies favored by TV, and the thinness of competitive "big" TV entertainment, should carry this period into the foreseeable future. High-definition electronic imaging may replace century-old chemical imaging in theaters. Individual on-demand screening of cable and videocassette films drawn from the whole of motion picture history may further fracture once-huge audiences attending single films shown on large screens in enormous theaters, further weakening motion pictures as public narratives reiterating common large social mythologies and diminishing the concept of films as rare and privileged states of mind. But the next phase in the evolution of film depends in all probability on cultural changes or crises not yet emerged, or emerged but not yet noticed.

PERSONAL AND CULTURAL MEANING

There are many reasons that films "mean," that is, seem meaningful to us. They offer ways to mirror and understand perplexing elements in our own personal, social, and political lives. For some of us, they also offer an experience of art, of a total experience where everything matters, two hours of significant and coherent life lived with senses heightened, in a finer tone. The particulars of any one film narrative always pose larger human issues and say things about them. On screen, what appears to be a cop is a cop, but also more than a cop: Cops can be an embodiment of the law, social authority, repression, protection, saintly dedication, cynical smarts, male power, female independence, conscience, an oppressive or protective parent, buddy, or friend, or other things, all in various combinations, depending upon how they appear and are used in the film.

A cop can also be two conflicting things, because any movie goer is always at least two things. A theatrical audience is an aggregate of individuals, each alone, yet also a group of people, a public body or small society. Each theater goer seeks to indulge the urge toward private personal pleasure, in which case cops may be repressive, and yet to acknowledge public necessity, which cops protect. These often conflict within one's personal or public values as well as between them. Theatrical films often subvert so-called responsible public values by appealing also to illicit, unconventional or antisocial private desires, or vice versa, generating tensions between them and usually mediating those tensions in some ways. But they do so in public space. For this reason, a theatrical film seen on TV alone in a living room can seem different (like a porn film seen in a courtroom), and different people seeing the same film in a theater see different films.

All films create meaning, on the screen as texts, to be interpreted, and in the conditions of their reception, felt by each individual. But whatever their nature and whatever the conditions of their reception, there is no reason to theorize as we often do that all images moving in rectangles generate or "construct" their overall meanings the same way. Our expectations on entering the theater or turning on the tube, and our previous experience or our personal desires, largely determine what we wish to see, can see, and actually see. Educational documentaries, news reports, adventure films, melodramas, comedies, commercial advertising spots, talk shows, game shows, and music videos each meet different expectations, are read differently, and are designed to be read differently. Whatever the patina of realism or fantasy the films may exhibit, they each carry different forms of truth, result in different conditions of belief, and elicit different responses.

Yet narrative films especially have the power to absorb our attention more fully, often, than events occurring to us in actual life. This is odd, because for the most part such films are concerned with specific fictional people resembling other people of small or no concern to us in actual life. Films convey a significance for us far beyond their particularity as fictive newsreels, biographies, histories, or fascinating gossip. This poses what was once called the problem of the "concrete universal," concern for why particular imaginary events generally matter to us. We need to ask why we care what happens in certain movies (and couldn't care less what happens in others). Why do we go to the movies when we could be living our own lives in our own time and space? Why do we go to the movies as a *way* of living our own lives? We have many reasons. We need to sort them out, to keep aware of them as we come aware of the many things happening to us while we watch the many things happening on the screen. The first two were discussed earlier—vicarious experience and identification:

Vicarious Experience. Film extends our participation in the world into other places we have never been and might not wish to go except in imagination, and a film is a travelogue into a world gratifyingly unlike our own, one where meaning finally reveals itself.

Identification. By common processes of identification, sublimation, and transference, in a safe location and in various degrees, in the dark, people go to the movies to try out being other people. This kind of imaginary role play would seem to be essential to our growth and maturity; in prefilmic days other forms of stories and narratives served, as well as role modeling within the community.

The other reasons explaining our movie experience need longer examination.

Analogous Experience

A part of a film and sometimes all of it, especially its plot, can present itself as a specific example of a larger kind of the significant experience it represents. It can be seen as a symbolic action, or as an objective correlative for other similar experiences, as a microcosm of all equivalents of similar shape, physical, psychological, or moral. How a film portrays a particular experience says things about those other similar experiences.

Every film presents **a** world, none present **the** world. Each can be regarded as a simplified model providing a coherent way for us to sort out and see clearly the entangled events and contingencies of the worlds we actually inhabit, where no questions are ever posed as clearly or answered as definitively. We respond appropriately to events in a film even when we cannot consciously identify the larger or similar real-world analogous issues. The particular **manifest content** we see on the screen conveys a hidden **latent content,** invoking for us an inner world of stressful concern we usually carry into the theater unexamined, perhaps even unacknowledged.

Paradigms   Films present to their audiences **paradigms** or representative examples of kinds of predicaments, of kinds of responses to those predicaments, and of kinds of consequences following from those responses. These are readily translatable into other similar examples, and audiences may instinctively translate these examples into personal equivalents without even knowing they are reading the one as the other.

Intellectual analysis can read these tales as **allegories** by abstracting their specificity into general categories (one unfaithful wife can stand for all, or even for the abstract moral quality infidelity, as can a jealously suspicious husband, given his lack of faith in his wife). Bergman's *Cries and Whispers* (1972) is a psychomachia of physical and also spiritual selfishness, each its own punishment, and of physical and also spiritual generosity, each its own reward. Each of these moral states is personified in each of four women gathered in an ancestral house (Bergman likened it to a single human heart), where one of them (Agnes, the sacrificial lamb) and the spiritual generosity she exemplifies both lie dying. The

In Juzo Itami's *Tampopo* (1987), the characters' amusing obsession with creating perfect noodles for their customers provides a satiric paradigm for any similarly single-minded Japanese dedication to the manufacture and marketing of consumer products, with interlude sequences that broaden the references further.

family's unity and psychic unity itself—we all contain all four moral traits—is diminished by that death. Adventure thrillers in the United States commonly give special allegorical resonance to their battles between good guys and bad guys (most abstractly, good versus evil) by making the good quality modest determination, for example, and the bad quality arrogant carelessness. Which wins out, and how, carries as hopeful a message as the fable of the Tortoise and the Hare.

Or we can read films less intellectually as attractively exaggerated equivalents for our own situations. Prison films for example are famously popular with people who feel they have little authority or control over their own lives, teenagers, or factory workers, or people caught up in heavily bureaucratic hierarchies. How the main character accommodates to these restrictions yet preserves some kind of individual freedom and dignity, by surrender, sly conformity, defiance, or outright intimidation, provides knowledge of the range, problems, and results of the options open to such people. At the least prison films can provide minimal recognition and perhaps compensatory fantasies for people who feel similarly trapped in their own circumstances. Two corollaries follow from this paradigmatic way films carry meaning:

1 No films of absorbing interest to audiences are ever merely "escape" films. They provide alternative, attractively displaced ways to think and feel our way through present problems, seemingly impersonally. If a film seems to be pure "escape" in its appeal, one can always ask "escape to what, and therefore from what?"; we will always find informative answers to these questions. Thirties "white telephone" high-society films such as *My Man Godfrey* (1936) seem to offer only escape to economically harrassed members of the audience during the Great Depression. We can see now that by concentrating on the frivolously free folkways of the very wealthy, such films merely eliminate concern with some difficult problems, such as earning a living, in order to concentrate attention undistracted on others no less difficult, such as finding romantic love. And not far below the surfaces of such films—see also *It Happened One Night* (1934)—lie implicit allegories of class conflict and class reconciliation against which Fritz Lang's allegory of capital and labor, head, heart, and hand in *Metropolis* (1926) seems crude. We reenact in movies various dramas of our early family lives, relations with friends, or street or work experiences, repeatedly working out our unresolved problems in various ways, coming to terms with them. If we cannot guiltlessly resent parents, or defy bosses with impunity, we can always resent and defy oppressive prison wardens. At the same time, a prison film's plot can help exorcise from our supposedly older, mature, and liberated selves any haunting sense of imprisonment we still carry within from childhood. Few people care about prison reform as such, but since we all live within imposed limits, rules, and proprieties, subject to other people's self-indulgent or sadistic tyranny, prison films remain popular, preserving their paradigmatic relevance to all. Such escape fantasies help us to deal with our own lives' realities; they are not merely places we go to get away from them.

2 All films carry and convey the ideological assumptions governing their culture, their makers, and the processes by which they are made. Some films are overtly political; the director Costa-Gavras for example, in many political thrillers from *Z* (1969) through *Missing* (1982) and *Hanna K.* (1983), despises the wealthy reactionaries who control unjust governments and admires the rebels who protest or revolt against them, yet shows bitterly that reactionary power will prevail. But a film's political ideologies need not be presented overtly. The principles generating the significant form a story will take, and even the shot strategies available to the cinema's apparatus, are value-laden. The values originate in the ways a culture organizes itself and achieves the support or acquiescence of those comprising it. These established power relationships support ideologies we experience as deeply-held beliefs.

That films concern themselves with individuals seen to be solely responsible for their own lives and bearing the burden of their own choices, for example, implies by **ellipsis** or exclusion that family, communal, or social or political action is irrelevant; it can even imply an obvious untruth, that we make our own lives unaided and live alone. Unlike virtually everyone in real life, characters in movies often seem to belong to no social or family group (or one at most): They rarely seem influenced by nearby relatives, friends, or associates, and they rarely seem to feel bound and accountable to others. Marxists believe that this definition of ourselves as isolated individuals is an ideological consequence of our private competitive market economy. This isolation certainly reflects something of the ideological position of the young adults who comprise most movie audiences: They are nearly liberated from the families that reared them, not yet the heads of their own families, and not yet habituated to the possessions and cross-tangled community and peer relationships that bind most of us.

There are similar ideological implications in our sexual politics. That a woman in a World War II melodrama such as *Woman of the Year* (1942) or *Mildred Pierce* (1945) is necessarily unfulfilled when she chooses a personal career over marriage and housewifery implies by **overdetermination** or exaggeration that no woman can so-choose rightly, or can combine both a career and a marriage. Such gender differentiation, men fulfilled by their work and women by their men, is an ideological consequence of our predominantly patriarchal culture, discouraging women from competing with men and encouraging their dependency on men. Again, a shot/reaction shot strategy repeatedly showing men gazing appreciatively at women, and not vice versa, invites men in the audience to define themselves as those who look and women as those who are looked at, rarely vice versa, again confirming male privilege, with many consequences for the sexual behavior of both genders. Some theorists believe that control of "the gaze" is control over the subjectivity of those gazed at, that we feel ourselves to be what others see us, with women's self-images therefore subject to what men choose to see.

Again, most U.S. films assume that a monogamous, heterosexual, materially prosperous nuclear family provides the highest happiness anyone can attain, a haven against anxiety and loneliness in the heartless world outside; audiences accept this idea with its bourgeois ideological consequences because they themselves incline to believe it (even people who are unmarried, or frequently divorced). Our films usually reinforce this assumption, and social critics therefore look especially closely at films which seem also to subvert it (Douglas Sirk's for example, or Hitchcock's).

In reality all societies are complex and multiple; we each inhabit

many subcultures and live by many contradictory ideological commitments. Films are designed to try to satisfy as many people and convictions as possible. Thus they often contradict or subvert themselves, or
transgress against dominant ideologies. The major or persistent genres
usually mediate between these conflicting beliefs, resolving them, com-
promising them, or confusing them in ways that seem least to de-
stabilize our society's habits and arrangements. These genres take into
themselves and redefine and discharge as fantasy enactments those
discontents which might otherwise have radical social or personal
consequences.

Parables Films can present **parables,** or tales carrying in narrative
form some moral or psychological truth seen in the relationships between
the characters, their choices, and the consequences, explicitly withheld
but implicitly revealed. In such cases we say they carry a "moral lesson,"
one which can be abstracted and stated as such, an illustration of right
behavior in difficult circumstances, or of wrong behavior, with an implied
invitation to do likewise or an implied warning not to. This is sometimes
called the film's "theme," though the broad word "theme" applies as
well to other unifying narrative concerns when it is used at all. *Fatal
Attraction* (1987) had several exemplary lessons, warning husbands that
casual sex threatens domestic security, warning single women against
overwrought emotional dependence on men (some think against sexual
independence), and counselling wives that contrite errant husbands
can be forgiven, even rescued in order to preserve that highest good,
the child-rearing family.

Meaning through Substitution Films present experiences and meanings by comparison or substitution, especially in their smaller elements.
Some critical theorists borrow from literary theory the traditional overlapping rhetorical terms **metaphor** (presenting one area of experience as
if it were another, a girl as a flower, or a city as a jungle), **metonymy**
(naming something by an abstract attribute, the specific by its intangible
general category), and **synecdoche** (naming the whole by a part, or a
part by another part, a whole wealthy society by its "white telephones"
for example). These figures of comparison and substitution are usefully
employed in analysis of the ways smaller elements of a film signify
larger meanings: in a Western a railroad track can signify encroaching
industrialism, or the unbending path of oncoming fate, and a single
image of an unshaven "ranch hand" can signify careless, nonconforming
potentiality for violence. In *Rear Window* (1954) an early pan across a
leg in a cast, action photos, a photo of a racing car and one of its

In this brief synechdoche, the part declares a whole argument wordlessly. In *High Noon*, the mayor had betrayed Kane by arguing that if he would only leave town, there would be no trouble. Now, as the four assembled gunmen walk down the street to confront and kill the sheriff, one pauses, smashes the glass front of a woman's clothing shop, takes a bonnet, and hangs it by its ribbons alongside his crotch. Another gunman asks him, "Can't you wait?"

wheels hurtling out of control, a smashed camera, a magazine cover photo of a beautiful woman, and that photo's negative, tells us by implication the main character's profession and professional status, how he broke his leg, how he met the woman, her profession and status, and even what incompatibility of life-styles may be separating them. In a sense all filmic experiences are metaphors to be read, and no corporate accountant's abiding private pleasure in six-gun walkdowns, in submarine crews attacked by depth charges, or in mad scientists threatening the world is merely "escapist" or altogether inexplicable.

Public Ritual

A film provides occasion for living through processes of affirmation, denial, or challenge we feel essential to the preservation of public order and the meaning of our social lives, even performing for us acts of propitiation to safeguard us against powerful governing forces beyond our control, which we fear we may have offended. In this sense seeing a film is a semireligious rite, and a movie theater is a kind of secular church, temple, mosque, or synagogue, returning and reconciling us to a universe of moral and ideological covenants and obligations, faiths essential to us even though eroded by daily experience. Here the traditional genres figure heavily: A film displaying a wartime mission properly accomplished not only serves as a parable for right behavior for other soldiers (or anyone else performing difficult actions on behalf of a threatened community), such a film dramatizes and thereby generates in each viewer an equivalent process of selfless self-suppression in favor of the public good, each member of the audience ritually tested in imagination and arriving at a similar confirmed commitment. *Casablanca* (1942) in this sense not only depicts a tough-guy cynical individualist enlisting for the duration of the war, it provides ritual occasion for like-minded individuals in the audience to sacrifice whatever their personal indulgences and rededicate themselves to higher public purposes.

The recurring enactment in U.S. films of assurance that crime does not pay, and that virtue is eventually rewarded and vice punished, reassures many in the audience that this is so by carrying them through successive stages of doubt, anxiety, reaffirmation, and finally, justified conviction; statistics, if not frequent personal experience, steadfastly inform us that crime does pay, but faith in a world of retributive justice remains essential to our traditional religious commitments, our childhood family expectations (where the claim that "It isn't fair!" is always expected to have weight), and our practical sense of social necessity. We seek out rituals to confirm ourselves in that faith despite the evidence of our eyes. Like hymn singing, public participation in a film helps return us to true belief, whether or not that belief is true. Some films ritually depict that a witty and clever scoundrel may be forgiven if harmless to others, confirming us in that alternative faith.

At the same time, Freudian theorists find that by **projection** and **transference** various suppressed and unacknowledged traits in ourselves can be figured as those of others, especially of characters in films whom we can then blame, male fears and desires concerning helpless eroticism generating for example the recurrent destructive vamps and scheming women of films noir. Moreover, the anxieties generated by certain films serve out ritual punishment for our backsliding from our own convictions. Hitchcock's protagonists punished for crimes they have not committed, or sexually active babysitters slaughtered by mad slashers, allow us occasion to acknowledge our own guilty secrets—however trivial or serious—as someone else's, and to be punished vicariously for them. This provides a kind of purgation, even a feeling of moral regeneration. Sitting among like-minded people at the movies, we can all feel better and safer on leaving the theater.

Ritual purgation. In *The Best Years of Our Lives* (1946), World War II over and its instruments of war maimed and scrapped, a one-time bombardier who has failed to fit back into civilian life walks among them as metaphorical forms of himself, to comprehend his own cast-off condition, forget his own former glory, and begin again. His travails and those of two other returning veterans are designed to shape the equivalent journey to self-comprehension and a stable civilian life of millions returning from the war when the film was released.

Private Ritual

Like children playing with toy cars, guns, or dolls, we go to the movies seeking to participate imaginatively in situations and actions preparing us for possible future personal experiences, or compensating for those we know we shall never have. These anticipation or compensation fantasies provide rehearsals for new experiences, so they will not altogether addle us when we encounter them; they provide as well the fulfillment of private desires we dare not enact because we are inadequately endowed with the necessary physical or moral qualities or opportunities, or we fear the consequences, or we are inhibited by other nobler convictions. Such desires may be sexual or vengeful, generous or villainous; in theaters we can commit to any and live them out imaginatively because in theaters we are in fact committed to none of them. Proponents of pornographic films argue that they provide a safety valve in fantasy for individuals who might otherwise act out sexual desires in actual life; opponents counter that pornography catalyzes such desires for enactment in actual life; both may be right, the affected viewers either way cancelling each other out among the cohorts studied, or more probably neither is right (there is no good evidence for either). Such fantasies are always anyhow available to anyone's unaided imagination; what movies provide is both a kind of public sanction to indulge specific private imaginings in the presence of others similarly inclined and specific psychodramas for imaginary enactment of similar inclinations (as in our dreams, which films in many ways resemble).

Profundity

Communion with certain profound minds expressing themselves in film, the auteurs who in this century have largely replaced theologians or scholars as the interpreters of our culture and our lives, draws certain film goers. We are occasionally inclined to seek in film what we also find in "high" culture such as great literature or classical music, and many find in religion, a profound yet respectable way to reconceive the nature and value of our lives as nobler and ultimately more important than they seem, and we honor the sages who speak their own profundity to us through such arts. Most filmmakers are not philosophers or even especially wise; they are highly skilled professional entertainers who tell us what we already know, or less, or what we would like to believe. Yet many say important and difficult things by creating worlds that show those things, and some filmmakers—Bergman, or Bresson among other Europeans, Ford and Hawks among other Americans—at times present dramatic visions of considerable weight and profundity. We can argue whether, for example, any films or for that matter novels present meditations as profound as those in Beethoven's last string quartets, because music presents us with complex relationships and moods, not articulated verbal ideas. But many films do justify the humanistic belief that great minds express themselves through great art and that we are enriched and illuminated when we participate in their work, given access to levels of meaning in our experience we cannot reach on our own.

Art

Some film audiences look for the experience of art, of a significant and coherent formal work heightening and refining our sensibilities, for the sake of that experience. We go to the movies for some of the same reasons we attend concerts, museums, stage dramas, operas, and ballets, and people of various classes and cultures attend sporting events, bullfights, parades, and circuses. We want to see something extraordinarily difficult, complex, or new marvellously achieved, and to test and strengthen our ability to understand their subtleties. Other art forms speak to us in various ways, as films do. Like films other art forms also provide mostly commercially salable *kitsch*, undemanding, instantly gratifying experiences. But all the arts share one thing especially: In a given medium, whether sound, substance, paint, or photographed images, whether formed on the human body like dance, or formed from several media like drama, kinds of experience are provided which are different from everyday experiences, inviting and rewarding concentrated attention. Within each art form various sensuous and conceptual codes come together to elicit a distinctive perceptual event, not for the sake of personal or social utility, doctrinal truth, or ideological assertion or subversion, but for its own sake. **Films, like the other arts, offer purely aesthetic pleasures, the gratifications of light, color, music, and human feeling arranged in spatial and dramatic form for endlessly revivified contemplation and further discovery.** What survives when our personal or social needs are otherwise met, depleted, or irrelevant is film as a feast for the senses, the sensibilities, the emotions, and the mind, an available intensified condition of existence we cannot live in for long but prefer not to live without. We may not all attend concerts, museums, and theaters, but we all go to the movies for some of the same reasons others attend other works of art.

Such aestheticism sets its own standards for evaluating a work. The wider and more profound the range of experience the work contains, the more concentrated the experience, the more we see complexity brought into coherent unity or orchestrated diversity, the greater the work. Presumably, the greater the work, the more complex and powerful our response to it, certainly the more refined and discriminating. John Ford's discomfiting *The Searchers* (1956) can be judged a finer work than his ingratiating idyll *The Quiet Man* (1952) by this view, because it incorporates into itself some meaner, far more difficult issues. These standards can conflict with other ways we view such works. Film being a popular art, its ideological values are never altogether secondary to its aesthetic values. In Riefenstahl's *Triumph of the Will*, for example, the art deco arrangements of massed Nazis and their flags create strong visual pleasure only to the degree that we suppress, as we can, our knowledge that those dedicated masses will soon devastate Europe and bring misery to millions of people. Film being less than a century old, there are not many great films equal in profundity of vision to some great works of literature, painting, sculpture, or music. But there are some, and there are many splendid films equal to many.

Whatever its other functions, a film like any other work of art can outlast the times and audiences it first addresses, providing its distinctive modes of feeling and perception to future times. When later generations for whatever **their** reasons also find viewing it extraordinary, even privileged, it becomes a classic in the traditional meaning of the word. In film industry jargon, it has "legs" (for long runs).

Films are human achievements with extraordinary power to create comprehension of what it means to be human, in the form and imagery by which we otherwise also comprehend ourselves. In profound as well as trivial ways, whether we are enlightened or "merely" entertained, we are defined by the films we comprehend.

Analysis and Interpretation

In the languages which are the subject of this book, using the conventions which are also its subject, films "say" things about common human experience, what it means to be alive. Their temporal structures—beginnings, middles, and ends—array their interactive experiences as "texts" or "essays" on the screen, commenting on something. A film **review** will answer certain questions about a film in order to guide potential customers toward or away from the box office: What kind of film is it? What are the particular pleasures or problems in watching it? What in the story or performances is notable? What is not? Meanwhile a review never reveals how the plot problem is resolved, "spoiling the ending" for suspense seekers. We all come aware of these matters while we watch a film, registering though rarely trying to articulate them. Film **criticism** is far more extensive in its concerns, beginning as tentative speculation while the film reveals itself, then engaging in earnest as we leave the theater, the entire film available for analytic commentary.

There are two main ways we can attempt interpretation, or engage in textual **hermeneutics.** One is to read these texts as they unspool before our eyes, diachronically, the film considered to be the experience of watching it, over when the film is over and we can contemplate the full filmic, dramatic, social, and moral implications of what we have seen. In this case one set of meanings will emerge, usually the film as a form of parable, its narrative development a primary carrier of its meaning.

But we can also read a film text in simultaneity, synchronically, the two hours' experience available in the mind all at once immediately after the film ends, examining it by recovering various parts in memory, earlier parts even after later. We cannot recover in mind the entirety of the experience, but such "deconstruction" and selective reconstruction and reinterpretation of a film is routine when we replay parts of the film in our imaginations and on our VCRs for our own pleasure, and can be performed with increasing skill by those who practice it. Synchronically, causes in a film can be seen as their consequences, a gangster's later betrayals in Martin Scorsese's *GoodFellas* (1990) seen to be implicit in his earlier acts of devoted loyalty; synchronically, isolated but similar images and actions can be reviewed as forms of each other, like different shots from the inside looking out in *The Searchers* (1956); synchronically, characters can be seen arrayed in patterns even though they may never meet in the plot, like the secondary characters in *Casablanca* (1942), who range in a single spectrum from the sentimentally helpless to the cynically opportunistic, all serving as foils to Rick, who is ostensibly all these things. The film can then be interpreted differently, as a coded value system rather than a process. Popular genre films, with their concern to satisfy all who view them, can especially be seen to be supportive yet subversive, confirming the audience's conventional beliefs yet also undermining them. Each opposing argument can be sorted out by deliberate critical analysis when the film has ended.

This kind of selective recovering and recombining of different elements in a film yields meanings often not apparent when the film was playing as a voyeuristic experience occupying two consecutive hours in a multiplex. The more inclusive the analytic process, the more cognizant of relevant features in the film's text (including the way the film presents itself), the more some seemingly insignificant features are seen to be highly relevant, and the closer we arrive at the intricate statements implicit in a film text's design. When films have something to say but seem baffling when they have ended—however deeply moving—this kind of critical act can reveal what they are saying. A dense film returned to in mind, and perhaps after some thought returned to in the theater or on the VCR, reveals more of itself with each viewing. The same ticket bought at the box office provides vicarious experience in the theater and more thought afterward, if the film has something to say we didn't already know.

All good art eventually nudges our comprehension of things we didn't know, and all films are artfully designed, made by artisans if not artists. But some are also art in this classic sense, whatever their popularity for whatever other reasons. Great art is not necessarily forbiddingly inaccessible at first view, and even some schlock blockbusters turn out to be films successive generations preserve in memory and mind, revisit, find increasingly profound, and will not let die. This book has been designed to provide greater access to all of them.

THEORETICAL STUDIES

Academic discourse differs from most other kinds in its methodological self-consciousness: it knows, or should know even as it speaks, what its governing assumptions are, and how its intellectual procedures match up to them. Any such sets of presuppositions and procedures can be separately studied. If **film criticism** is the study of films in various relationships to each other, their arts, and their cultures, **film theory** is the study of the various presuppositions and procedures implicit in film study. In theory, it guides and informs criticism; but like philosophy (defined once as "the criticism of abstractions"), it can take on autonomy and refer thereafter only to itself.

Film in Universities

Filmmaking was once learned by informal apprenticeship within the industry, though it was also taught in a few colleges and universities. Film history was the province at first of a few inspired buffs associated with museums. Of tens of thousands of films, those selected and saved as most artistic, typical, or notable were largely the films those first curators singled out. Film criticism was a branch of journalism, not taught at all, and film theory emerged eventually from art criticism, communication theory, philosophy, social theory, and psychology. But most higher education devoted itself to the higher arts comprising high culture, the established classics in the various arts and some more recent works resembling those masterpieces. With a few notable exceptions films were thought mere manifestations of low or popular culture, mechanically contrived and commercially packaged substitutes for the older, preindustrial, individually handmade manifestations of folk culture. Even after World War II academic humanists and social historians tended to think an absorption with film self-indulgent, a hobby for off-hours.

Thus the academic study of movies, called "cinema studies" for maximum prestige, is less than forty years old. Its acceptance as a respectable discipline is barely twenty years old; in many institutions the jury is still out, and in many countries—including Japan—the issue has not yet even arisen. Those who prowl their library shelves for film reference books or special studies will see that most have been written only during the past twenty years, and the more scholarly or daunting studies only during the past ten.

Theory Then and Now

Though no longer in its primitive or pioneering phase, the entire field is still relatively young, and many kinds of film study still bear traces of their origins in many different disciplines. Without a burdensome but stabilizing past to govern it, the field's leading edge has pressed on from issue to issue, following and sometimes leading various other disciplines and trends while searching for its own usable projects and methodologies or adapting others'. During the past two decades specialized concerns within film study have proliferated, many with half-lives of only a few years. But many have enriched film studies, and still do, even as the field has moved on to more recent concerns.

This viewer's guide has been marked by this ferment. Even its effort to retain common language is tasked by the various specialized terminologies film scholars and theoreticians use in an effort to speak with precision (although at times they are accused of masquerading precision). Mechanistic terms and metaphors derived from French rationalism tend to dominate discourse along with the concepts they define, implying that human processes are precisely, rationally, and exhaustively analyzable, and replacing the earlier organic and at times obscure metaphors of German phenomenology. Theoretical discourse often proceeds deductively, like philosophical discourse, without necessarily testing itself against actual films or actual experience (itself a theoretical construct), tripping out among its own implications. Thus theory often oversimplifies issues and often obfuscates them.

Of course much that film studies examines **is** obscure. We do not know enough about human social consciousness, self-perception, or its unconscious underpinnings if any, to be utterly clear about anything that happens when we look at a film or think of one, and what we do know soon turns trendy. Of their nature we may never be able to know certain things, because observing ourselves alters whatever we observe. No matter. Though film theory has been the most difficult and solemn branch of film study, with the boldest claims and often the shortest attention span, it is nevertheless essential to sophisticated thinking about film. By making explicit its underlying assumptions, relating itself to larger systems of thought, and looking for its own intellectual consistency, film theory keeps film history and criticism honest. If often driven by strong ideological commitments, to affirm or excoriate forms of Marxism, feminism, existential relativism, or commodity capitalism, and if its philosophical detachment (itself another dubious notion, viewed theoretically) is often pretentious, theory does help recognize unacknowledged or unresolved problems, and it frequently proposes methodologies for coping with them. As film studies has achieved respectability among the older disciplines, its theoretical component has grown less militant or defensive and recently less terminologically impenetrable. The following brief account of its wars, triumphs, and battlefields suddenly deserted for others unavoidably misrepresents. But it may also clarify.

Classical film theory arose from a need to conceptualize an emerging art and its peculiar characteristics especially during the century's teens and twenties. It argued whether films provide self-enclosed experiences or imitate reality (Arnheim, Kracauer), and examined film as participatory phenomena collaboratively created by the audience in the presence of the artist's work (Munsterberg, Kuleshov, Eisenstein). The theoreticians tended to be German or Russian intelligentsia familiar with post-Hegelian philosophic discourse, though Hungary (Balasz), France (Delluc), and even the U.S. (Vachel Lindsay) participated. They were fascinated to define the nature, possibilities, and especially the obligations of this new art form, and conducted their debates in intellectual journals of a rigor then unknown to the U.S. World War II silenced the proponents, or sent them into exile.

Post-war film problems and concerns (called "problematics" in theoretical jargon), were those of the 1950s and 1960s, when cinema consciousness ramified in print while responding to the cinematic innovations of the French New Wave. This consciousness was strongly influenced by then-current literary and dramatic theory stressing textual exigesis; this theory attempted to define a canon of "classic" films resembling certain literary models, reflecting to some extent the philosophic concerns of the classical theoreticians of the 1920s (what is cinema essentially?). To some extent, despite all this, film theory's social conscience began responding to the Civil Rights movements of the sixties. Its "projects" in those decades were not dissimilar to those of scholars and critics in the traditional arts, and their familiarity helped film enter the academy for formal study. The first film article printed in the august journal of academic literary scholarship *PMLA*, for example, traced a theme-defining cluster of images through successive drafts of the script of *Citizen Kane*, as was often done with drafts of poems and novels.

Later film problems and concerns surfaced in the 1970s and 1980s, when film studies established itself in American, British, and French universities and took on a life of its own. Women established themselves on faculties in larger numbers, found no patriarchs already occupying the field, and took over much of it themselves; knowledge of the subject proliferated and refined itself, and film culture outside the academy also became respectable. A generation reared in late-sixties social activism saw films as ideologically loaded public discourse rather than autonomous art, manifestations of social and psychological processes rather than artfully designed objects, and film studies altered accordingly. The predominant shifts in concern were brought on by feminist theory and criticism, which adapted psychoanalytic theory to its purposes and among other things opened to broad analysis the huge issue of the gendered and empowered "gaze." Academic film journals established themselves and took on a vitality which now influences study even of the traditional arts.

Problem Areas

Film Historiography   The earliest accounts of the origin and development of motion pictures presented the story of the development of a new art form. As such the story singled out for notice the innovations of certain pioneers who enlarged the expressivity of cinematic language and set examples for others, such as D. W. Griffith (who did not, as he claimed, invent insert close-ups), or German Expressionist filmmakers who adapted post–World War I expressionist painting, or Ingmar Bergman for bringing to film his profound if obscure personal religious searchings as well as his canny instinct for dramatic form. Film history mainly defined auteurist and national characteristics it saw on the screen, and also tended to stress watershed moments in the progress of the art (as, for example, Warners taking the plunge with Vitagraph to initiate sound films). These initial impressions and stories began to break down as film archives and studio records became increasingly available, known, and used. Histories and biographies of studios, producers, and technologies, a more detailed knowledge of cinematic apparatus (as well as the concept), and better understanding of the economic history of the motion picture industry gradually replaced earlier historical accounts based on critical observation. Historians are now unconcerned with canon formation, but study film as they find it. Hollywood films dominate all other national film markets, especially those in the third world, excepting Japan and India, with their own huge film industries, and a few countries such as Brazil, Cuba, and Senegal with their own few original filmmakers. That hegemony now has added to it the increasing domination by U.S. film historians of the histories of those alternative film traditions.

Textual Criticism   At first film criticism did what literary criticism had been doing, recognize and interpret individual films as complex but coherent objects well-shaped to generate refined and intense experiences and valued for that shape whatever their systems of belief. The more difficult films, those of the avant-garde or of filmmakers uninhibited by mainstream conventions, often foreign filmmakers, and those with the most intricate structures, tended to require and receive the most attention and interpretation. This kind of mediating commentary, explaining a text's rationale to the bewildered, came to be considered the primary task of film criticism. Adapted theories of literary New Criticism dominated, stressing that all texts are stand-alone "verbal icons" existing independent of their readers' ideological commitments or "doctrinal adhesions," to be read in their complex unity, without concern for their moral or social implications, or even for their author's intentions.

Such concepts of art especially satisfied the existential or relativist streak in twentieth-century modernism, with its desire to believe that moral value and meaning is attributed to objects or actions, never inherent or "essential" in them. Instead of its moral righteousness or its social utility, a work could be valued for its esthetic qualities: order, harmony, variety, significant form, or structured dissonance, for example. But during the sixties and seventies cultural studies dethroned the notion that texts can be written or read in a moral or social vacuum. Such a notion was found to be epistemologically naive, since a work made of signs, signifiers, or symbols does not "mean" anything independent of the culture investing those symbols with meaning. In addition, the notion seemed both politically arid—ignoring all concern with the power relationships creating the work, implicit in it, and perpetuated by it—and elitist and undemocratic—with proper readings of any texts, including film texts, the privilege of the few people who are educated to perform the required intricate acts of exigesis. The notion of films formed in moral vacuums was intimidating to viewers because it required that they suppress all personal or idiosyncratic responses to the film not justified by careful critical analysis. Gradually, **reception theory,** concerned with how we read a text, supplanted concern to read rightly a supposedly autonomous text.

One will more frequently encounter these days some form of **reader response theory,** often democratically permissive and validating anyone's personal, even quirky perception of the film, and often finding worthy any interesting conceptual structures derived from those perceptions. Earlier structuralism looked for the primary and primal forms of dramatic and human engagement echoed in the work's surface arrangements, the eternal tensions expressed in temporal or arbitrary language, guided especially by the French anthropologist Levi-Strauss and the commentator on Russian folk tales Vladimir Propp. Westerns, and even screwball comedies, were found to reenact certain archetypal tribal rituals so-viewed. **Poststructuralism** is more concerned with parts than wholes and with the surfaces by which the work manifests itself. **Semiotics** or the theory of signs looks to see what processes, interactions, and cultural codes are bound up in an image or an action, ultimately how meaning is generated and transmitted. **Deconstruction** finds that all such signs and signifiers (previously, "symbols") are significant only by virtue of their textual contexts, being themselves essentially arbitrary and meaningless. For deconstruction meaning is created by perceivable **difference** wrought by recurrences in the text, readers are themselves "texts" inscribed by the work, and the universe of signifiers creates both the work and its readers, though readings "against the grain" may subvert a work's primary design. As with reader response theory, a certain amount of free-spirited creativity in response to the text is not out of place, and a great critic is the necessary and sufficient condition of great creative artistry.

The formal and material conditions of filmmaking are now studied mainly by film historians who provide detailed production histories, not by critics. Personal, psychological, or intellectual influences on a film's creators tend to be ignored altogether, or dealt with by publishing uninterpreted interviews. The text of the film is the critic's sole essential informant, and when it enters the public domain it can be read many ways for many things additional to the unified single thing its formal integrity supposedly defines. Earlier textual criticism looked for and found paradox, tension, or irony within a work, two distinct and even incompatible points of view held in stasis, reconciled, or sustained in dynamic instability. Poststructural textual criticism looks for and finds ways in which the text's way of working upon its reader is subverted or transgressed by other ways, while the collaborative transaction between the text and its viewer takes place.

Ontology—the Status of the Image   Historically movies have always been thought a representative art to be measured against a reality the camera passively photographs and the image resembles. The **ontology** or real existence of the images in movies depends upon how exactly the movie represents (or because this is obviously impossible, "suggests") what it ostensibly shows. A good film is truthful or believable or realistic, faithful to its source, and a bad one is not. Italian neorealism is to be preferred to theatrical French poetic realism because it invokes more immediately a world we can all recognize as our own. From this assumption **mimetic** criticism follows, which measures a film's world against an ostensible external standard, the events as also portrayed by historians, biographers, diarists, or novelists, a real world "redeemed" by its photographed equivalent. Propagandists sometimes assume that the world being photographed is being recommended to the viewer as a preferable version of our own and have added to a film's mimetic fidelity an additional requirement, that it show the world as it should be, better, not as it is. Thus, films which show men terrorizing women are part of the patriarchal conspiracy against women, encouraging misogyny, and films which show workers cheerfully dedicated to their tasks are presumably good for a socialist or feudal economy and for social stability. The philosophic and other problems encumbering mimetic criticism render it finally difficult or impossible to sustain, though it provides attractive short-term ways to account for our responses to films. Even *Star Wars* (1977) and *A Nightmare on Elm Street* (1984) have been praised by naive theorists for their "realism."

A second and alternative set of assumptions declares that photographic images create a new world altogether out of photographed scraps of the old, many of them made to be photographed and otherwise nonexistent. Because a film on a screen generates a sense that such a separate world exists by itself, commentary proceeding from this assumption is called **generative** or **formalist** criticism. This criticism includes the common identification of films with dreams, or at least waking dreams induced in the audience, and values expressionistic power over mimetic verisimilitude; how a film makes you feel is more important than how accurate it is. Because films so regarded are fantasies or a distinct kind of created experience called "art," not otherwise representing anything outside themselves, they must be judged for their formal characteristics, their power and consistency rather than their truth. These films don't lie about the world, because they don't affirm anything. Textual criticism especially prospers under a formalist regime.

A third group of assumptions argues that a film is a **dialectical** process, a collaborative hallucination stimulated by events on the screen which are, in turn, recognized and then recreated out of the viewers' memory of similar events as film language reshapes them. This associationism or some equivalent allows films to be considered catalysts for communal reveries, opening the way for psychoanalytic examination of the audience's states. Associationism is especially useful to **semiotic** understanding of films, comprehending how they mean what they mean, because it situates precisely the two places where meaning and value are infused or imposed on the images, in the filmmakers' and then in the viewers' prior equivalent experiences in their common culture. The viewer always finally governs how the image is read, clearly or confusedly.

Auteur Theory   Originally a "politique" or policy by which *Cahier du Cinema* critics could attack mediocre or mannerist French filmmakers, auteurism or "author-ism" stressed film as the personal expression of one person's unique sensibility, values, and creative vitality, that person being the director or *metteur en scene* (maker of the *mise en scene* or look of the film). A director/auteur's distinction is seen in the way his or her work evolves yet holds consistent, like handwriting, and it may be weighed among the major contributions to human cultural consciousness. Auteurism is relatively uninterested in the auteur's personal life apart from filmmaking, or in filmmaking apart from the films as they appear on the screen (though a director's implied screen personality matters). An auteurist book studies the films and their characteristics chronologically or topically but attempts few or no biographical explanations. Obviously polemical and intending to be argumentative, auteurism created pantheon lists of worthwhile directors, including many U.S.

studio directors often thought to be hacks (Hawks and Ford among them), and auterism created other lists of outcasts not really worth discussing (such as John Huston). Above all it attributed anything odd or interesting in a film to its director. It is true that directors can usually (not always) veto what they cannot approve while a film is being made, that a director sets the tone on a set, and that some—mainly European— directors maintain total control over the work from its first gleam in their own eyes to its definitive screening. But film is a collaborative art, and studies of cinematographers, set designers, and other contributing artists make it clear that credit cannot safely be attributed to anyone without knowing the film's production history (which now supplants some auteur studies).

Auteurism at first authorized the academic study of directors who seemed to resemble established European men and women of letters,

Jean Renoir's profound humanism crosses boundaries of class, nationality, and even gender. Here in *Grand Illusion* (1937), British soldiers dressed in women's clothing for a prison camp show break off to sing the French national anthem to a German audience, when Jean Gabin triumphantly announces that a French town has been retaken by the Allies. The moment is short-lived: the town is repeatedly recaptured by the other side until nothing much remains, and the soldiers are punished for their empty gesture. More to the point is a costume rehearsal's moment of reverence when they are reminded of the feminine companionship they have been denied by the war.

Dreyer and Renoir accepted as the filmmaker equivalents of novelists such as Mann and Kafka, and Bergman rightfully declared to be Strindberg's heir. Methodologies for studying the evolving or collected works of single authors were well-established and familiar to academics. Thus auteurism, together with a common belief in the importance of textual exigesis and the common belief that great artists speak representatively for their culture, helped ease film study into university studies. Once there, auteurism directed attention to the profundity and stylistic subtlety of many popular Hollywood filmmakers in an industry far more diversified than had been credited. This in turn helped ease the way for academic study of other forms of popular culture, such as TV and advertising, and for other theoretical concerns.

Genre Theory Early attention to great films or to the films of great filmmakers did not account for the genre films which were most of the commercial industry's product, nor for the prominence of genre films in any U.S. filmmaker's output; the problem was exacerbated by the nature of sixties films, which were often combinations of several genres or radical transformations of one. The studio genres, or kinds of films the studios themselves categorized as such for budgeting purposes, provided one way to group individual films for contextual study, stressing their similarity to each other as well as their individual variations on shared settings and themes. Other contextual groupings proliferated and were also called "genres": subgenres such as "monster films," subjects such as "war," component concerns such as "women," auteur studies such as "Hitchcock," and star configurations such as "Bogart" or "Garbo." To discuss films in their resemblances to other films seemed in many ways arbitrary.

An unsolved problem was a tautology common also to genres of art history and literature: A genre consists of films with certain similarities by which we recognize the genre ("horses appear in Westerns, which is why Westerns have horses"). Another was that contextual criticism, seeing films in some explicit relation to each other, authorizes any viewer's random association of like with like at the movies, whether the association aids discrimination or is otherwise informative. Interest developed in a film's **intertextuality,** its referential relationships with other films, from the casual references one film may make to another to wholesale borrowings or "appropriations." But film genres still seemed an especially significant form of intertextuality. One attempt to define the term "genre" divided films into families of resemblance, all films with enough similar traits being declared to be members of a single genre. This was not perfectly satisfactory either: Among commonly listed "screwball comedies," each has many traits in common with the next most similar, but the first and the last in this Wittgensteinian daisy chain may have nearly nothing in common.

This book's discussions of genre employ a theory adapted in part from both structuralist and linguistic theory when it refers to a particular genre's deep structural or archetypal concerns and its surface structural or signifier concerns. A Western is for example a film examining the individual's role in bringing civilization out of wilderness among its deeper concerns, and celebrating the taming of animal nature rather than mastery over machines in its surface signifiers, such as horses. Films constituting a genre can share similar **semantic** characteristics on the level of words or icons, similar **syntactic** characteristics defining how the words are arranged, and similar subjects they address with their semantics and syntax. So seen, Peckinpah's *Straw Dogs* (1971), a contemporary film about a professor of mathematics threatened by village louts in England, is a syntactic Western with a few simple semantic substitutions (such as cars for horses, and pubs for saloons). So seen, many of Kurosawa's Samurai films are Westerns with superficial semantic substitutions, of swords for guns, and Tokugawa-period Japan for the post–Civil War West in the United States. This is why *The Seven Samurai* (1954) translated so easily into *The Magnificent Seven* (1960) and how *Star Wars* so closely resembles swashbucklers such as *Captain Blood* (1935).

Social Signifiers and Social Significance   Clearly films reflect or represent in certain ways the beliefs and attitudes of their own times. In time of war there are war films, and the years immediately following World War II gave us the McCarthy period in politics, the age of anxiety in literature, and film noir among movies, all these recapitulating fears of self-betrayal. It is less clear that all films provide access to a "collective unconscious" of their times, as fantasies shared by large groups of people. A pioneering study derived Hitler's rise to power in Germany through the fears and desires expressed by German films of the preceding decades. But the study used obscure as well as popular films to make its point and selected only films that supported its point while ignoring others.

Some studies of films and society hang from their own tautological bootstraps ("a film reveals that its age was what the film reveals it to be"). Others may misread who or what speaks through the film. The 1946 *Duel in the Sun*'s ending seems to reveal archetypal sexual torsions suppressed by our common consciousness. But in its own time the ending was mocked as merely silly, and Selznick's attempt to buy the film's audiences failed. It may be that audiences repressed the film's difficult truth, or maybe they found its melodramatic excesses obvious and absurd. It may be that Selznick's casting of his wife Jennifer Jones in that film reflects his personal quiddities, not the culture's, like Blake Edwards' when he repeatedly casts his prim-seeming wife Julie Andrews into sexually kinky roles. In the absence of other evidence the only representative social or psychological truths a film surely reveals are those governing its production.

There are theories that films impose on their audiences their producers' commitments to the ideologies of consumer captialism, providing the ruling class a powerful means of social control; conflicting theories claim that movie manufacturers merely sell people what they want to buy, and that the fantasies of consumer capitalism—such as *Pretty Woman*, whose success surprised everyone—happen to be high up on film consumers' want lists. Films do provide social analysts with access to certain darker desires and fears, but they need to be read cautiously. Marxist theorists provide some guidance but can be criticized for assuming that mass culture is a monolith which traps public desire into support for a monolithic status quo. An alternative theory of dynamic disequilibrium argues that all societies and psyches are pluralistic, multivalent, incongruously in conflict with other parts of themselves, and shifting in their desires and loyalties, in turn ensuring systemic instability, which in turn ensures continuing social adjustment if not radical change.

Initially theorists concerned with social reform took note that films usually display the triumphs of powerful or successful people and that oppressed minorities and other relatively powerless groups of people are usually portrayed in ways that demean or dehumanize them. Early studies charted the evolution and variations in Hollywood films of different regional and minority stereotypes: the inhabitants of small towns and urban slums, blacks, native Americans, Jews, other ethnic groups, gays, and increasingly, women. These studies had different perceptions and social purposes but the same implicit title implying that screen reality too readily reinforces an undesirable social reality: "The Image of . . . in Film." Theories of mass culture conflict over whether media actively propagate these stereotypes in support of the dominant classes (whites, WASPS, homophobes, and/or men), but identifying them does help make readers conscious that they *are* stereotypes and discourages filmmakers from insulting and possibly injuring people by using them further. Studying changing social stereotypes in films also provides a way to study the culture's governing and changing convictions and ambivalences. Some social theories developed originally for understanding how imperialist powers conceive colonized countries have been usefully adapted to study minority oppression within a majority culture. At the least, multicultural concern with the expressions and representations of nondominant cultures, classes, and societies enrich the dominant groups while seeming to "empower" the others, making our endemic ethnocentrism a bit more self-conscious and therefore a bit less arrogant.

Feminist Film Theory   Feminist film theory emerged as the woman's movement did from the larger Civil Rights movement of the sixties and took on such vitality that it still dominates the broader reaches of film study with its own concerns and influences other cultural studies as well. Feminist film study's concerns ranged from patriarchal male bashing to providing support for underassertive women bashed by men but settled early into examination of what might be the uniquely "feminine." The first "image of women in film" studies, largely of male images of women, were followed by others more specialized, for example of the problems posed by Katherine Hepburn (vulnerable yet liberated), Mae West (who camped herself as a sex goddess in scripts she herself wrote), Dorothy Arzner (the only U.S. woman studio director during the studio period), and the peculiarly Oedipal women of film noir (who

Marlene Dietrich as Lola Lola, in Josef Von Sternberg's *The Blue Angel* (1930) the ultimate fetichized femme fatale figment of the male masochistic imagination, a sex goddess who tempts and destroys. Early feminist criticism objected to the portrayal of women as "sex objects" to gratify the male gaze; more recent analysis is less judgmental.

A   B

The female gaze. Garbo's independence registered in the power with which her eyes addressed people, whether angrily as in this scene from *Anna Christie* (1930) (A), or with rapt devotion. When not assuming male prerogatives and staring intently at those close to her, she stared self-absorbed into the middle distance, as in *Camille* (1936) when asked to give up her lover (B). Mae West similarly looked men straight in the eye as well as up and down, frankly appraising their masculinity; here in *She Done Him Wrong* (1933) (C), which she coscripted, she invites the inexperienced Cary Grant to come up and see her.

use young lovers to rid themselves of older husbands). The first historical assumptions about women's roles were gradually corrected: The confined suburban housewives of fifties and early sixties films, for example, were seen to be not Victorian survivals, but one consequence when World War II veterans reentered the economy after surviving the war's male barracks fantasies, the earlier Great Depression's deferred domesticity, and the comparatively liberated period earlier still. Suburban houses imprisoning women and children became "domestic spaces" where women govern absolutely. Hollywood films soon modified their conceptions of women (now rarely "girls"), especially of working women and single parents, and of male-shared rituals such as sex, marriage, and divorce. Screen characters now tend to reflect the feminist movement's and women film producers' largely urban and professional conceptions of women's independence and predicaments.

Psychoanalytic theories of repression and gender difference were similarly advanced then revised. What at first seemed to be crude "phallocentric" repression of women by an exclusively governing male patriarchy took on more elaborate scenarios according to various class, regional, and cultural gender roles, and protest that with pornography men fantasize and demean women as filmed or actual sex objects has led in turn to examination of male visual fetishes. Women's "lack" in Freud's terms, with its implications for male castration fears and female penis envy, has been found a source of the fetichized sex goddesses of the classic period and analogized with the screen's lack, since screen images similarly affirm the presence of absences. Lacan's theories especially concerning mirroring and self-imaging have helped understanding of film as a "dream screen."

During the seventies, an important conjunction of psychoanalysis and Marxism advanced the thesis that films being made by men, the power to look, both in and at films, is dominated by the "male gaze" with its own masculine patterns of desire, effectively reducing women's pleasure in films to "women's films" such as melodrama, or to imaginative play in men's roles. This thesis has been modified by closer attention to how women respond as actual spectators. Distinctly masculine characteristics are beginning to be more precisely differentiated from those found distinctly feminine within other concepts of ungendered "human" characteristics. But by calling attention to who or what directs looking, gazing, and viewing in cinematic experience, to how the viewer is altered while viewing, and to the older existential problem of how one is altered by the knowledge that one is being seen, the thesis opened out a whole new set of issues now under study in all the imaginative arts and opened whole new ways to see critically what happens in films. Whatever theory's repeatedly abandoned constructs, this is the kind of thing it does best.

Glossary of Film Terms

abstraction a picture's formal characteristics, its lines, shapes, masses, shadings, colors, textures, and their relationships, stripped of all representational meaning and signifying nothing; also, particular ideas when stripped of their particularity and restated as general categories and principles

Academy ratio the "golden mean" relationship of a picture's width to its height established by the Academy of Motion Picture Arts and Sciences, 4 to 3, standard before 1950 and still used for TV

A.C.E. American Cinema Editors, the guild to which many professional film editors belong

A.S.C. American Society of Cinematographers, the self-selecting guild or union of most of the best (in Britain, B.S.C.)

acting the art of playing roles as if they were people, according to type and a film's dramatic needs

action (discourse) events in the order in which they occur on the screen, gradually revealing the story of those same events supposedly happening chronologically in the film's world

actors artists who discipline their bodies and mannerisms to create the illusion that they are other people in other situations, shot by shot, according to cinematic and dramatic necessity

ADR editor the technician who operates "automatic dialogue replacement" dubbing or looping machines

aesthetic experience any experience engaged in for its own sake and not for its moral virtue or social utility, usually provided by works of art but sometimes also by life

aesthetic values the variety, coherence or dissonance, texture, intensity, and range of sensations, ideas, and experiences brought into formal unity in a work and experienced as such, quite apart from a work's other values such as conformity to a moral code, to a program of social reform, or to a concept of truth

aleatory by chance, random features of a work expressing similarly spontaneous, accidental, or arbitrary arrangements in life

allegory a story in which the characters each represent an abstract moral, psychological, or philosophical trait or quality, so their dramatic relationships reveal the nature of other more abstract kinds of relationships

ambient sound "live" background sounds creating the illusion that we are seeing and hearing a real world, such as the sounds of distant birds or cars, supposedly incidental but in fact functioning to enhance the drama

American shot a three-quarter shot showing a human figure from the knees up, implying the ability to move at will, so-called by the French

analogy anything simple and familiar used to explain anything complex and unfamiliar because the two things share certain similarities

analytic montage editing that analyzes parts of a supposed continuity of time and space onscreen as if it were examining it, not creating it, revealing significant details in an ongoing sequence, for example, by inserting close-ups into a master shot

anamorphic lens optics that horizontally squeeze a very wide image onto standard gauge film, then horizontally expand it again when that film is projected in a theater

animation drawings, clay figures, and sand swirls, or various objects seemingly "animated" or brought to life, made to seem to move by photographing them one frame at a time, with slight changes in position introduced between frames, then projecting these frames at regular speeds

answer print a trial print struck by the lab from the original negative when it has been cut to match precisely the edited work print supplied by the editor, not yet color-balanced but with an optical sound track, ready to screen for investors, preview audiences, and others

antagonist any character or force opposing the protagonist's desires, making for difficulties or dramatic conflict; in U.S. films usually though not always a bad guy

art any significant and formally coherent work we feel enriched to witness, or anything at all regarded solely for its aesthetic qualities

art director (production designer) the artist who selects or designs the sets, settings, locations, and props seen in the film, in accordance with the film's visual style

art documentary a nonfiction film appreciated more for its style, or for its aesthetic qualities, than for its subject, message, or truth

aspect ratio the screen's width in relation to its height, classically 1.33 to 1, more recently widescreen's 1.85 to 1, or, if an anamorphic ratio, 2.35 to 1

assistant director one of several director's helpers as needed to assist with set-ups, secondary shots, car or crowd cueing and control, preliminary rehearsals of lesser performers, or other directorial chores

associational flashback   a character's recollection seen on screen, occurring because a sight, sound, gesture, or word in the present seems similar to something remembered from the past

auteur   a film's "author" or primary creative sensibility, supposedly the director, a term originating in French critical policy directed against impersonal films, now supporting the cult of the director as superstar

avant-garde films   art films extending or violating film conventions in new ways, made by individual artists for their own noncommercial reasons, usually challenging viewers to find for themselves the appropriate ways to look at them

back light   lights illuminating the main image from the rear, sculpting it from the background with highlighted edges, as with haloed hair

background music   off-screen extra-diegetic music heard during the film, not originating within the action but accompanying that action in order to heighten its dramatic power

backstage musical   a genre depicting the fictive staging of a real musical entertainment, the plot usually showing how ambitious and talented people can become successful by planning to please others and then doing it

best boy   the gaffer or chief electrician's principal assistant

best boy grip   the key grip or head stagehand's principal assistant

big caper film   a form of gangster film showing a team of skilled, usually admirable professional thieves gathering to plan a fabulous crime, then pulling it off

bio-pic   a biographical picture dramatizing the personal life of some historical figure or recent celebrity, or a partial or complete fiction about some such person, usually inspirational but occasionally disturbing

bit players   relatively unknown professional actors hired for a day or two to play brief minor roles in a film

black comedy   a comedy in which the clowns' follies cause serious consequences, or a melodrama populated by destructive but amusing clowns, with the audience's usual moral response to the sight of people in trouble suppressed or suspended

blind bidding   theater owners negotiating to exhibit films not yet seen, perhaps not yet completed, to assure themselves product especially during school holidays

block booking   renting a packaged bundle of films regardless of their appeal, in order to secure the exhibition rights to one particular film

blocking   a director's primary responsibility, planning the positions and movements of actors, objects, and cameras during a shot, so the actors can "hit their marks" taped on the floor, remain in focus, and perform with maximum dramatic effectiveness

bounce light   light reflected off reflector panels, diffusers, ceilings, or light-colored walls, making a scene seem more evenly lit than otherwise

buffoon   a witless or clumsy character constantly making a fool of himself, the deserving butt for other people's scorn, jokes, or amusement

burlesque   a form of satire mocking lofty aspiration, pretentious superiority, upper-class manners, and intimidating sexuality by treating them all in a low, familiar, and vulgar manner, often laced with physical abuse; also, the turn-of-the-century stage variety shows which did just that

cameo   a brief appearance of a well-known star in a small role, sometimes uncredited

camera   a portable device for recording whatever images are in front of it, consisting of a lens, a shutter, a film strip coated with light-sensitive chemicals, and some means for transporting the film strip past the lens for successive intermittent exposure to light, one frame at a time

camera obscura   a "dark room" in precinematic days, where images from outside passing through a small aperture could marvelously reappear on a flat surface within

camera operator   the camera assistant who rides with the camera and actually works it during a take, as the cinematographer directs

camp   a term originally referring to genial or jealous mockery of gender mannerisms, usually by subtly exaggerating while imitating them; later, similarly bemused mockery of any other kind of stylized behavior

canted camera shot   a shot made with the camera slanted off its vertical axis, showing a world somehow gone awry

caricature   a character who appears ridiculously out of proportion because one physical, psychological, or moral trait has been grossly exaggerated

cast   all the people seen onscreen playing known or anonymous characters

cast against type   hired to play character traits very different from those customarily played, violating audience expectations for that actor

casting agency   a company used to supply a film with its lesser cast and extras

causal flashback   past events shown by the film to explain how the present state of things got that way, a temporal reversion within a framing action

celebrity   a person known and usually admired by many people, who has become part of their shared consciousness and therefore seemingly larger-than-life, sometimes celebrated only for having become a celebrity, any original accomplishments forgotten

center line   an imaginary line perpendicular to the camera's line of sight, basis of the 180-degree rule, determining the "picture plane" or plane of the action parallel to the screen, never crossed between shots without risking the viewer's sense of spatial relationships

character actor   an actor with the many skills and techniques needed to play roles distinctly differing from each other and from the actor's own character, unlike actors who play variations on themselves or their established screen images

characters   dramatic figments in human form with carefully selected traits who resemble people and are so-regarded by the audience, participating in the dramatic action and often seeming to initiate it

charisma   literally "divine grace," the extraordinary appeal of any political leader, screen character, actor, or celebrity who seems able to exemplify and gratify the intense desires we project upon them

choke shot   a tight close-up of a face cut off at its chin and forehead, usually conveying great contained intensity

choreography   a plan for a dance, precisely directing the dancers' postures, gestures, movements, and sequences of movements from its beginning to its end, serving the same functions as a dramatic script or a musical score but rarely written down

cinema verité   a form of documentary or nonfiction film laying claim to "cinema truth" (the term translating the Russian *kino pravda*), seeking to avoid all artistic dissimulation and to show the event as it was as photographed, the image's flat lighting, jerkiness, and misfocusing testifying to its authenticity

CinemaScope   the trade name for Twentieth Century Fox's anamorphic lens process, creating a very wide screen image by squeezing the image horizontally in the camera and then expanding it again during projection, now used casually as a generic term for any anamorphic process

cinematographer (director of photography or DP)   the artist and technician responsible for the film's lighting and photography, an expert with lights, lenses, cameras, film stocks, and photographic processes who designs and tests different effects until they match the director's intentions for the film, then oversees the actual shooting

clapboard   a slate with a hinged clapper on top for labelling the beginning of each take visually and aurally, for later synchronizing of the film with the sound track

clapper-loader   the camera assistant who tags each take with a clapboard, and also looks after the film magazines

classical film   critics' term for films in the prevailing Hollywood studio style, with continuity editing creating a credible screen reality, sets reinforcing that impression, plots built on lines of action finally resolving whatever the conflicts posed (whatever their incompatibility in the real world), and characters who elicit strong audience identification

climactic structure   plot construction based on a single problem or issue posed at the outset, developed through conflict and complication in a "rising" action, climaxed irreversibly near the end, and resolved or fully comprehended after the climax, the structure assumed by virtually all drama and storytelling in the Western world for the past three thousand years

climax   that moment or scene near the end of a dramatic action when conflicting characters or forces confront each other, whatever is at issue becomes fully known, and whatever will come of it is finally determined, sometimes called the "obligatory scene"

close-up   a shot made with a camera position or lens setting filling the screen with the image of any object the size of a human face or smaller, generating strong viewer attentiveness and feelings of intimacy

closed-frame composition   masses and shapes in a shot formally arranged within the frame's rectangle, so that a viewer's eye repeatedly returns to compositionally privileged details, as if there were no off-screen space and the frame at that moment contained a sufficiently complete world

closure   a sense of finality felt as the action ends, with the plot problem resolved, other issues adequately settled, and the outcome of the characters' supposed lives thereafter sufficiently predictable; recently some ambiguity or uncertainty in these matters has been preferred by some film goers

clown in comedy, the lone character, peculiar in appearance and behavior, who deliberately or unwittingly acts out the audience's repressed fears and desires, serving therefore as both their hero and scapegoat, the originator and the object of their laughter

colorizing electronically processing videos of black and white films so they will broadcast as if they were murky color films with dramatically inept tinting

comedian comedy a kind of comedy in which the performer remains visible even while playing a character, the familiar comedian seen deliberately pretending to be a familiar fool

comedy a major genre portraying varieties of fools in their folly, inducing in the audience distanced recognition, mutual relief from anxieties, and amused laughter

commercials short TV advertisements designed to enhance product recognition and sales, edited vigorously and broadcast repeatedly in order to overcome an audience's reflexive inattention, occasionally also played in film theaters

composite shots separate shots spliced together to create a continuing scene, without a master shot establishing and stabilizing the fixed space where the action takes place

composition the rectangular frame's patterns of lines, masses, and textures formed by the spatial relationships of the people and things making up the image

concept any new idea for a film, stated briefly as a gimmick, situation, setting, or series of opportunities for star actors, its novelty, familiarity, and commercial appeal sufficiently visible to put a gleam in a producer's eye

conflict the confrontation and struggle of opposing characters, forces, or principles basic to most narratives and all drama, defined usually by the relationship of a protagonist and an antagonist, in the United States by a good guy and a bad guy

continuity the spatial and temporal persistence and consistency of the world on film, created and ensured by the way the individual shots are made and then spliced together

continuity (script girl) the person who monitors every detail in shots meant to be seen in sequence, so mistakes and inconsistencies can be spotted and corrected

continuity editing the systematic sequential arranging of shots so that an action seen on the screen seems to be occurring in real time and known space

costume any clothing worn by anyone on screen, selected to help define that person's character, attitudes, and capabilities within the film world's applicable dress codes

courtroom film a genre portraying the drama of justice achieved, usually of innocence confirmed, by orderly and traditional public rituals and a certain amount of individual cunning

cover shot a "master shot" of a continuous action photographed without interruption, establishing relevant spatial relationships and protecting the planned narrative continuity in case other related shots are not usable

crane   a camera platform placed on one end of a long boom hinged at the other end, able to move the camera smoothly for considerable distances, vertically, horizontally, or both

crane shot   a shot displaying a flowing or floating movement up and across short distances, apparently liberated from gravity, the camera mounted on a crane

crew   all the technical and support people off-camera who help prepare and light the sets and shoot the film, at least five for any one shot, perhaps thirty for another

cross-cut   an edit cutting from one action to another simultaneous action somewhere else

cut   the spliced place between two frames where one shot ends abruptly and another begins, literally cut by the editor; also, the director's call to the crew to stop shooting

cutaway   a shot briefly interrupting one action to provide a glimpse of another also taking place

cutting continuity   a script written to guide the editor's rough cut assembly of selected takes

dailies   the "rushes" or previous day's takes hastily printed and screened to guide the director and other major technicians and artists in their next day's work, for selection of the specific take to be used in the edited film, and for monitoring of the production's progress by interested executives

day-for-night filters   filters placed over the camera lens to darken certain supposed night scenes shot in daylight for convenience

deconstruction   a system of criticism in which the meanings of parts and entireties of a work are shown in practice as well as theory to be elusive, imprecise, arbitrary, self-contemplating and self-subverting, regardless of the work's formal structure and declarations, especially focusing on the work as a mosaic of similarities and differences

— **deep focus**   critics' term for an image photographed with considerable depth of field, everything far and near seen in sharp focus whatever its distance from the lens

direct documentary   a nonfiction film showing a supposedly unmediated world, with no voice-overs or noticeable interviewers, as if it were not being photographed at all and its inhabitants were not even aware of being photographed

director   the film's chief artistic coordinator or authority, responsible for blocking the camera and cast and eliciting their performances, and for bringing in the film on time and within budget; usually oversees everything and often responsible for everything appearing onscreen

director of photography   the cinematographer, who designs and oversees the film's lighting and photography, assisted by lighting and camera crews

dissolve   a noticeable fading of one shot while another superimposed on it grows stronger and finally replaces it, quick or slow, the earlier shot seeming to dissolve into the later, signifying a change of time or place without loss of the action's momentum or meaning

docudrama (mock-doc)   fictive tales photographed using documentary techniques for the authenticity these techniques provide, or actual events reconceived, reenacted, and photographed as if fictions for the greater dramatic effectiveness of fiction

documentary film   any film consisting of images of the actual world, shot and edited to warn, inform, impress, or entertain its audiences with the supposed truth thereby revealed

Dolby sound   a patented process for reducing a sound track's background hissing and popping, making stereo and multisourced sound more pleasant and seemingly "realistic"

dolly   a camera platform on wheels, sometimes with a small crane as well, for slow, rolling shots toward and away from, but also alongside whatever is being photographed

dolly grips   the crew who hand-push the camera dolly during a shot

dolly-in   the camera entering into its own field of vision, moving closer to what it sees

dolly-out   the camera backing away from whatever it sees, distancing the viewer as well

domestic melodrama   a genre exploring women's desires and difficulties in their own homes, usually in traditional roles as nurturing wives and mothers, often stressing self-transcendence achieved through devotional self-sacrifice, often tear-jerking and therefore called "weepers"

doubles   pairs of similar characters seen in dramatic opposition or in tandem as foils to each other, each one's similar, complementary, or differing traits defined more clearly by the other's

dubbing   replacing sounds, voices, or languages on the sound track with others thought preferable, though maintaining their synchronicity with the image as far as possible

editor   the person who receives work prints of the film's takes, logs them, cuts and splices the preferred takes into a rough cut, then with the director trims shots and reconstructs sequences until a desired "final cut" of the work print has emerged

ellipsis   omission of anything already understood, in order to concentrate the story or because it couldn't hold up under too-close scrutiny

end credits   long lists of the lesser artists and technicians rolling up from the bottom of the frame, seen as the film ends and usually signalling that the action has indeed ended

episodic structure   plot construction in which a string of separate actions takes place, perhaps involving the same main character, each action concluded as the next one begins

escape film   any film sufficiently different in setting and concern from our own daily concerns, sufficiently free of our usual anxieties, and with sufficiently privileged or admirable characters for us to view it without being directly reminded of ourselves and our own predicaments

establishing shot   often also the "master" or "cover" shot, a medium or long shot establishing locations and various spatial relationships in a sequence, so these can remain clear in a viewer's mind even when offscreen during other shots

existential view   the belief found frequently in Europe after World War II, especially in films by New Wave filmmakers, that existence lacks any innate or essential purpose or meaning, that principles are delusions, and that freedom lies in deliberately choosing which illusions we will live by

experimental films avant-garde films using especially unfamiliar techniques or subjects, called "art" if they seem to succeed and "experiments" if they do not

explanatory flashback past events shown by the film to explain why the present seems difficult to understand, or why characters are behaving as they do, not necessarily a recollection in a character's mind or a causal explanation of present circumstances

exposition the information provided early in the dramatic action, usually indirectly, explaining whatever needs to be known about the story before the action began and the characters before they further reveal themselves

expressionism an artistic movement originating early in this century in Germany, presenting interior experience as if exterior, with the phantasmagoria of the mind and emotions such as fear, loathing, and perverse desire portrayed in grotesque and disturbing ways; in film, haunting sounds, unnatural or exaggerated sets, and low-keyed, single-sourced lighting surrounded by pools of darkness are among its hallmarks

extradiegetic critics' term for any world outside the film's own "diegesis" or ostensible reality, usually our own world in which we are viewing a film

extras unidentified cast members hired to play the anonymous people who fill out crowds, walk on streets, sit at bars, or otherwise provide human backgrounds

− **fade** a transition between shots in which the earlier shot darkens or brightens until the screen is blank, then the later shot reverses this process until it is fully visible, signifying a major break in the action, time passing in the interim

− **fade-in** a blank screen brightening until a new image appears

− **fade-out** a screen image darkening until it can no longer be seen

fantasy film the unpredictable, irrational, or magical set in a past or future world where our own natural laws do not prevail, the world as we can imagine it rather than as we know it

farce a comedy displaying energetic, irreverent, even zany disruption of sacred cows and restrictive social proprieties, political and sexual among others

fast motion (undercranking) shooting film at a slower speed than it will be projected, exposing fewer than 24 fps but projecting at 24 fps, achieving unnaturally accelerated motion, frantic or frenzied, for comic or subtly expressionistic effects

feature film since the twenties the film "featured" in advertising to attract audiences, usually with a developed plot, known stars, and a "feature length" running time of 90 to 120 minutes

feminist criticism the study of gender relationships and differences as they define women in film, women filmmakers, women spectators, women as perceived or "constructed" by films, and women's various relationships with a male-dominated culture and film industry, using psychoanalytic as well as historiographic approaches to account for the phenomena under examination

fill light   lighting used to soften the contrast between lit parts of an image and the shaded or shadowed parts

film criticism   informed commentary on films and the issues they raise, usually examining characteristics of film texts, interpreting them by an appropriate hermeneutic procedure, comprehending implications by some historical, psychological, or social body of theory, and sometimes evaluating the films to determine their presumed implicit worth, or valuating them to assign them an extrinsic moral, social, or artistic worth

film historiography   examination of the theories, assumptions, and kinds of information by which film history is written, as for example various historical accounts of film as an art form, a technology, an industry, a means of social control, or a medium of cultural or personal expression

film history   narrative or analytic accounts of what films and film institutions have been and are, how they work, the ways they change over time, and why

film noir   French term meaning "black film" now in general use, referring to U.S. films especially of the forties or early fifties, often made by expatriate European directors, with bitter or cynical voice-over narrations, plots displaying helpless entrapment or betrayal often by a femme fatale, sometimes sadistic violence, and often dark night scenes expressionistically lit

film review   timely advice to potential viewers telling what a film is like and whether it is worth seeing, restricted as criticism by its inability to discuss crucial questions of suspense, surprise, or outcome without "giving away" the plot

film stock   a flexible transparent strip spread with different light-sensitive emulsions, once with a flammable nitrate base but since 1950 an acetate base, perforated with sprocket holes along one or both edges

film theory   different intellectual structures adapted for examination of film viewing and film-related phenomena, themselves based self-consciously on different philosophical, linguistic, psychological, and social theories

filters   tinted or optically treated transparent lens covers used to alter the kind of light reaching the lens and therefore the kind of image filmed

final cut   last changes made in a film's editing for artistic or commercial reasons just before its release; the right to make or prevent such changes

flashback   any earlier time portrayed on the screen within a film's present time, usually as an interruption or digression in the main action, but sometimes providing the main action after a brief "frame story" introduction

flashforward   any future events shown within the film's ongoing account of events in time present

flip wipe   a transition between shots in which the later image seems to overturn the earlier, as if a page were turning

focus-puller   the camera assistant who rides the camera to refocus its lens as the camera or the action moves closer or further away

focus-through   blurring an image during a shot by taking it out of focus, then refocusing on something else; also called "rackfocusing" or "racking"

foil characters   minor characters who resemble yet differ significantly from a major character, who set off or reveal more clearly that major character's distinctive traits

Foley artist   the sound editor who creates or adapts and dubs onto the sound track various ambient or special sound effects

footage   the exposed film created during principal photography, not yet selected or edited

formalist criticism   a critical method assuming that film texts exist independent of the act of perceiving them, analyzing their formal structures in relation to each other, concerned with their representational or mimetic value only as these affect their formal strategies

four-walling   renting a whole theater, staff and all, for a set fee rather than a share of the box office receipts, to exhibit a movie which might otherwise remain shelved unseen

fps   frames per second, a measurement of the speed for exposing or projecting film, 24 fps being standard sound speed and 16 to 18 fps silent speed

frame   one still image on a strip of film (of 1440 seen each minute of a sound film); the rectangular outer rim of an image on screen, composing whatever is within it and defining everywhere else as "offscreen"

frame story   the plot's present action, within which a dramatized flashback or narrated action may occur, especially if the present action serves mainly to provide the occasion or excuse for the flashback

freeze-frame   the moving image made to seem a still photo because one frame has been selected and then repeatedly reprinted for screening

Freudian criticism   criticism which uses Freud's (or the later theorist Lacan's) concepts of the unconscious and the mind's other faculties, dreaming, mirroring, self-projection, the Oedipus complex, castration fears, penis envy, the primal scene, the pleasure principle, and various psychoanalytic procedures, to study the origin and nature of our fantasy uses for films

front projection   projecting a filmed background onto a screen from the front, then with reprocessing of the shadows photographing it again with actors acting in the foreground, producing a clearer overall image than rear projection

gaffer   the chief electrician in a lighting crew, overseeing everyone else

gag comedy   comedy based usually on a physical predicament or a series of them, showing in pantomime various elaborated structures of action as the clown copes

gangster film   genre about criminals who belong to or lead a gang, with its varying implications for violence, loyalty, and betrayal, showing ambitious crooks eventually thwarted by cops, the competition, or their own divided desires

genre   a group of films resembling each other because they share certain kinds of characters, settings, plots, and issues, constituting a kind of known language for examination of those issues

grip   strong crew member who hauls lights, equipment, or segments of sets where needed, or operates lifting machinery to do the hauling

hand-held camera   a portable camera carried by its operator, the image weaving and bouncing unsteadily, conveying a sense of spontaneity and, as with newsreel and documentary footage, a sense of authenticity

hard-core pornography   actual sexual acts, not simulations, filmed and then viewed for voyeuristic sexual gratification, to stimulate anxiety-free sexual fantasies

hermeneutics   any system of reading, analyzing, or interpreting a work's meaning and significance by close scrutiny of its form and language, including its visual language

— **high-angle shot**   a shot made with the camera looking down, as if superior to what it sees

— **high-key (realistic) lighting**   a lighting style in which all parts of the set and the screen are relatively evenly lit, suggesting a familiar world containing few surprises or mysteries

horror film   a genre in which the uncanny or seemingly supernatural threatens the helpless, vulnerable, or guiltily uneasy in order to provide a shape for fear to comprehend or to achieve its ritual exorcism

humor   a genial kind of comedy appealing more to sentiment than the mind, arising from characters whose mindlessly excessive traits or compulsions lead them into folly

identification   the process of imagining one's self to be a screen character, or in that character's predicament; understanding and sympathizing with a screen character's thoughts and feelings, to some extent merely enjoying being in the screen character's presence

ideology   an implicit governing system of values, beliefs, and assumptions shared by individuals and promulgated by institutions including the film industry and films themselves and considered self-evidently true and rarely challenged, providing a culture with its necessary enabling myths and convictions

improvisation   acting which arises spontaneously out of some situation or premise, without scripts, prearranged blocking, or premeditation; the resulting characters, dialogue, and skits

indispensability   a characteristic of an integrated work of art resulting from its unity or economy, each part essential and each contributing to each other as well as the whole

industrial documentary   an informational or propaganda documentary film designed to promote corporate purposes, paid for by that corporation

insert shot   a segment of an action inserted into a sequence for clarity or emphasis

integrated musical   a musical in which the musical numbers themselves explain the characters or advance the plot in ways the dramatic interludes do not

intellectual montage   editing shots to generate or comment on ideas, not primarily to maintain the spatial and temporal continuity of a "real" world

internal frame   a rectangle or other enclosing shape seen onscreen within the film image, such as a mirror, hallway, or doorway, distancing the viewer from whatever appears inside it by converting that inner world into yet another picture

intertextuality   the different ways films allude to other films, and what such filmic cross-references say

invective direct insult, liberated from our usual polite concern for the consequences and therefore liberating to witness, especially in a comedy

iris-wipe (or iris-fade) a circular diminution of the image, which grows smaller until it disappears

jump-cut an edit which wrenches or chops temporal or spatial continuity between shots, because things move or happen without adequate time for them to have moved or happened

key light lighting which selectively illuminates from the front various prominent features of the image, such as faces or hands, and provides the reflected gleam in an actor's eye

key grip the head crew member who supervises the grips in hauling of sets and equipment

lap dissolve (also, dissolve) a dissolve with the two images overlapped for a time, the earlier one fading as the later one becomes visible

latent content as with dreams a film's darkly hidden inner concerns, concealed by the manifest content's specific literal circumstances but also revealed by the manifest content when it is interpreted as an analogy, or as a symbolic displacement or objective correlative of those inner concerns

layered characters characters who are not what they seem on the surface but maintain complex motives within themselves and keep their own counsel

lens an optical system for transmitting light while bending it, focusing it, and changing its relationships in different ways

line producer a business administrator, usually representing the executive producer, who oversees a film's day-to-day production problems so the artists and technicians can concentrate on their own work

line-wipe a transition between shots in which the new image pushes the old one sideways along a straight line until the old one is entirely off the screen

linear structure a line of action or of plot construction in which events follow one another chronologically and follow from one another with linked causal logic, without interruption by flashbacks or digressive episodes

lip-synching dubbing dialogue or singing to match lip movements, or matching lip movements to prerecorded dialogue or singing

living dead films horror films in which the dead are returned to a semblance of life and become mindlessly aggressive, like zombies or vampires, arousing fear of the implacable as well as the supernatural

location a place some distance from the studio which looks suitable for exterior scenes, or, if especially authentic, for interior scenes as well

long shot a shot made with the camera some distance from the object viewed, showing at least a human form fully visible within the frame but sometimes showing a wide panorama seen by a camera even further away

looping recording or dubbing dialogue or singing to synchronize with short repeating "loops" of a film

low-angle shot a shot made with the camera looking up, as if the viewer were awed or cowed by what is seen

low-key (expressionistic) lighting lighting with strongly contrasted areas of light and shadow, often with one feature of the image lit from one side or below and the rest dark, creating a sense of lurking mystery

mad scientist films   a subgenre of science fiction or horror films in which a scientist conducts cruel or "unnatural" experiments, expressing our mistrust of mindless technological "progress" and of rabid rationalism divorced from human needs

mad slasher films   a subgenre of horror films in which a psychopath attacks and bloodily butchers unsuspecting people, especially young people, expressing the audience's vulnerability to sudden rage and its fear of physical mutilation, its uneasy wariness before perverse nonconformism, and perhaps also the guilt and need for symbolic self-punishment incurred during various transgressions of sexual, social, and moral codes

maguffin   Hitchcock's term for any arbitrarily chosen thing, secret, or state of knowledge—military plans for example, or industrial diamonds—some characters want badly enough to behave as they do, and other characters must therefore discover in order to understand what is happening

main title (opening) credits   lists of the principal businesspeople, artists, and technicians responsible for a film, appearing before or after the film's main title but before the primary action, though sometimes appearing overlaid on preliminary actions, or just after them

manifest content   the subjects and issues literally presented and at stake in a film or in a dream, a spade seen as such, figuring forth the latent content or suppressed inner concerns, perhaps a desire to uncover or dig up something long suppressed

Marxist criticism   criticism which derives a culture's and a film's ideologies, tensions, and systems of domination and repression from a Marxist analysis of the class interests of those who own, control, and exploit for profit a society's productive capabilities, in order to understand film as a mass medium, the film industry as a capitalist enterprise which manufactures commodities in its own interest, and films as those commodities bought and consumed, as well as subversions of them

master shot   in classical continuity editing, a medium or long shot of a complete continuous action, later broken up with insert shots, cutaways, match-cutting, cross-cutting, and so forth

match-cut   an edit maintaining a sense of smooth, continuing action from shot to shot, even though the second shot is from a different camera position

matte shot   a composite shot created in the lab of two shots made separately, perhaps of a close-up and a long shot, each partly matted or masked to accommodate the other, or perhaps an actual shot partially masked by a painting mounted near the lens

medium shot   a shot made with the camera seemingly near what it sees but not close to it, familiar but not intimate, showing a human figure from the waist up

melodrama   a large genre including thrillers, romances, and many other kinds of film, featuring powerful tensions and irreversible consequences, with life, death, goodness, evil, sacrifice, redemption, and other clear issues at stake, calling for strong emotional identification with the main characters

metaphor   an implicit comparison, something presented as if it were something else, for what that substitution can reveal about the original

method acting acting from a self-induced personal inner state equivalent to whatever the character is supposedly feeling or suppressing, so appropriate expressivity can manifest itself subtly in the character's voice, face, and gestures

metonymy any word, term, or image substituted for another one more categorical or abstract, the specific standing for the general

mickey-mousing cutting a sequence on the beat of its accompanying music, the image synchronized to the melody and the rhythm

mid-angle shot a shot made with the camera looking across, level, usually waist or chest high, creating a sense of familiarity

mike boom a long pole with a microphone on one end, held off-camera near actors to pick up their dialogue, kept near them as they move about

mimetic criticism criticism which studies films as truthful or distorted reflections or representations of the single reality we also supposedly inhabit

minimalist film a kind of avant-garde film barely and only presenting one subject, image, technique, object, or thing, uncomplicated and undistracted by any others

mise en scene a film's "look" or decor, as created by its sets, props, costumes, lighting, photography, and actors' postures and proximities, making up the film's visible universe and generating much of its mood and meaning

mock-heroic a form of satire which mocks our tendency to overvalue the familiar, trivial, and petty concerns of our lives, by treating them in the grand manner, as if they were noble or heroic

monologue a character's or narrator's lines spoken without interruption or expectation of a reply, often rather lengthy, rare in most films

montage the French term for editing, referring to any extraordinary or exceptionally artful sequence of shots, and also to the art of editing such a sequence

moral conflict a conflict between principles or characters, or within a character, each antagonist representing a moral quality, in U.S. melodrama some form of good opposed to some equivalent form of evil, though what any film considers good or evil may vary greatly

MOS "mitout sound," a notation on clapper slates and scripts that nothing will be recorded during a take, with any relevant voices or sounds to be added later

movement a tendency among certain filmmakers of a given time and place to adopt the same methods and goals, sometimes by deliberate agreement

multiple-trait characters characters each with many different complex psychological and moral characteristics, some perhaps at odds with others, common in everyday life but rare in film, where certain character traits function dramatically and all others are therefore irrelevant or distracting

music the controlled, expressive sounds and rhythms created by instruments designed and customarily used for the purpose, provided in order to reinforce moods and to guide an audience's responses

music director the person who selects, composes, and conducts all the music heard on the sound track

musical sometimes merely a series of musical numbers, as in a variety, review, or concert film, but more often a plotted genre featuring occasional songs and dances, usually celebrating simple pleasures and common transcendent feelings, or lamenting them, above all those of courtship, romance, and the achieving of desirable goals

narrative time the chronological time presumably elapsed between the beginning of a story and its end, usually a few days, sometimes several centuries

naturalism the belief common in the decades after Darwin, especially as film narratives first developed or during the Great Depression, that we are creatures of nature subject to natural laws, our destinies determined by the blind workings of heredity and environment, with no significant control over either

negative cost what a film's completed negative and answer print actually cost to produce, its "above the line" costs including one-time contracts for artists and its "below the line" costs for overhead, technicians, and equipment all calculated in, before the film incurs additional distribution and marketing costs

negative cutter the individual, usually employed by the laboratory, who carefully cuts and splices the film's negative to duplicate precisely the work print supplied by the editor

neorealism a movement originating in Italy as World War II ended, associated with filmmakers such as Rossellini, De Sica, and Visconti and influential on many others; it used gritty newsreel-like photography, actual settings, and sometimes nonprofessional actors to portray the ways ordinary people confront or endure extraordinary situations

New Wave a movement originating in France in the late fifties and flowering during the sixties, associated with filmmakers such as Chabrol, Godard, Truffaut, Resnais, and Rohmer and influential on many others, it explored ways to make personal but realistic-seeming films, explicitly cinematic in method and existential in outlook; the term has since been applied to the German film renaissance of the 1970s and to the Australian surge of local talent of the early 1980s.

news feature a story or "sidebar" which provides additional information in greater depth about some one characteristic of an event

newsreels film clips showing current events, usually ending with an amusing feature, common in theaters before television

nickelodeons the long, narrow storefronts that became the first movie theaters during the first decade of this century, serving until "movie palaces" with their large holding areas for waiting audiences began to be designed and built during the second decade

noise the layers of random-seeming sounds heard in a film, as if from an actual world, contributing to the illusion that the film's events are taking place in an actual world

nondiegetic sound accompanying sound, not attributable in any way to on-screen or offscreen sources in the film's world

nontransposability a characteristic of an organic work of art's formal integrity, each scene, sequence, element, or part seen to be essential and effective where it occurs and meaningless if moved anywhere else

objective correlative   critics' term for a work regarded as a functional catalyst, able to generate in its audiences certain ideas and feelings equivalent to others felt earlier by other people in other circumstances

obligatory scene   a work's anticipated climax, the payoff for all earlier uncertainties and tensions, when plot issues are finally settled one way or another

180-degree rule   the principle of continuity editing stating that a camera should not change its angle of vision between shots more than 180 degrees, never crossing a "line" defined by the earlier shot's angle of vision, or characters and objects will seem inexplicably to have reversed themselves

one-shot   a shot of one person only, who is then felt to be isolated even when conversing with someone else

ontology   the branch of philosophy that studies being, essence, or existence, what **is** apart from what seems and how we know it (epistemology), or what it's worth (ethics and esthetics), a term sometimes used to refer to a film's "reality" or to the relationship of a film's images to some ostensible reality somewhere else

open-frame composition   a loose arrangement of compositional elements in a frame, or because of camera movement a flow into the frame of various other compositional features, so the screen always implies a further world offscreen and the rectangle is never quite formally composed

out-takes   any film footage shot but not used in the film's final edited version, including scenes later cut out, alternative takes, and trims cut from the takes actually selected

over-the-shoulder shot   a shot over someone's shoulder often still visible at the bottom of the frame, looking at whatever that character supposedly sees, usually another character in medium shot or close-up; this shot combines the implied communality of a two-shot with the implied isolation of a one-shot and avoids the subjectivity of a POV shot

overdetermined   critic's term for anything exaggerated or laid on thick, overstated to show firm conviction or to drown out certain persistent doubts or uncertainties

pan   a camera's horizontal pivot across a panorama or wide scene while otherwise immobile on a tripod, creating the impression of a head turning deliberately to inspect a field of vision

pantomime acting   the primary acting technique of silent films, sometimes exaggerated but sometimes subtle, using facial expressions, gestures, and body language to convey emotions and ideas without speaking

parable   a specific narrated tale providing general moral guidance by example or analogy

paradigm   any all-inclusive model for the systematic, orderly consideration of a single group of experiences we usually can't examine carefully because in life they are hopelessly entangled with many other experiences and undiscriminated; film narratives often provide simple paradigms for comprehending complicated problems

parallel-cut (cross-cut)   an edit to another action taking place simultaneously somewhere else

parody   a mocking imitation of a director's or genre's habitual artifices, exaggerating them and indirectly commenting on their audience's entrancement by them

period   a length of time in film history when films share certain distinctive characteristics, film production is conducted in certain particular ways, or film audiences demonstrate preference for certain kinds of films

phenomenological time   various time periods as they flow and merge in fantasy, recollection, and the sensible present, our actual experience of duration as consciousness provides it

pixillation   swift, spastic, or jerkily artificial movement made by stop-motion photography or by cutting out a given number of frames per second and then splicing the remainder together

play or pay   a contract clause guaranteeing payment to a filmmaker whether or not the film is completed and released

plot   a series of problematic events in the film as they seem to the main characters who cope with them, revealed to the audience as they are initiated, complicated, and finally—if at all—resolved

police procedural   a crime detection film in which the detective is a professional police officer, usually stressing dogged teamwork and faith in society's institutionalized due processes, though not infrequently the hero is a maverick who behaves like a renegade private eye

postproduction   all the phases of film production remaining after the basic footage has been shot—editing, dubbing and mixing of voices, music, and other sounds, completion and insertion of special effects, etc., until a finished negative ready for printing emerges

poststructuralism   term for a critical school which studies indeterminacies, paradoxes, and dissonances in a work, and in the reader's or viewer's perception of it

POV shot   a shot from the point of view or line of sight of a character, the camera seeing what the character supposedly sees

preproduction   all phases of film production before the shoot, or principal photography, actually begins, including script development, casting, set construction, and preliminary discussion of the film's look and feel with the major artists and technicians involved

presold   a film already well-known to large potential audiences, because based on a best-seller, notorious controversy, or headline news event

press kit   informational packets about a film and the people involved in making it, prepared by publicists and sent to reviewers and journalists to encourage favorable reviews and free publicity

principal photography   the main phase of film production, creating the acted footage which will become the film

prison film   a film genre concerned with individual survival under severely constrained circumstances or when subject to arbitrary persecution, usually set in a penitentiary or P.O.W. camp which serves as a paradigm for the lesser and more diffused constraints of daily life

private eye film   a crime detection film in which the detective is a lone professional, usually stressing faith in individual toughness and resourcefulness as opposed to faith in law enforcement organizations

process shots   matte shots, special effect shots, and others produced in a laboratory by manipulating images, emulsions, exposures, and film stocks

producer   the business executive who brings together the various artists, technicians, subcontractors, and financiers required for the film to be made, then during production oversees the film's schedules, costs, and contracts

production designer   the art director, who selects or designs locations, sets, settings, and props in accordance with the film's agreed visual style

profound characters   characters with deep and complex motives and purposes which can be glimpsed in their behavior though they themselves may not be aware of them, extremely rare in film as in all drama, though common enough in everyday life

projector   a fixed or portable device for displaying images on a flat screen in quick sequence, by shining a bright light through a film strip containing those images and focusing it with a lens, transporting the film between intermittent projections of each frame onto the screen, twenty-four times each second during the sound era

projection and transference   psychoanalytic terms for ways we attribute our own inadmissible and suppressed traits, desires, and needs to other people

projection positives   release prints of the movie made from the film's negative, playable on standard theater projectors

props   "properties," such as lamps, statues, and telephones, the appropriate furniture and bric-a-brac of a characters' usual surroundings, placed here and there on the set as appropriate or needed

protagonist   almost always the major character of a drama, the "hero" who seems to initiate the action or is most affected by it, though sometimes not an individual but a group, tribe, society, culture, or dominant idea

psychomachia   a film's characters considered as allegorical personifications of different psychological or moral traits found in a single individual, so that conflicts between those characters represent conflicts between those traits within any one individual

rack focusing   "racking" or refocusing on something closer or further away, so the first clear image blurs as the second becomes sharp

reaction shot   usually a quick insert shot or cutaway in medium shot or close-up, showing how a key character or a group of people are reacting to whatever we have just seen, often to suggest how we should react

reader response criticism   a range of critical approaches stressing the integrity of any reader's or viewer's engagement with a work, no matter how attentive or subjectively partial, since the work comes into existence only while it is being read, exists afterward only in the minds of its readers, and is used imaginatively as they see fit

real time   clock time, unchanging as a metronome or the movement of stars on which it is based, the objective time we inhabit quite independent of the subjective time that inhabits us

rear projection   a studio process in which a previously filmed background such as a city street seen from a moving car is projected onto a screen from behind then rephotographed with actors in front of the screen as if riding in a car

reception theory   concern with the theoretical issues raised by the different ways people see, interpret, and judge films while in their presence and how they reconstitute them afterward

recurrence   the repetition common to all time-bound oral literatures as well as films, of phrases, motifs, events, angles of vision, or images, serving to accumulate and concentrate significance by including memory of the earlier event in the meaning of the current similar one, while the ongoing work unfolds or unspools without allowing time for reflection

red herring   in a crime or mystery film, a misleading clue distracting attention from others, seemingly important but later found not to be

reflexivity   a film's references to itself as a film, to its own processes, or to other similar films, reminding audiences that a film is no more than it seems

ritual   a carefully repeated real-life scenario we follow devotedly or religiously, to safeguard our convictions or to purge them, as in certain ways when we go to the movies

romantic comedy   comedy concerned with the heart's deepest needs, usually with a couple who misconceive themselves and each other but learn after ludicrous and chastening ordeals that each does provide what the other most needs

rough-cut   previously selected takes tentatively spliced together in their intended order, the film crudely assembled though each shot's precise length and position has not yet been determined or confirmed

running gag   the same gag or joke repeated several times in the course of a comedy, for the pleasures of surprise yet familiarity, tricking viewers while reminding them that the whole event is an agreeable artifice

rushes (dailies)   the previous day's takes hastily developed for screening and critical examination by the director, cinematographer, producer, actors, and others

satire   mockery with a moral purpose, to expose human foibles and excesses, to punish the guilty with laughter, and to inhibit with ridicule any others similarly inclined

scene   a single continuous action, perhaps one master shot but more often made up of many shots spliced together

schlemiel   Yiddish term used in show business and elsewhere to describe a blundering, incompetent clown, who can't get anything right

schlimazl   Yiddish term used in show business and elsewhere to refer to a helplessly unlucky clown, one who often serves unwittingly as the butt of other people's blundering

school   the recurring stylistic and thematic ways in which the artists of a nation or a region tend to express their particular concerns and values

sci-fi   a film genre exploring the implications and anxieties of postindustrial culture, usually dystopian or pessimistic, usually set in some future when a current technological phenomenon has become commonplace and people are living with its social consequences

screenplay   once called a "photoplay," a film script, usually written in master scenes in a prescribed form, each scene identified as "exterior" or "interior" and "day" or "night," with all the dialogue provided and the essential actions described, but with much else left to the director and players

screwball comedy   a fast-paced and irreverent form of romantic comedy made frequently during the 1930s and occasionally since, at least one of the romantic couple apparently free from conventional inhibition, the other in need of such liberation

scriptwriter   the author of the film's screenplay, whether original or adapted from some other work, often writing in collaboration with other writers or the director

second unit director   the director of a small crew, perhaps with some lesser players, which goes somewhere else to shoot certain necessary shots while the film's main action continues to be shot as and where scheduled

semantic meaning   meaning seen to derive primarily from words or shots themselves, not from their syntax or arrangement with respect to each other

semiotics   study of the theory of signs, signifiers, significance, and the social codes which constitute these languages and inform behavior

sentimental comedy   comedy comprised of characters who are essentially good at heart, well-meaning if temporarily misguided, and therefore sympathetic even when foolish

sequence   the spliced shots and scenes making up a single significant dramatic unit

setting   the time and place where the action occurs and the implied range of options and moods appropriate to that time and place

shallow focus   what is seen by a lens with a short depth of field, the image sharp a certain distance from the camera and otherwise blurred, thereby focusing a viewer's attention on one particular part of the screen

shock or collision montage   editing which follows Sergei Eisenstein's example, with successive shots opposing different directions of motion and different shapes, creating violent juxtapositions

shot   in criticism, a take, the film from a single continuous, uninterrupted run of the camera, after it has been edited for the finished film; in filmmaking, more casually, any take whether or not edited

shot/reaction shot   three shots commonly linked, the first showing a person looking, the second, that person's POV showing what is seen, and the third, showing the person's response

shot/reverse shot   two shots commonly linked or repeated, each aimed nearly 180 degrees opposite the other, frequently used to show two people talking and listening to each other in successive over-the-shoulder shots or one-shot close-ups

sight gags   comic pantomiming of various physical predicaments, often involving props and elaborated strenuous activity, the audience's comic perception achieved without recourse to language, rare in sound comedy but primary in silent comedy

single-trait characters   characters defined by one dominating psychological or moral trait who have no others at all, frequently the case with secondary or foil characters, and with clowns or buffoons

slapstick   a form of aggressive physical comedy involving violent abuse of other people, or blundering collisions and pratfalls, named for the special paddle used by stage clowns to beat up on each other

slow motion (overcranking)   speeding up the camera to expose more than 24 fps but projecting the film at 24 fps, providing unnaturally retarded movement, languorous and dreamy, perhaps nightmarish

snuff films   films other than wartime newsreels which supposedly show people actually murdered on camera, supposedly made to provide voyeuristic thrills, but in all known cases fraudulent

soft-core pornography   films showing intimate sexual acts being simulated as if actual, rarely with a significant dramatic point at issue, mainly for voyeuristic gratification

sound   everything heard while a film is being "seen," rarely noticed as such and therefore often subliminal in effect, including the voices, music, and noises carefully mixed on the sound track

sound effects   the "SFX" and Foley sounds mixed onto the sound track, created to "accompany" various images as if they were originated by those images

source music (diegetic music)   music supposedly originating from a visible on-screen source within the film's implied world, as if played by a character, a band in a night club, or an orchestra heard on a radio

source sound (or diegetic sound)   sound that seems to originate in the world created by the film, including industrial cacophonies caused by machines and the sounds of the wind, waves, and birds heard near a seashore, almost always added after shooting

spaghetti Western   familiar term for the slow, mean, remorselessly cruel Westerns made in Italy by Sergio Leone and starring Clint Eastwood, and for some of their imitations

special effects   any visual or auditory trickery making the unreal seem real and the fantastic seem actually to be happening

stand-ins (camera doubles)   people of approximately the same build and coloration as the stars, hired to sit or stand in the stars' positions and be lit and measured during long, boring technical setups for a shot, so the stars can loiter elsewhere until the director is ready for them

star quality   an actor's rare usually indefinable but nevertheless undeniable ability to seize and concentrate an audience's attention whenever he or she is on screen, to achieve strong audience identification or merely to seem utterly fascinating

stars   actors who for various reasons prove especially appealing to film audiences, who therefore provide "bankable" assurance that their films will attract audiences, and who are therefore highly paid to perform in them

Steadicam   trade name for a portable camera hung counterbalanced from a harness worn by its operator, providing smooth movement even during "hand-held" shooting

stereotypes   socially sanctioned type characters, often insulting or derogatory but sometimes admirable, thought by prejudiced, ignorant, or naive people actually to exist in the real world

story   everything that happens or has happened, implied or actually seen, rearranged for retelling into its chronological sequence, whatever the order in which the film revealed it

storyboard a shot sequence drawn in comic-strip format, displaying clearly the camera positions and setups, backgrounds, and blocking for each shot

special effects editing editing which requires special processing such as dissolves or mattes, or which otherwise calls attention to itself

structuralism a critical school deriving from a branch of cultural anthropology, reading films as special-case postindustrial variants of primal ritual tales such as those of primitive cultures, in which a culture's contradictory commitments can find modes of reconciliation

structuralist films sometimes applied to films especially responsive to structuralist analyses but more often a category used for avant-garde films that declare their own organization in time, by being self-evidently cumulative or symmetrical for example

studio originally any film company owning most of its own production facilities such as sound stages and laboratories, set-construction shops, dressing rooms, and offices, contracting with artisans, technicians, artists, and executives, and maintaining established procedures for making and marketing films; more recently a term used by management groups who rent such facilities and by the rental facilities themselves

stunt doubles specialists who know how to perform the stars' dangerous actions on screen without getting hurt, and are hired to do so

style the implicit way a film chooses, arranges, and presents all its resources, all these together making up its distinctive "look," or "feel," an attitude toward its subject as well as the subject itself

styled acting as in dance, mime, operas, or swashbucklers, deliberately elaborated gestures and use of voice, for grand or subdued, graceful or studied effect

subjective time duration as it seems to us while we live it, its pace sometimes creeping and sometimes flying, different from phenomenological time, our mental reshuffling into present consciousness of various memories and fantasies, and different from clock time, which ticks on as impersonally as the earth rotates whether we notice or not

sublimation psychoanalytic term for the ways unacceptable and suppressed desires—aggressive or sexual, for example—can express themselves in acceptable behavior of a different kind altogether, thought to be a powerful motive behind making movies and responding to them

subplot a secondary plot usually reflecting and commenting on some concern of the primary plot, with a secondary character as a protagonist echoing or serving as a foil to the primary protagonist

subsidiary sales other sources of income apart from box office returns, such as record sales, tie-in toys, videocassette rentals, and novelized scripts

supporting players all those members of a cast who are seen less frequently than the ones playing leading roles, a term which assumes that their task is somehow to "support" or display the leading players rather than to fill out a film's dramatic requirements along with the leading players

surface characters characters who are exactly what they first appear to be, no more nor less, often familiar types who carry no mysteries nor uncertainties within themselves

surrealist films films made by some of the prescriptions and artists of the surreal and Dada movements of the 1920s, most notably by Luis Bunuel, Salvador Dali, and Rene Clair, to defy sardonically the customary relationships of bourgeois material reality by yoking the strange together with the familiar, used more recently by artists such as Maya Deren to invoke unconscious processes and display the irrational truths of dreams

swashbuckler adventurous tales of courtly swordplay and elegant courtship in palaces and pirate ships, when presumably men were more daring, women more romantic, and the world gloriously closer to the Renaissance

swish-pan a fast horizontal pivot of the camera, blurring anything seen in passing, used as a transition between shots while sustaining their momentum

sword and sorcery a fantastic adventure genre resembling the swashbuckler and also the Arthurian legends, set in a mythical medieval time when magic and desire have not yet been hemmed in by probability and natural law

symbol any thing or act seen to model, present, or represent the meaning of its own larger implications, a term once used frequently by critics, now used sparingly because several other semiotic or rhetorical concepts such as metaphor or metonymy account more precisely for the enlarged significa-tion of objects and events

symmetry a mirror image along an axis, all on one side of that axis appearing to be a reverse image of all on the other side, plots ending as they began, or images composed to appear similar on either side of the screen

synechdoche a rhetorical term for the process of signifying the whole by a part of that whole, or by another part of it, a cowboy signified for example as a ranch "hand" or as a hired "gun," or visually by his hat or saddle

syntactic meaning meaning derived primarily from the arrangements of words in sentences or shots in edited sequences

take a single uninterrupted and unedited run of the camera, one of many made for each shot, each tagged at its beginning with a clapper-slate

take-out ratio the ratio of all footage exposed during production to all footage appearing in the completed film, rarely less than 10:1

talking head a lengthy medium shot or close-up of someone speaking, un-broken by cutaways, inserts, reverse shots, reaction shots, or other more cinematic interruptions

technical acting acting which uses the customary associated gestures, postures, and other outer manifestations of feelings to imply them for the character, whatever the actor may in fact be thinking or feeling at the time, usually opposed to method acting

teleological view the belief that life and all things living have some ultimate purpose or function to fulfill, move toward that significant event, and take their meaning from it, usually opposed to an existential view

telephoto (long) lens a lens system which narrows the field of vision and so seems to enlarge whatever it sees, but at the same time flattens the relative distances seen, so that very distant objects seems almost as close as nearby objects

textual criticism   a form of hermeneutic criticism which assumes the autonomy of a text independent of perception, whatever appears on the screen in some sense existing as such, and which then subjects its structures, components, and implications to formal exegetical analysis

30-degree rule   the principle of continuity editing stating that a camera angle should always change by at least 30 degrees between shots or else not at all, or the edit will seem jerky or jump-cut

3-D   a process of binocular filming creating the illusion that objects seen are moving in three dimensions, the third being distance from the viewer, one of several attempts to differentiate theatrical films from television during the 1950s

three-quarter shot   a medium long shot showing a human figure from the knees up, implying readiness to move about, called by the French an "American shot"

three-shot   a shot of three people occupying the same frame

thriller   a kind of adventure melodrama with apprehension and suspense arising from a protagonist's physical danger over an extended period of time

tilt up (or down)   during a shot, pivoting a camera vertically from a fixed position and height, as if someone were looking up or down

time-loop plot   a paradoxical action portraying time travel into the past in order to cause or change the present

tracking shot   the camera moving smoothly on tracks, trucks, or dollies toward but more commonly alongside whatever it sees, while whatever it sees may also be moving

tragedy   the classical form of drama in which a character confronts a dilemma, makes a choice, and endures the consequences

trailer   an advertising short for an upcoming film, with brief clips, shown in theaters along with the current film

travelling shot   one in which the camera's position changes to follow an action, in one of many ways

treatment   an elaborated plot and character outline for a script not yet written, usually in narrative form with commentary

tripod   a three-legged camera platform of variable height for shots from a fixed position, with the camera attached to a "head" which is able to pan or tilt smoothly should these movements be required

two-shot   a shot of two people occupying the same frame, sharing the same space

type casting   hiring an actor to play only familiar roles similar to those the actor played earlier

type characters   dramatic characters with a few familiar recurring traits, who reappear in films under different names and guises because audiences like to see them, because they provide preestablished dramatic economy with audiences already familiar with them, or because writers can't create any other kinds

unintegrated musical   a musical in which the songs and dances are incidental to the plot's requirements, entertaining the audience but not essentially advancing the action

unity a peculiar condition of art, rarely of anything else, in that all its particulars seem to work with each other to define or elaborate some one thing

unity as organic form a work's structural integrity, with each characteristic important to every other, all essential and none unnecessary or missing

unity of action the plot's single concern, with an issue, problem, or character, from its opening through to its end

unity of place the classical idea that a work should take place in one locale, rarely helpful to films, which can roam widely, though useful to naturalistic theater where the characters all anyhow occupy a narrow, limited world

unity of time the classical idea that a dramatic action should be concentrated into as brief a span of time as possible, or should seem so

unsourced (off-screen) sound accompanying sound, not attributable in any way to a supposed source within the film's world, though appropriately enhancing the audience's sense of that world

valuative flashback a sequence inserted into an action portraying earlier events in order to explain why something in the present seems especially precious or worthless

verbal comedy jokes, jests, quips, puns, witty turns of phrase, and insults, all forms of comedy deriving from how words are used

vicarious experience indirect experience, imaginatively participating in someone else's experiences by proxy, one reason that people go to the movies

voice-over an unattributed off-screen voice, commenting on whatever is being seen

voices the sounds human beings make when conversing or vocally expressing themselves, different from all other sounds and carrying radically different implications whether heard or overheard

wardrobe the place costumes are kept, the costumes themselves, and the person who supplies them as needed; any clothing seen in a film no matter how ordinary or bizarre

Westerns the classical frontier genre, pitting self-reliant individualism against anarchic impulse with the establishment of justice or some form of new community at stake

wide-angle (short) lens a lens system that shows a wide field of vision, with images that therefore look more distant than they are, distorted when seen close-up

wild (live) sound sound actually recorded while the shot is made, often of poor quality and unusable if recorded outdoors on location but serving nevertheless as a guide for dubbing and editing, and as a reminder of dramatic intentions

wipe substitution of one image by another as if one were pushing, flipping, or squeezing the other off the screen

wit a form of quick intellectual cleverness, usually expressing itself by finding patterns of similarity among words, things, predicaments, and people

work print positive prints of the film's takes, provided for the editor to cut and splice shot by shot when assembling the film, so the negative can remain untouched until the editor arrives at a final cut

wrap completion of principal photography, a moment usually celebrated with a party for the cast and crew

zoetrope one of many nineteenth-century persistence-of-vision toys, using a spinning cylinder with slightly differentiated figures drawn on its inside, so they seem to move when glimpsed through successive slits in the cylinder's side

zoom lens a lens system which can smoothly change the field of vision's size while maintaining focus, in effect changing itself from wide angle to telephoto and back, creating the impression that the camera and therefore the viewer's attention are drawing closer or moving further away

Index

Page numbers in boldface refer to glossary definitions.

Laurel, Stan, 106, 117, 125
Lavender Hill Mob, The (1951), 96
L'Avventura (1960), 21
Lawrence of Arabia (1962), 159
Layered characters, 103, **213**
Lean, David, 11
Lee, *Spike*, xi, 59
Left Handed Gun, The (1958), 134
Lemon (1969), 156–157
Lens, 37–39, 43–49, **213**
Leone, Sergio, 137
Les Mistons (1957), 34
Lethal Weapon II (1989), 42
Levi-Strauss, Claude, 190
Levinson, Barry, 95
Lewis, Jerry, 106, 124
Lights and lighting, 49–50
Lindbergh, Charles, 159
Lindsay, Vachel, 188
Line producer, 9, 69, **213**
Line wipe, 79, **213**
Linear perspective, 59, 64
Linear structure, 93–96, **213**
Lip-synching, 19, 80, **213**
Little Big Man (1970), 137
Little Caesar (1930), 138–139
Living dead films, 143, **213**
Lloyd, Harold, 124, 126
Location, 2, 9, 15, 19–20, 49, 57, 68, 80,
    109, 202, **213, 226**
Loews Theaters, 4
Lombard, Carole, 81
Loneliness of the Long Distance Runner,
    The, (1962), 164
Lonely Are the Brave (1962), 137
Long shot, 28–29, **213**
Looping, 13–14, 19, 79–80, **208, 213**
Lorentz, Pare, 148, 152–153
Losey, Joseph, 84
Low-angle shot, 30–31, **213**
Low-key lighting, 50, **213**
Lubitsch, Ernst, 79, 123
Lucas, George, 19
Lumet, Sidney, 98
Lumière, Auguste, 27, 87, 120, 167
Lumière, Louis, 27, 87, 120, 167

M (1930), 129
M*A*S*H (1970), 82, 122
M*A*S*H (TV), 32, 122
McCabe and Mrs. Miller (1971), 137
McCarthy period, 162, 195
McCrea, Joel, 92
McLaglen, Victor, 23
McLaren, Norman, 40
McTiernan, John, 50
Mad Max (1979), 144
Mad scientist films, 143, **214**
Mad slasher films, 143, **214**
Magnificent Obsession (1954), 131
Magnificent Seven, The (1960), 195
Maguffin, 94–95, **214**
Main title credits, 5–19, **214**
Maltese Falcon, The (1941), 12, 52, 103,
    117, 140, 151

Man Who Shot Liberty Valence, The
    (1962), 137
Manhattan (1979), 47, 54
Manifest content, 174, **214**
Mann, Anthony, 117
Mann, Thomas, 194
Marat/Sade (play), 93
March, Frederick, 56
Marlowe, Philip, 103, 117
Marnie (1964), 104
Married to the Mob (1988), 6
Martin, Dean, 106, 124
Martin, Steve, 21
Marx Brothers, 158
    Groucho, 122
    Harpo, 126
Marxist criticism, 196–197, 199, **214**
Master shot, 29, 70, **214**
Match-cuts, 76, **214**
Matte shot, 87, **214**
May, Elaine, 29, 113
Meaning, 172–185
    allegory, 174–176, **202**
    analogy, 174–179, **202**
        metaphor, 178, **214**
        metonymy, 178, **215**
        parables, 178–179, **217**
        paradigms, 174–178, **217**
        synechdoche, 178–179, **224**
    difference, 190
    ideology, 176–177, **212**
    personal identification, 22–25, 101, **212**
    ritual enactment, 179–182, **220**
    semantic, 119, 195, **221**
    semiotic, 190, **221**
    syntactic, 119, 195, **224**
    vicarious experience, 20–22, 173, **226**
Medium Cool (1969), 150
Medium shot, 29, **214**
Meet John Doe (1941), 36, 68, 81, 96
Méliès, George, 87–88, 120, 167
Melodrama, 130–131, **214**
Memphis Belle (1990), 20, 154
Memphis Belle, The (1943), 154
Meshes of the Afternoon (1943), 158
Metaphor, 178, **214**
Method acting, 111, **215**
Metonymy, 178, **215**
Metro-Goldwyn Mayer (MGM), 8
Metropolis (1926), 62, 143, 176
Mickey-mousing, 85, **215**
Mid-angle shot, 30, **215**
Midnight Cowboy (1969), 130
Midnight Express (1978), 140
Mike boom, **215**
Mildred Pierce (1945), 97–98, 159, 177
Miller, Glenn, 159
Miller's Crossing (1990), 24, 138
Mimetic criticism, 191, **215**
Minimalist film, 156–157, **215**
Miracle, The (1948), 170
Mise en scene, 11, 43–64, **215**
Missing (1982), 176
Mitchum, Robert, 103
Moana (1925), 152–153